Revolutionary Monsters

REVOLUTIONARY MONSTERS

Five Men Who Turned Liberation into Tyranny

DONALD T. CRITCHLOW

REGNERY
HISTORY
Washington, D.C.

Regnery History™ is a trademark of Salem Communications Holding Corporation
Regnery® is a registered trademark and its colophon is a trademark of Salem Communications Holding Corporation

Cataloging-in-Publication data on file with the Library of Congress
ISBN: 978-1-68451-124-2
eISBN: 978-1-68451-149-5
Library of Congress Control Number: 2021943476

Published in the United States by
Regnery History
An Imprint of Regnery Publishing
A Division of Salem Media Group
Washington, D.C.
www.Regnery.com

Manufactured in the United States of America

10 9 8 7 6 5 4 3 2 1

Books are available in quantity for promotional or premium use. For information on discounts and terms, please visit our website: www.RegneryHistory.com.

To William J. Rorabaugh, my friend since graduate school at the University of California, Berkeley.

To Dean Riesen, Dan and Carleen Brophy, and David and Bob Katzin—good friends all.

CONTENTS

INTRODUCTION
The Revolutionary Mind   ix

CHAPTER 1
Lenin: Monster as Dictator   1

CHAPTER 2
Mao: Revolutionary Destroyer   31

CHAPTER 3
Castro: Megalomania Empowered   67

CHAPTER 4
Robert Mugabe: Monster of Zimbabwe   107

CHAPTER 5
Khomeini: God and the State   135

CONCLUSION
Lessons Learned?   173

Acknowledgments   179
Selected Readings   181
Notes   193
Index   201

Introduction:
The Revolutionary Mind

Many young people today are infatuated with revolution, but for those who fled Communist dictatorships, revolution is a serious matter. People who have experienced the chaos and terror that comes with political upheaval often ask such things as: "Why aren't young people better informed?"; "What's happening in our schools that students are learning this?"; or "Why aren't our youth being taught about the nature of these oppressive regimes?"

Revolutionary Monsters provides a warning to those beguiled by the siren call of revolution. The lessons of the tragic revolutions in the twentieth century are all too apparent in the failures of the former Soviet Union, China, Cuba, Zimbabwe, and Iran. A myriad of books can be found on each of these failures. Exceptionally diligent scholars have detailed them. Memoirs by those who suffered under these regimes offer heartbreaking, terrifying accounts of human suffering and the deaths of millions. *Revolutionary Monsters* also provides a grim account of these failed revolutions. The book asks an apparently simple question: What motivated leaders such as Lenin, Mao, Castro, Mugabe, and Khomeini—revolutionaries who transformed their societies—to create such monstrous, brutal, and oppressive regimes? Each of these men in his own way called for creating the "New Man." They were convinced that a new age in history—one of equality and social perfection—was about to begin with the overthrow of the existing government.

Revolutionary Monsters recounts the tragedy of dictatorship in our age of alleged "enlightenment." The book is short, with the intention of being read by those who know little about the human tragedy of history. The assumption behind *Revolutionary Monsters* is that facts can replace vacuous rhetoric about "liberation," "equality," and "freedom." These words should impart a deeper meaning to those cautious ones who realize the imperfections of the world and human nature, even while understanding that progress, albeit often uneven, should be sought. To speak, though, of "imperfections of the world and human nature" hardly captures the tragedy of revolution (and war) in the twentieth century. *Revolutionary Monsters* presents the dialectic of revolution as liberation transformed into oppression, freedom into tyranny, and idealism into tragedy. Individual men and women, not nameless social forces, drive history. With little knowledge of history, the young are easily persuaded by the romance of revolution and the acceptance of destruction as a path to human perfection.

The modern revolutionary mind is enraptured by millennialist visions of a perfected society. Those who succumb the most to revolutionary logic take on a terrorist mentality. These revolutionary monsters assume the roles of prophets acting in a corrupt world that cannot be reformed or bettered gradually; heaven on earth arrives only through destruction of the existing world order. The modern revolutionary believes with fanatical conviction that the old order needs to be destroyed. Violence is necessary to fulfill the prophecy. Terror is an instrument for achieving and maintaining power. This apocalyptic vision, in which the new world order springs out of the old, relegates individuals to treatment as abstract entities that either stand on the side of revolution or on the side of reaction.

In the twentieth century, millions of people have died at the hands of revolutionary monsters who came into power calling for the liberation of people from their oppressors. Mass murder within these revolutionary regimes was not a coincidence. Terror is instrumental to the modern revolutionary—mass murder follows without apology. Terror is employed to maintain power within the regime and is used against the revolutionary's internal and external enemies. The Islamic Republic of Iran, for example, executed tens of thousands of alleged enemies of the state and today maintains order through a regime of mass arrests, torture, and imprisonment. Support of international terrorism against the American infidels or Zionist Israel has followed without qualm.

Today, the word *revolution* connotes upheaval, but its origins begin in modern usage as an astronomical term, employed by the Polish scientist Copernicus, who in the early sixteenth century used the word in its Latin sense to describe a recurring, cyclical movement of planets. The word meant planets' revolving back to a preestablished point. In this sense, *revolution* meant restoration. When the word began as a political term, it too meant restoration. The Glorious Revolution of 1689, which brought William and Mary to the throne in England, was seen as a "restoration" of ancient liberties. The American Revolution, less than a century later, demanded the restoration of liberties and the universal rights of Englishmen. It was the French Revolution that introduced to the modern world a revolutionary vision in which the old order is destroyed to create a new world, a new millennium for humankind. The modern concept of revolution denoting the destruction of the old order through violence and terror found articulation in the French Revolution.

The French Revolution came in the age of democratic revolutions that followed the American Revolution. Revolutionaries found, however, that the American model was not easily replicated. Those French officers who had fought in the American Revolution had been warned, "You will carry our sentiments with you, but if you try to plant them in a country that has been corrupt for centuries, you will encounter obstacles more formidable than ours. Our liberty has been won with blood; yours will have to be shed in torrents before liberty can take root in the old world."[1]

The French Revolution began when King Louis XVI of France convened the Estates General in May 1789 for the first time since 1614. The

Estates General represented the clergy, the nobility, and the commoners. In June, the Estates General transformed itself into a National Assembly, which undertook to abolish slavery, placed the Catholic Church under state control, and extended the right to vote. The French Revolution began as a claim to restore the ancient powers of the Estate, but under the threat of counterrevolution, social unrest, and war with Austria, Britain, and Prussia, a Reign of Terror began in 1793 with the establishment of the Committee of Public Safety, headed by Maximilien Robespierre and his Jacobin faction. Under Robespierre, a wave of violence was unleashed to root out alleged counterrevolutionaries.

Robespierre personified the modern revolutionary mind. Upon his rise to power, a new calendar was declared, churches were ordered closed, and Christianity was replaced by the deist Cult of the Supreme Being. At least sixteen thousand people were executed during the Reign of Terror by revolutionary tribunals in trials in which procedural guarantees for the accused were removed. Robespierre personally ordered nine hundred arrests. The Terror ended when opponents, fearing for their own lives, arrested and publicly executed Robespierre and ninety other Jacobins. The Revolution had devoured its own children.

The French Revolution set the contours for modern revolutions by seeking to eradicate social classes in the name of equality. This demand for social equality contrasted with the American revolutionaries, who sought political, not social, equality. The American revolutionaries believed that social equality was impossible given human nature. The American Revolution was a political revolution to ensure liberty and rights through constitutional representative government. The Founding Fathers distrusted direct democracy and the passions of the *demos* ("the people"), easily aroused by demagogues. Voices of artisans (with few exceptions), women, and blacks were excluded at the Philadelphia Convention in 1787. The new Constitution benefitted white males but set forth ideals of liberty for what followed: the continued expansion of suffrage, the abolition of black slavery (after a bloody Civil War), and the importance of the rule of law in which all, rich and poor, are to be judged equally.

Without doubt, the American Revolution unleashed a spirit of egalitarianism across the new nation, as political and social elites were challenged. Republican simplicity was demanded in speech, dress, and manner. In Boston, gentlemen and ladies were mocked by the lower orders for signs of elitism such as wearing powdered wigs and silk stockings. In upstate New York, land rentiers seized property, and in Western Pennsylvania backwoods farmers rebelled when the federal government imposed a whiskey tax. Yet, these manifestations of social equality were limited. The Founders, while committed to republican values, distrusted the passions of the people. Above all else, they feared power, the domination of some over others. They understood that majorities could become tyrannies. They believed, however, that power is a natural aspect of government. Power within government could only be made legitimate through a compact of mutual consent. If left unconstrained, government power, they believed, would degenerate into tyranny, oligarchy, or mob rule. The new federal government was to serve as a referee adjudicating various sectional, economic, and social interests of the nation. The coercive powers of government were to remain relatively weak, although necessary to national trade, territorial expansion, immigration, relations with Native Americans, and diplomatic relations with other countries.

This fear of power as a threat to liberty and a sense of human limitations—so aptly expressed by Alexander Hamilton, who declared, "Man, after all, is but Man"—precluded social revolution. All Americans understood that social inequality existed within their own society and were repulsed by deep social inequality in Europe. Yet, as William Penn, the founder of the Pennsylvania colony, observed, America was "the best poor man's country." Later critics accused the Founders of the American Republic for not addressing social questions concerning black slavery or the treatment of Native Americans and women. The American Founders sought political order on the assumption that political stability, the rule of law, and a representative, constitutional order allowed for the opportunity for social advancement, at least for the citizens of the new republic. It is worth noting that successful revolutions in the late twentieth century, seen in the Polish and Baltic state revolutions, were political revolutions, not social revolutions.

The French Revolution embodied the modern revolutionary concept and practice that social justice could be implemented through the expression of the "general will" of the masses—articulated through enlightened revolutionary leadership. French revolutionaries spoke of the will of the people—expressed through people's communes and "societies" such as the Jacobin clubs. Later, the Bolsheviks spoke of the power of the Soviets. Modern revolutionary states have proclaimed themselves "People's Republics," no matter how dictatorial the regime. The "general will" became an abstract concept that implied unanimity of opinion and excluded difference. A divided will—the will of the people as it actually exists—was logically inconceivable.

But how was the "general will" to be determined? The answer proved, in reality, to be whatever the revolutionary elite decided to call the "general will." Dissenters opposed to the "will of the people" became enemies of the state. The very concept of the "general will," as well as the practice of revolutionary terror, presupposes a hostility to individual opinion or individual rights. Lenin, Mao, Castro, and Mugabe claimed to speak on behalf of the interests of the people as a whole. Khomeini and the Iranian revolutionary clergy avoided the problem of consent by denying popular sovereignty altogether. Only God was sovereign, and the Supreme Leader of Iran spoke for Allah. The resulting secular and religious revolutionary regimes found an ingenuous way to place the will of the people in a single voice: the dictator.

The French Revolution set another model for social revolution in the modern era: liberation for those who suffered social inequality. Compassion, not reason, drove the call for revolution. The consequence was the glorification of the masses, the poor and the oppressed. Modern social revolutionaries speak as liberators for the oppressed and the downtrodden. Vengeance against the oppressors is called for in the revolution. As a result, revolution becomes an act of vengeance. As one French revolutionary declared, "Vengeance is the only source of liberty."[2] Because misery knew no bounds in the old regime, vengeance in the revolution need not be restrained. A delirious rage characterizes the modern revolution as the anger of the mob is unleashed. Revolutionary terror is justified in the pursuit of liberation. The delusion of achieving complete social equality embraces the shedding of blood.

Revolutions are by nature upheavals, but there are many examples of revolutions occurring with minimal bloodshed. As historian Richard Pipes observes, there were no mass killings in the Glorious Revolution in England in 1689 or the American Revolution of 1776—and indeed, the overthrow of the Russian czar in February 1917 occurred without terrible bloodshed. What followed in the Bolshevik Revolution and subsequent modern revolutions was the shedding of blood on a massive scale, however.

A revolutionary mentality that willingly accepts the execution, torture, starvation, and imprisonment of tens of thousands of people is unfathomable to most average people. Evil is difficult to understand. Richard Pipes observes that it takes a certain kind of personality to "massacre vanquished enemies . . . and prisoners of war, the kind of personality that would boast, as did a triumphant Lenin in 1920, 'We did not hesitate to shoot thousands of people, and we shall not hesitate to do that [again], and we shall save the country.'"[3]

Lenin, Mao, Castro, Mugabe, and Khomeini were zealots in their secular (or, in Khomeini's case, religious) faiths. They shared a faith that society could be remade with a will to power that benefits them personally. In this way, they conflated ideology and personal power so that the two became inseparable. The destiny of history weighed on their shoulders; they believed that without them all would be lost. The magnitude of this arrogance is measured in their crimes against humanity. These revolutionaries created a reality within their own minds and a demand for power set in terms of their own morality. The world was divided in their eyes between the enlightened and the unenlightened, true believers and infidels, revolutionaries and reactionaries, the state and the enemies of the state. Theirs was a world of light and darkness, black and white, salvation and damnation.

These revolutionaries proclaimed themselves as instruments of history. Their obsession with the "necessity of history" and the fulfilment of prophecy casts over their minds a magical, poisonous spell that no antidote exists to remedy. As they brought the blade of history to murder thousands, they remained confident of their self-anointed roles as the saviors of mankind. The hubris of proclaiming oneself a savior astounds the average person, but it defines the revolutionary mind. The grandiosity of their dreams of liberation and the grim reality of the nightmares that followed in pursuit of their delusions provide a lesson for us in the tragedy of history. These revolutionaries rallied the masses in the name of freedom, only to become worse than the rulers they replaced. Revolutionary regimes became washed in the blood of the very people they had called to freedom.

Yet, as they betrayed the revolution, these monsters created cults of personality to ensure that their grip on power was maintained. And surprisingly many are still willing to see in the tyrant only benevolence, wisdom, and compassion. The tyrant emerges as a kind of folk hero, as myths are created through propaganda, subtle and crude. No number of arrests or executions, no degree of political repression, no extent of economic deprivation persuades the masses that their revolution has been betrayed. Of course, it's best in an oppressive regime not to even think such thoughts or voice criticism of the revolutionary regime and its supreme leader. Admission that the revolution has been betrayed or that a better world does not await is understandable; less excusable are those outside the country who apologize or deny mass executions, massive starvation, and continued oppression within the revolutionary regimes. Lenin, Mao, Castro, Mugabe, and Khomeini found ready apologists and deniers of their crimes in the Western media, foreign governments, and international bodies—until reality could no longer be denied.

Revolutionary Monsters captures the psyche of modern social revolutionaries willing to unleash devastation, suffering, and death in pursuit of constructing the New Man, the New Society, and a New World unchained from the past. What do these twentieth-century revolutionary minds share in common other than a belief in the necessity of revolution? When do these revolutionary minds turn from liberation to tyranny? Are tyrants produced in the revolutionary process, or were these monsters simply awaiting a revolution so they could emerge?

Revolutionary Monsters presents a collective biography of five modern-day revolutionaries who came into power calling for the liberation of the people only to end up killing millions in the name of revolution: Lenin (Russia), Mao (China), Castro (Cuba), Mugabe (Zimbabwe), and Khomeini (Iran). This book explores basic questions about the kind of person who joins a movement to liberate "the people," only to become a tyrant worse than the regime replaced by the revolution—the kind of personality that allows a revolution to be personified and projected into a cult to be worshiped. To do so, the book dissects the shared common mentality of modern-day social revolutionaries that allowed them to envision themselves as prophets of a new age. These leaders shared messianic views that a new world could be created either through socialism, pan-Africanism, or religion. Ironically, all were students of history yet sought to throw off the restraints of history.

These revolutionaries shared a deep faith in the perfectibility of men. In their claim of historical necessity, they denied the lessons of history—mankind's fallen nature. Their hubris lay in their claim that without them in power, the New Society and the creation of the Perfect Man would not be achieved. Their claim reveals a kind of pathological narcissism, a pattern of fantasized and behavioral grandiosity, an intense need for admiration, and a demonstrable lack of empathy for those they made suffer in order to achieve that "Perfect Man." They were narcissists attracted to messianic beliefs that allowed for tyranny, dictatorship, and cultism. They shared a ruthless bloodlust in their pursuit of power. They accepted the necessity of violence and terrorism. Altruistic ideals and the necessity of revolution provided them a rationale for violence.

Lenin, Mao, Castro, Mugabe, and Khomeini offer supreme examples of narcissists holding messianic beliefs. Others might have been included—Adolf Hitler, Benito Mussolini, Kim Il-sung, François Duvalier, Ho Chi Minh, or Hugo Chávez—in this book. Lenin, Mao, Castro, Mugabe, and Khomeini were chosen as subjects because they best represent the monstrous manifestation of the revolutionary mind across continents. *Revolutionary Monsters* offers not an encyclopedic account of tyranny in our age but a selective didactic warning: perfection in a finite world is impossible. To seek perfection is to find only tragedy.

The lust for power presents a consistent theme in history. The revolutionary mind sees power, and ultimately absolute power, as necessary for the creation of the perfect world. An arrogance develops (or is revealed) in the revolutionary leader who posits that he embodies the revolution. Without him the revolutionary regime will fail. The leader becomes the personification of the revolution itself. As a result, a cult of personality emerges early in the revolutionary process. The cult of personality promotes the leader's humble origins as a "man of the people" and the embodiment of the aspirations of the people. The leader cares not for his own wants, lives a simple, even austere, life, and lives only to serve his people. Power is held only as if by divine right of the revolutionary. This divine right of the revolutionary ruler is derived from the logic of history.

Not every self-proclaimed messiah becomes a dictator. But given the right social and political conditions, a narcissist adhering to a messianic ideology can bring untold suffering to humanity. This is an immutable lesson of history. These monsters wore the masks of liberators, hiding the malevolence of hubris that comes when men attempt to create heaven on earth. Their regimes lead us to recall words found in the Book of Revelation: "And he cried out in a mighty voice: 'Fallen, fallen is Babylon the great! She has become a lair for demons and a haunt for every unclean spirit, every unclean bird, and every detestable beast.'"[4]

CHAPTER 1

Lenin:
Monster as Dictator

As bands played the revolutionary "Internationale," tens of thousands of people lined the streets of Moscow to watch Vladimir Lenin's coffin carried to rest in the Red Square on an extremely cold morning, 35 degrees below zero Fahrenheit, on January 27, 1924. The leader of the Communist Revolution was dead. Later, in a morbid feat of mortuary science, Lenin's body was embalmed and placed on permanent display in a new mausoleum in the Red Square. It became a place of pilgrimage for the Communist faithful, and statues, mementos, and souvenirs of Lenin were on display. Lenin's body remains on display, even after the collapse of the Soviet Union in 1991. But the lines waiting to see Lenin's preserved body are shorter today.

Lenin's legacy to his country was one-party rule, a police state, a failed economy, and Joseph Stalin. Lenin saw in Stalin a protégé and heir apparent. Lenin turned on Stalin only after a series of strokes forced Lenin into retirement and he realized his former protégé no longer cared about his opinions. The final straw came when Stalin was rude to Lenin's wife Nadezhda Krupskaya. In 1923, Lenin dictated his final testament, urging party leaders to remove Stalin as general secretary of the Central Committee of the Soviet Communist Party. Following Lenin's death, Stalin carefully suppressed publication of Lenin's last words by limiting their availability to a tight circle of party officials. In 1925, an American journalist named Max Eastman got hold of the document and published it in the West, but few in Russia even knew of it. By this time Stalin had consolidated his authority, suppressing dissenting voices just as Lenin had.

Vladimir Ilyich Lenin came to power in Russia in October 1917. His intent was the elimination of all political opponents: socialists, liberals, and reactionaries. His method was terrorism. His goal was a dictatorship. When opponents complained against the use of violence and repression, Lenin replied, "Surely you don't think we'll come out as winners if we don't use the harshest revolutionary terror?"[1]

Shortly after coming into power, Lenin's Bolshevik government issued a decree dissolving the courts; a year later, another decree invalidated existing laws. Freed from legal shackles, the Red Terror campaign began in 1918. Within two months, there were at least 6,185 summary executions. (By comparison, between 1825 and 1917, Russian courts had issued 6,321 death sentences.) Lenin utterly rejected the idea that the Communists should eliminate capital punishment, declaring, "Nonsense, how can you make a revolution without executions? Do you expect to dispose of your enemies by disarming yourself?" He added that a resolution to abolish the death penalty would be a sign of "impermissible weakness, pacifist illusion, and so on."[2]

In December 1917, he established a secret police force, the Cheka, which became an instrument of terror to arrest, imprison, torture, and execute opponents of the Bolshevik dictatorship. The Cheka occupied the Lubyanka building in Moscow, making "Lubyanka" a byword for torture and terrorism. The Cheka was reported to have scalped people, cut off their limbs with hacksaws, impaled people on stakes, rolled them in spike-laden barrels, and burned victims alive in furnaces. One method of torture, called "the glove," involved putting a victim's hand in boiling water and peeling off the skin to form a glove. Lenin always supported, regularly employed, and never doubted using terrorism to advance his totalitarian aims.

Terror as an Instrument of Power

Terror was woven deeply into the fabric of the Communist regime. Lenin dismissed critics who said he was imprisoning and executing the innocent along with the guilty. "I judge soberly and categorically," he said. "What is better—to put in prison a few dozen or a few hundred inciters, guilty or not, conscious or not, or lose thousands of Red Army soldiers and workers?"[3] As Lenin's commissar of justice, Isaac Steinberg, observed, terror was essential to the regime for "the purpose of mass intimidation, mass compulsion, mass extermination."[4]

After a failed assassination attempt against Lenin in September 1918, the regime intensified its persecution of ordinary Russian citizens. Anyone suspected of being an "enemy of the people" became a target of leather-coated Cheka officers. Lenin directed his Cheka police to arrest dissidents and send them to Siberian work camps, the beginning of the notorious gulag prison system. Lenin called for mass execution of kulaks (wealthier peasants). He directed the Red Army to hang them and to leave them hanging as a warning to other peasants who would not submit utterly to the new regime.

That new regime was personified by Lenin, and a cult of personality was built around him. Hundreds of thousands of pamphlets were distributed throughout the country describing Lenin as the "apostle of world communism" and "the invincible messenger of peace, crowned with the thorns of slander."[5] One pamphlet written by the high party leader Grigory Zinoviev declared, "Such a leader is born once in [five hundred] years in the life of mankind."[6] Photographs of Lenin were circulated everywhere, including as replacements for religious icons and portraits of the czar in peasant huts. He became the Workers' Christ. This cult of personality around Lenin distorted in varying ways how historians have portrayed Lenin, Trotsky, and Stalin.

While historians differ in their interpretations of the full contours of Leninism, they all agree that Lenin erected a Communist police state.[7] That is a simple historical fact. Marxism provided Lenin with pseudo-scientific laws of progress that rationalized his total power and the necessity of perpetuating the Communist Party's total power. Leon Trotsky and Joseph Stalin shared Lenin's faith in terror as an instrument to maintain the "dictatorship of the proletariat" in Russia. The views that Stalin's use of terror "betrayed" the revolution and that Trotsky was somehow a different kind of Communist miss the nature of the Bolshevik Revolution itself.

It was Trotsky, not Lenin or Stalin, who said, "Repression in the interest of achieving economic goals is a necessary weapon of the socialist dictatorship," and it was he who called for the conscription of workers into an industrial army.[8] As a revolutionary leader in Russia, Trotsky showed no compunction in executing socialist opposition. He smashed a revolt by sailors in Kronstadt who dared call for the reestablishment of political parties, the end of press censorship, and the reinstitution of a representative assembly. As head of the Red Army, Trotsky conducted a campaign of terror against uncooperative peasants, burning entire villages and executing village leaders. The severity of his actions shocked even fellow Communists, but Lenin defended him. Once Trotsky declared himself a Bolshevik in 1918, he never wavered from advocating for a totalitarian state, which justified Communist terrorism. At the Thirteenth Party Congress in May 1924, shortly after Lenin's death, Trotsky declared, "Comrades, none of us wants to be or can be right standing against the party. In the last analysis the party is always right, because the party is the sole historical instrument that the working class possesses for the solution to its fundamental tasks."[9] He admitted that the party could make "occasional mistakes," but party loyalty was an ironclad conviction of the Communist.

Trotsky, ever arrogant, later accused Stalin of betraying the revolution through bureaucratic careerism. But Stalin, of course, was more than a grey, mediocre bureaucrat; he was a Marxist-Leninist revolutionary committed to preserving Bolshevik power. His support within the Communist Party came from "his tenacious dedication to the revolutionary cause and to the state's powers," as one of his biographers observed.[10]

Stalin was a committed, devout, and ruthless Communist both before the October Revolution and afterwards. As a revolutionary political organizer, working in the oil-producing city of Baku, Stalin willingly involved himself in criminal work for the party, including kidnapping, robberies, running protection rackets, and ordering assassinations. As one of Stalin's fellow revolutionaries recalled, Stalin showed "great zeal in organizing the assassination of princes, priests, and the bourgeois."[11] Stalin was the robber-in-chief of the Bolsheviks, and Lenin was attracted to Stalin's ruthlessness and loyalty to the party.

Stalin achieved, at monstrous cost, the collectivization of agriculture. Yet the war on peasants began under Lenin. When relatively wealthy peasants—and wealthy in this case meant owning over eight acres—resisted turning over their grain to Bolsheviks, Lenin called for war: "Merciless war against the kulaks! Death to them."[12] With his usual vitriol, he called them bloodsuckers, leeches, and vampires.

The language the Communist Lenin used against the kulaks is similar to the language that the National Socialist Adolf Hitler used against the Jews. That is not a coincidence. Lenin, Stalin, and Hitler were all committed to party loyalty and obedience, the elimination of dissenting factions, and an ultimate, global clash of ideologies. During the Second World War, Stalin aligned himself first against the National Socialists, then with them, then against them again, after Nazi Germany's invasion of Soviet Russia. But even when he was allied with Great Britain and the United States, he believed in an inevitable, ultimate clash between Western capitalist democracy and the Communist world. Partly in preparation for this international showdown, Stalin instigated an anti-Jewish purge of the Communist Party, known as the "Jewish Doctors Plot."[13] Begun in 1951, it ceased shortly after Stalin died in March 1953, but had it proceeded, it could have paralleled the National Socialist policy of deporting Jews to labor camps. Terror, for Stalin, as for Lenin, as for

Trotsky, was a way to maintain total party control; and the party had to be in control, because it was the engine of progress.

Perfecting Humanity

Lenin and his fellow Marxists represent one offshoot of the Enlightenment, with the idea that science and scientific planning made possible the perfection of society and humanity. In the English-speaking world, this hubris was tempered by the Anglo-American tradition of limited government, unalienable rights, and the rule of law, all held together by a fundamentally Christian view that humans are naturally imperfectible.

Communists, on the contrary, thought that man's perfectibility had essentially no limits. Trotsky wrote, "Man will become incomparably stronger, wiser, subtler. His body will become more harmonious, his movement more rhythmic, his voice more melodious. . . . The average human type will rise to the heights of Aristotle, Goethe, Marx."[14] Lenin, Trotsky, and Stalin were certain that they were instruments in bringing about this new world order, and to achieve it they put no limit on the terror, repression, executions, and forced starvations that were required to eliminate class enemies and opponents of Communist progress.

Marxism, though couched in terms of economics, was advanced, in many cases, by leaders who had little practical knowledge of economics. Marx's patron, Friedrich Engels, was a successful businessman, but Marx himself was a ne'er-do-well journalist who lived off his mother-in-law and Engels. Neither Lenin, nor Trotsky, nor Stalin—until they came to power—had ever worked for a living. Lenin supported himself with party funds and his mother's handouts. Trotsky, too, received handouts from his family. Stalin's income derived from party funds and criminal enterprise, including extortion and robbery.

Lenin and Trotsky believed that the Russian Revolution would ignite a working-class upheaval across Europe. Stalin, a former seminary student, took the more realistic view that world revolution was not imminent. It had to be consolidated in Russia and then promoted through subversion. But all three were agreed that there should be no restraints on the party's power to advance its cause of human perfectibility. The individual and individual rights were meaningless; what mattered was the party and its totalitarian authority.

The Young Lenin

At Stalin's direction, later Russian hagiographers portrayed Lenin as coming from a peasant family. In reality, he was born in 1870 to a comfortable, well-off family in the provincial town of Simbirsk in southeast Russia along the Volga River. Simbirsk was a small city of unpaved streets and modest homes, with a few pretentious winter residences of provincial gentry. Lenin's childhood home on Moska Street was a substantial house in the smart area of a town of thirty thousand inhabitants. (He was born Vladimir Ilyich Ulyanov and only as a revolutionary took the alias and pseudonym "Lenin," probably derived from the River Lena in Siberia.) His father, Ilya Ulyanov, was a school inspector who rose to the rank of state councilor, which allowed him to wear a uniform and to declare himself minor nobility. Lenin's mother came from a wealthy family (her father had been a physician), and the Ulyanovs spent their summers at her family estate (which included a farm worked by peasants) at Kokushkino, a province located a couple hundred miles away from Simbirsk. Lenin's father was a deeply religious Russian Orthodox Christian. His mother was an indifferent Protestant with possible Jewish ancestry. But they were united in considering themselves enlightened, reform-minded liberals.

Lenin displayed intellectual brilliance even as a young boy. He revealed a certain cruel streak as well. He was a prodigious reader. He was especially influenced by his reading of Harriet Beecher Stowe's *Uncle Tom's Cabin*, which reinforced his family's liberal values. He stood at the top of his class in all subjects. Although described by classmates as cool, distant, self-centered, arrogant, given to bragging, and without many close friends, he could be convivial and charming when he chose to be. It is an irony of history that the headmaster of his high school was Fedor Kerensky, the father of the man he would later oust from power.

Two shocking events seem to have had a profound impact on Lenin. The first was the death of his father in 1886 at the age of fifty-four. His father had suffered a stroke and, before he died, had renounced his faith and may have gone slightly mad. In 1887, his older brother Alexander was executed for plotting to assassinate the czar.

Until this time, Lenin had shown little interest in politics. The brothers had not been particularly close. Alexander, in fact, was repulsed by his younger brother's arrogance and sarcasm. But Lenin had looked up to Alexander as a brilliant student in mathematics and science, and he competed with him for academic recognition. He also followed Alexander's political path.

Alexander had been a student at St. Petersburg University, taking a degree in zoology. At school, he was introduced to the writings of Karl Marx, which were popular among liberal-minded Russian students. Alexander took the next step when he joined a student terrorist cell. He was arrested in March 1887, after police intercepted a letter revealing his involvement in a plot to kill the czar. At his trial, Alexander refused to ask for clemency. He declared in a prepared statement, "Terror is the only form of defense, the only road individuals can take when their discontent becomes extreme."[15] He was sentenced to death. His mother, who attended the trial, pleaded with officials to spare her son's life, but to no avail.

The family remained relatively well-off, but they were now social pariahs, a slight that young Lenin felt deeply and that turned him against both bourgeois society and what he regarded as unreliable, hypocritical liberals. He later wrote, "From the age of [seventeen], I began to despise the liberals. . . . [N]ot a single liberal 'canaille' in Simbirsk came forward with the slightest word of sympathy for my mother after my brother's execution. In order not to run into her, they would cross to the other side of the street."[16] From this day on, his mantra was, "The bourgeois . . . they will always be traitors and cowards."[17]

The family left Simbirsk, moved to its estate in Kokushkino, and lived in a mansion. At the estate, Lenin enjoyed the life of a country squire and immersed himself in his brother's political library. In 1887, thanks to the influence of headmaster Fedor Kerensky and his mother's promise that he would behave himself, Lenin gained admission to the Imperial Kazan University. In his first term, however, he was expelled for participating in a student demonstration. His mother pleaded for Lenin to be readmitted, but her request was denied, as was Lenin's request to study abroad.

His mother finally convinced the authorities to allow Lenin to study law at St. Petersburg University as an external student. He crammed the four-year course into four months, obtaining high marks. He found a low-paying job as an assistant barrister with a liberal-minded lawyer in Samara; he still required financial support from his mother. In the summer of 1893, Lenin and his family moved to St. Petersburg, where Lenin deepened his connections with Russian revolutionaries and helped organize the Union of Struggle for the Emancipation of the Working Class, a study group that intended to teach revolutionary ideas to the workers.

Joining the study group was Yuliy Zederbaum, later known by his underground name Julius Martov. Martov, like Lenin, was an alienated intellectual obsessed with the French Revolution. Martov's heroes were Robespierre and Saint-Just, leaders of the French Terror in the 1790s. He admired Louis Auguste Blanqui, who believed that a dictatorship led by a small band of conspirators operating in the name of the working class was the only way to achieve a socialist revolution. Later he recalled that he held in his youth "this primitive Blanquist conception of revolution as the triumph of abstract principles of popular power valid for all times, resting firmly on the support of the 'poor,' not embarrassed by the means."[18] Martov and Lenin became best friends, until Martov broke with Lenin in 1903 over Lenin's concept of a highly centralized party. While in St. Petersburg, Lenin meet Nedezhda (Nadya) Krupskaya, a young activist and daughter of an army officer from the minor nobility.

They were later married while Lenin was in exile. She became his lifelong comrade, private secretary, and caretaker, so devoted to him that she even tolerated his taking a mistress.

On December 9, 1895, the police turned up at Lenin's apartment and arrested him for subversive activities. He was eventually sentenced to three years of Siberian exile, which only enhanced his credentials among his fellow revolutionaries. His three-year exile ended in late January 1900 on the condition that he not live in any major Russian city or university town. In late July 1900, Lenin left Russia for Western Europe.

Ideological Origins of Leninism

Leninism arose during a time of terrorism. In the twenty-five years before Nicholas II's abdication from the throne in 1917, an estimated twenty thousand Russian officials—high-ranking military officers, ministers, provincial governors, and senior civil servants—were assassinated by terrorists. Although Lenin claimed to be an orthodox Marxist, he was more of a generic revolutionary who employed Marxism to justify terrorism. As literary critic Edmund Wilson pointed out, Lenin was an ideological opportunist. Wilson observed, "The theoretical side of Lenin is, in a sense, not serious; it is the instinct for dealing with the reality of the definite political situation which attains in him the point of genius. He sees and he adopts his tactic with no regard for theoretical positions of others or for his own theoretical positions of the past; then he supports it with Marxist texts."[19]

Lenin drew heavily on Russian revolutionary writers, in particular from famed anarchist Mikhail Bakunin; Bakunin's one-time protégé Sergey Nechayev; Pëtr Tkachëv, an early Russian Marxist theorist who proposed mass terror against priests, the police, and landlords; and Nikolai Chernyshevsky, whose 1863 novel *What Is to Be Done? Tales about New People* was written while he was in prison for disseminating radical ideas. As literature, it has little merit, but as a revolutionary tract it proved immensely popular and influential. Lenin pored over

Chernyshevsky's novel and became such an admirer that he kept the writer's photo in his wallet and took Chernyshevsky's title, *What Is to Be Done?*, for a pamphlet he published in 1902 calling for the creation of a Marxist political party that would be the vanguard of a workers' revolution. Lenin later recalled, "It was only Chernyshevsky who had an overwhelming influence on me. . . . Chernyshevsky's great service was not only that he showed that every right-thinking and really decent person must be a revolutionary, but something more important: what kind of revolutionary, what his principles ought to be, how he should aim for his goal, what means and methods he should employ to realize it."[20]

Chernyshevsky's hero in *What Is to Be Done?* is Rakhmetov, a militant, ascetic revolutionary, who rejects traditional family, marriage, and established religion and calls for a "new people" of scientifically informed revolutionary intellectuals who understand that the old order must be violently overthrown, that "good" and "evil" are relative terms to be weighed on a utilitarian scale of how they advance the cause of revolution, and that by these means the new people can direct society toward a cooperative utopian future. For a generation of Russian university students, *What Is to Be Done?* offered them an anointed place in history. Lenin recalled, "After my brother's execution, knowing that Chernyshevsky's novel was one of his favorite books, I really undertook to read it. . . . It's a thing that supplies energy for a whole lifetime."[21] Lenin drew from Chernyshevsky's character of Rakhmetov a role model for how to change the future.

So did the real-life terrorist and murderer Sergey Nechayev. Nechayev was a young teacher when he began reading revolutionary tracts and associating with student radicals. He soon wrote a tract of his own, *Catechism of a Revolutionist*, published in 1869. The tract declares that the first duty of a revolutionary is to accept that he is a doomed, consecrated person with "no emotions, no attachments, no property, no name. Everything in him is wholly absorbed in the single thought and single passion for revolution." The revolutionary knows from the "very depths of his being," in his thought and deeds, that he has broken ties with "the civilized world with all its laws, moralities, and customs, and with all its generally accepted conventions." The revolutionary "despises and hates the existing social morality in all its manifestations." The revolutionary should have no friendships or attachments, except only to those who have proved themselves, through action, dedicated to the revolution. The purpose of the revolution is a social transformation that destroys the "entire State to the roots and exterminates all the state traditions, institutions, and classes." What follows is to be decided by future generations. He concludes, "Our task is terrible, total, universal, and merciless."[22]

Nechayev arrived in Moscow in 1869, claiming to represent a well-organized, secret revolutionary organization called the Worldwide Revolutionary Union. It did not actually exist, but with that imaginary authority, he was able to form a small terrorist cell. When one of its members, a young worker, questioned the existence of a larger organization, Nechayev accused him of being a police spy. The terrorists lured the young worker to a park where they beat, strangled, and shot him. Nechayev was finally arrested for the murder and sentenced to prison, where he died in 1882. Lenin admired Nechayev's single-minded dedication to the destruction of the old order.

Lenin's thought was simple: though a workers' revolution was inevitable, the revolution needed to be accelerated, imposed, and maintained by a ruthless Marxist political party. That party needed a vicious, conspiratorial leader (a man like him) who saw beyond the people's obvious class enemies—the church, the monarchy, capitalists, and reactionaries—to their real enemies: the liberals and trade union leaders who claimed to sympathize with the revolution but who were weak and could not be trusted.

Creating a Vanguard Party

From the summer of 1900 and for the next seventeen years, Lenin and his wife lived in Western Europe (in Switzerland, Germany, and England). In Switzerland, Lenin met with Russia's leading Marxist theoretician, Georgy Plekhanov, and with his help became a leader of the underground Russian Social Democratic Labor Party, editing the party's newspaper, *Iskra* (*The Spark*), and penning many articles under the pseudonym that would become his name, Lenin. *Iskra* was smuggled into Russia and distributed by underground agents.

In 1902, Lenin published *What Is to Be Done?*, which, in its call for the creation of a centralized vanguard party of hardened revolutionaries, was a direct attack on social democrats in Europe and Russia who thought progress could be achieved through trade unions and liberal or socialist mass political parties that looked to reform capitalism. Lenin declared that capitalism could not be reformed. Capitalism was by nature evil. There could be no compromise, no "middle ground," between reaction and revolution, and true revolutionaries could not accept "this worship of spontaneity" that left revolution in the hands of the workers themselves.[23] No, he insisted: "The history of all countries shows that the working class, exclusively by its own effort, is able to develop only trade union consciousness," but not true revolutionary class consciousness. "Class consciousness," he asserted, "can be brought to the working class *only from without*."[24]

For Lenin, the vanguard party had to work "as theoreticians, as propagandists, as agitators, and as organizers" to rally the masses to revolution.[25] Members of the vanguard party had to be professional revolutionaries, trained in the "art of combating the political police." That meant the party itself had to be conspiratorial in structure.[26] These professional revolutionaries would require "a stable organization of leaders." It had to be a "powerful and strictly secret organization, which" would concentrate "in its hands all the threads of secret activities, an organization which of necessity" would be "centralized." A strong revolutionary organization would avoid "making thoughtless attacks" and understand when and how to strike against the capitalists and reactionaries.[27]

Leninism put the party first and foremost. Its members deserved privileged status. They were the revolutionary elite. They were the architects of a program for the salvation of mankind. They deserved absolute obedience. It was the party that, with its tools of organization and mass terror, could make the "Russian proletariat the vanguard of the international revolutionary proletariat."[28] Marx had thought of Russia as a precapitalist society that was too backward for a socialist revolution. Lenin, however, proclaimed that the vanguard revolutionary party could make Russia the engine of Communist revolution.

Bolsheviks Emerge

In 1902, the Russian Social Democratic Labor Party and its affiliated party organizations had about 3,500 members. Most members were under the age of 24.[29] Not all of them agreed with Lenin's call for a centralized vanguard party. Some believed that a mass party along the lines of the German Social Democratic Party was more likely to advance the cause of socialist progress. Lenin's old comrade, Julius Martov, took umbrage at Lenin's call for a smaller, more disciplined party. Martov asserted, "In our eyes, the labor party is not limited to an organization of professional revolutionaries. It consists of them plus the entire combination of active, leading elements of the proletariat."[30] He declared that Lenin was proposing a dictatorship of one party. Lenin replied, "Yes, there is no other way."[31] In a party vote, Martov's formulation for inclusive party membership won, 28 votes for; 22 against.

This was a major setback for Lenin, but he countered by campaigning for his allies to take control of the Central Committee. The election for Central Committee members was the next day, and Lenin's faction won. He then turned to securing a majority on the editorial board of *Iskra*. He proposed reducing the editorial board from six members to three: Martov, Plekhanov, and him. Plekhanov disagreed with Lenin that Russia was ready for revolution, but he admired Lenin's devotion to revolution and supported him.[32] When Lenin's motion came to the floor, Martov's faction left the convention in protest, leaving the field to Lenin and his allies. Lenin's faction proclaimed themselves the majority party, the Bolsheviks, while Martov's faction became the minority, the Mensheviks. Though Plekhanov had supported Lenin, he later found himself outnumbered on the editorial board of *Iskra*. Plekhanov realized too late that he had taken into his arms a young Cassius—a man driven by power who did not care that Plekhanov thought of him as a theoretically immature revolutionary.

Following the conference, Martov's Mensheviks denounced Lenin as "un-Marxist."[33] Rosa Luxemburg, one of the most influential Marxists in Germany, joined the anti-Leninist critique.[34] Lenin, who loved polemical exchanges, called the Mensheviks and their allies "traitors" and "cunts."[35]

Revolutions: 1905 and 1917

In late January 1905, a Russian Orthodox priest, Father Georgy Gapon, led a peaceful march of petitioners to the square in front of the czar's Winter Palace in St. Petersburg. The city had been effectively shut down by mass labor strikes, and the petitioners were coming to the czar with a list of grievances. Troops guarding the palace ordered the marchers to halt. When they did not, the troops opened fire, killing more than a hundred and leaving another hundred wounded. A Russian general strike was called. A workers' committee, the Soviet, was formed, and Leon Trotsky, a fiery orator, emerged as a leading figure. Across the country revolution spread: workers erected barricades, and there was fighting in the streets. But by the end of 1905, the czar's troops had finally crushed the revolution. In October, as a concession, Czar Nicholas II granted the establishment of a congress, a Duma. The first Duma convened in May 1906. The Duma's powers were limited, but the body gave force to demands for universal, direct, and equal suffrage, and widespread land reform.

At the start of the 1905 Revolution, the Bolsheviks numbered an estimated ten thousand paid members. Criminal enterprises and donations from wealthy supporters kept them well-funded, but the Bolsheviks had little influence within the working class and nearly none among the peasantry. Lenin concluded that the 1905 Revolution had failed because the vanguard party did not take charge. He saw the creation of the Duma as a weak palliative to quiet the workers.

Lenin repudiated the idea of peaceful progress through democratic means. He denounced the Mensheviks' postrevolutionary strategy of building legal trade unions, conducting educational programs and clubs for workers, and supporting reformist legislation in the Duma. He saw the Mensheviks and their social democratic allies in Germany—with their focus on constitutional reform, universal suffrage, welfare provisions, and better working conditions—as betrayers of Marxism. Still, social democratic parties were growing at a staggering pace across Europe. The Bolsheviks, in contrast, while loud and violent, were a tiny and powerless faction. History appeared to have passed Lenin by.

Then came a world war. When Germany declared war on Russia in August 1914, Lenin was living in Austrian-controlled Poland. Threatened with arrest as a Russian agent, he fled to Berne, Switzerland. There he convened a conference of Bolsheviks to declare their opposition to the imperialist war and to denounce socialist leaders who supported their countries' war efforts as betrayers of the working class.

While Lenin preached revolution, Russia's armies were suffering horrible losses, and civil discontent was rising. In March 1917, in the wake of general strikes, with the police unable to control mass demonstrations and protests, and with mutinies in the ranks of the army and the navy, Czar Nicholas II abdicated. With the fall of the Romanov dynasty, which had ruled Russia since 1613, the entire country teetered on the verge of collapse.

Petrograd, as St. Petersburg had been renamed in 1914, became the epicenter of the revolutionary struggle between the Petrograd Soviet and the legislative Duma. The Duma formed the official provisional government, but the Petrograd Soviet declared that the Duma's authority depended entirely on the Soviet's consent.

Lenin was desperate to return to Russia and take charge of the revolution. He knew there could be no lasting alliance of the socialist parties
in Russia, especially as the provisional government insisted on carrying
on the war. The Bolsheviks had to seize power now, and to do so, Lenin
made common cause with the German high command. German officials
understood that Lenin had a "lust for power," but in March 1917, they
helped smuggle Lenin and his entourage into Russia via Finland, with
the understanding that Lenin would remove Russia from the war, allowing German troops to be redirected to the Western Front.[36] Little did the
Germans realize they were unleashing a monster.

Forty-seven years of age, not in the prime of health, Lenin returned
to Russia intent on overthrowing the provisional government led by the
liberal Prince Georgy Lvov, who served as prime minister, and the socialist Alexander Kerensky, who served as minister of justice and was soon
to become minister of war. Kerensky was a brilliant orator, with allies
among the more moderate members of the Petrograd Soviet, and when
Lenin arrived in Petrograd, Kerensky offered to meet with him, hoping
to rid Lenin of "the lens of his own fantasies" and convince him to work
with the Duma.[37] Lenin declined the meeting. He correctly saw Kerensky
as a hero of the moment, but of a moment that would pass.

Unlike Kerensky, Lenin was not a charismatic speaker, but he was
bold and direct and active. He told his followers, "The crisis has matured.
The whole future of the Russian Revolution is at stake. The honor of the
Bolshevik Party is in question. The whole future of the international
worker[s'] revolution for socialism is at stake."[38] He accused the provisional government of being under the control of robber barons and
imperialists and castigated Mensheviks and socialists for cooperating
with it. He called his opponents "blockheads," "bastards," "dirty scum,"
"prostitutes," and "silly old maids." He spoke at mass meetings; he wrote
in party publications; he politicked within the Bolshevik Central Committee. His fierce denunciations of his opponents suggested that he was
a strong man, willing to wield government power in the interests of the

people, unlike the establishment-liberal Prince Lvov and the vain, foundering, liberal-socialist Kerensky.

In the spring of 1917, Lenin issued his April Theses, which demanded that the provisional government withdraw from the European war, nationalize the banks and industry, expropriate all agricultural lands, and abolish the police and the army. He also called for the provisional government to be overthrown and replaced by a "commune state" in which workers would control the factories and peasants the land.

With the war going badly and the Bolsheviks leading violent mass riots against the government, Kerensky, who replaced Prince Lvov as prime minister in July 1917, cracked down on the Bolsheviks, ordered an investigation into their German connections, and issued orders for Lenin's arrest, prompting Lenin to flee to Finland. But Kerensky's reassertion of the provisional government's authority was undercut by an attempted military coup by General Lavr Kornilov in September 1917. The Petrograd Soviet responded to rumors of the impending coup by organizing the Committee for the Struggle Against Counterrevolution. Leon Trotsky was placed in charge of organizing the defense of the city. Arms and munitions were distributed to Bolshevik militia forces. Bolshevik agitators infiltrated the ranks of Kornilov's men, leading to mass desertions, and the coup failed. Kerensky had Kornilov arrested, declared himself commander in chief, and formed a 5-member directory to oversee the provisional government. By this time more than a million and a quarter troops had deserted the army. All discipline in the army had vanished, and Lenin knew that his revolutionary moment had come. He wrote, "The government is wobbling. We must *smash* it! It would be death to wait." The coup came on October 25, 1917 (in the Julian calendar, still in use then in Russia), through an armed insurrection in Petrograd. Subverted by the Bolsheviks, revolutionary sailors and military troops refused to defend the provisional government. Red Guards under the direction of Trotsky seized government buildings and then the Winter Palace. Effectively, the October Revolution was a coup d'état, with the Bolsheviks seizing power. Kerensky fled to Finland and eventually found his way to the United States, where he became a fellow at the Hoover Institute at Stanford University.

The New Regime

Lenin promised the people land, peace, and bread. He did not promise them "bourgeois, parliamentary democracy," because he despised it. In a speech to factory workers, shortly after the Bolshevik takeover, he said, "When 'democrats' rule, you find plain, straightforward theft. We know the true nature of democracies."[39] The Russian writer Maxim Gorky wrote dozens of newspaper columns warning of Lenin's dictatorial intents, noting, "Lenin and his comrades-in-arms think they can commit any crime in the pursuit of power."[40] He was right.

Lenin and Trotsky consolidated Bolshevik power in every way they could. They arrested ministers of the provisional government, took control of the Petrograd Soviet, and plotted the destruction of the soon-to-be-formed Constituent Assembly, a democratically elected legislative body that Lenin could not simply outlaw without facing mass opposition. Elections for the assembly had been organized before the Bolshevik seizure of power in October. Bolsheviks won only a quarter of the seats in the new assembly, but the Bolshevik strategy for subverting the assembly was insidiously clever. Lenin and his followers declared that the "bourgeois" assembly should accede its power to the Soviets ("All Power to the Soviets" was their slogan). When the assembly convened on January 6, 1918 (in the Julian calendar), Bolshevik members shouted down their opponents, and outside the assembly the Bolsheviks had organized mobs and pro-Bolshevik military units. When the assembly adjourned that evening, the Bolsheviks surrounded the building so that there could not be another session, and the assembly was effectively dissolved. In its place, Lenin created an all-powerful Communist Party Central Committee that put every function of government under party control, laying the foundation for a vast totalitarian system.

In December 1917, Lenin authorized the formation of a secret police, the Extraordinary Commission for Combating Counter-revolution and Sabotage ("Cheka," from the letters of the Russian acronym). Cheka was given the powers to arrest, interrogate, and execute enemies of the revolution and cooperated with the Revolutionary Tribunals, which had the authority to hand down sentences without appeal. Lenin appointed as the head of Cheka Felix Dzerzhinsky, a Polish Bolshevik who had spent years in prison for his revolutionary activities. In June 1918, Cheka was directed by the party to shoot prominent counterrevolutionaries; arrest liberals, right-wing socialists, and Mensheviks; and put under surveillance Red Army generals and officers. In 1918, independent newspapers were abolished, putting them all under Communist (as the Bolsheviks now called themselves) control, and Cheka was given responsibility for censoring the press, movies, and telegraph messages. A violent suppression of religion was fundamental to the revolution. Under Lenin's orders, more than thirty bishops and more than a thousand priests were killed; churches, synagogues, and mosques were destroyed; and thousands of religious leaders were sent to the concentration camps that the Communists had started organizing. In April 1921, Lenin approved the building of labor camps in the far north capable of holding ten to twenty thousand inmates.

Fearing a German attack on Petrograd, Lenin ordered the capital to be moved to Moscow in March 1918 (as it was before Czar Peter the Great). In January 1919, the Communist Party established two inner subcommittees, the Political Bureau (Politburo) and the Organizational Bureau (Orgburo). The Political Bureau was composed of six members, including Lenin, Stalin, Trotsky, and Grigory Zinoviev.

As he tightened his hold on power, Lenin faced extraordinary challenges: ending the war with Germany, winning an ongoing civil war, confronting the so-called "national question" (as former parts of imperial Russia broke away), resolving an economic crisis, and addressing widespread food shortages. As typical, Lenin responded by centralizing power, invoking totalitarian authority, and instituting terror. In April

1918, Lenin introduced War Communism. All industry was brought under state control. Food from the provinces was forcibly requisitioned (the state's control of food distribution was treated as a real or potential weapon). Bolshevik political commissars were appointed to army units to ensure the loyalty of commanders and troops and to keep them at a fever pitch of Communist zeal in a campaign of Red Terror against the regime's opponents. Trotsky said, "We must put an end once and for all to the papist-Quaker babble about the sanctity of human life."[41] Nothing was to restrain the Communists from destroying their class or political enemies.

One of those restraints was the war against the Central Powers. Lenin assigned Trotsky to negotiate what became the Treaty of Brest-Litovsk, signed March 3, 1918. Lenin regarded the treaty's terms as a strategic retreat, conceding to the Central Powers everything they demanded, but freeing the Communists to win the civil war within Russia itself.

In April 1918, Lenin issued a booklet, *The Current Tasks of Soviet Power*, arguing for the necessity of Communist Party dictatorship. He wrote, "But dictatorship is a big word. And big words should not be thrown up into the wind. Dictatorship is iron authority, authority that is revolutionarily audacious as well as rapid and merciless in its suppression of both exploiters and hooligans." He asserted that "guilt for the torments of hunger and unemployment is born by all who break labor discipline in any factory, or any farm, or any enterprise." He declared that the dictatorship needed to discover the guilty, arrest them and "punish them pitilessly."[42] In August 1918, Lenin followed up his injunction by telling party members in a letter that an insurrection in five kulak districts should be immediately and brutally suppressed in the interests of the whole revolution. He ordered the hanging of "no fewer than one hundred known kulaks, rich men, bloodsuckers." These hangings, he ordered, should be a public spectacle so that "the people might see, tremble, know, shout: they are strangling to death the blood-sucking kulaks."[43]

The "national question" was especially vexing for the Bolsheviks, who proclaimed themselves an internationalist workers' party. The Bolshevik's only answer was to ruthlessly crush nationalist opposition where they had the power to do so. In February 1918, for example, Communists in Russian Turkestan massacred approximately fourteen thousand Muslims and requisitioned food from the peasants, creating a famine in which an estimated nine hundred thousand people perished.

Religion, nationalism, traditional customs—the Communists considered these hateful remnants of the old regime, obstacles to the creation of a Communist utopia. To eradicate them, the Communists focused on a massive program of indoctrination and propaganda. Schools were given new Communist curricula, with every topic from history to biology rewritten from a Marxist perspective. Teachers and university professors who failed to accept the Communist line were removed. Communist youth organizations were established. Communists assumed control not only of Russia's newspapers, but also of its publishing houses and theatrical companies. In every institution, Communist officials were appointed to ensure that the party line was followed.

Communists especially targeted Christianity, which offered the most comprehensive alternative way of looking at the world. The Communists were committed to the destruction of all traditional religion. They intended to replace the worship of God with the worship of the party. Within months of taking power, the Communist state seized all church and monastic funds; religious presses were banned; priests were forced to register with the state; and all church and seminary property was transferred to the state. These policies were followed by more ruthless measures. Lenin saw in the terrible Russian famine of 1921–22 a perfect opportunity to strike against the church. In a letter to his right-hand man, Vyacheslav Mikhailovich Molotov, Lenin wrote, "It is now and only now, when in the starving regions people are eating human flesh, and hundreds if not thousands of corpses are littering the roads, that we can (and therefore must) carry out the confiscation of church valuables with the most savage and merciless energy; not stopping [short of] crushing any resistance."[44] A massive propaganda campaign was initiated to promote atheism. Within a decade, the Russian Orthodox Church had been consumed by the party, Roman Catholics eliminated, and old Protestant sects repressed.

The Chimera of World Revolution

Lenin's understanding of world affairs often bordered on the preposterous. In March 1919, he foresaw "soon the birth of the World Federal Soviet Republic."[45] Trotsky, who was no less delusional, proposed forming a calvary corps of thirty to forty thousand horsemen to invade India, insisting, "The path to Paris and London lies through the cities of Afghanistan, the Punjab[,] and Bengal."[46] World revolution, Lenin was convinced, was necessary to preserve the new Bolshevik state. He created the Comintern (the Communist International) in March 1919 as an agency for world revolution. He ordered the Finance Commissariat to make available millions of rubles to sponsor the world revolution. Secret funds were funneled into Communist parties across the globe, including in the United States, aided by agents like Armand Hammer.

From Lenin's perspective, the world was aflame with revolution. British workers were on strike; in the United States, the city of Seattle experienced a general strike, and in Boston the police had gone on strike. Lenin viewed Germany as the keystone to the collapse of European capitalism. Following the abdication of Kaiser Wilhelm II, leaders of the German Social Democratic Party formed a coalition government under Friedrich Ebert, a forty-seven-year-old former saddler and trade union leader. Lenin denounced this German Social Democratic government, calling for its overthrow just as he had called for the overthrow of the Kerensky government in Russia. He supported the revolutionary Spartacus League, headed by two of his former opponents, Karl Liebknecht—son of Karl Marx's friend, Wilhelm Liebknecht—and Rosa Luxemburg, a former Polish revolutionary who had migrated to Germany. Lenin sent agents to assist in an insurrection.

Meanwhile, in Bavaria, socialists under journalist Kurt Eisner over-threw the government and declared the People's State of Bavaria. In January 1919, Eisner's inept government was soundly defeated in district elections. Eisner's assassination a short time later by a right-wing nation-alist caused the socialist government to flee. Chaos ensued as workers and soldiers rioted. In April 1919, a coalition of Communists and anar-chists declared a Bavarian Soviet Republic.

Elsewhere, revolutionaries in Hungary announced the formation of a Communist state, and in Moscow, the *Communist International* predicted that within a year "the whole of Europe" would be Communist.[47]

Yet things were going less well for the Communists than it seemed, especially in Germany.

On January 6, 1919, the Spartacus League had attempted to over-throw the socialist government in Berlin. Rosa Luxemburg worried that Germany was not yet ready for a revolution, but Russian agents pressed the Spartacus League to act. Luxemburg was right. German defense minister Gustav Nolte mobilized anti-Communist military units, the Freikorps, and crushed the revolution. Liebknecht and Luxemburg were captured and summarily executed.

The Bavarian Soviet Republic, established after the assassination of Kurt Eisner, proved short-lived, lasting just six days. It was a farce from its conception. Headed by a young, radical playwright, Ernst Toller, the government proved utterly inept. Cabinet posts were given to volunteers. The Roman Catholic cathedral in Munich was seized and rededicated to the "Goddess Reason." The new head of foreign affairs, Franz Lipp, wrote in reply to a congratulatory letter from Lenin that the revolution was going well, except that the previous government had stolen the lava-tory key and he had no access to the toilet. Next, Lipp declared war on Switzerland, declaring, "[I am] certain that we will be victorious. Fur-thermore, I will ask the Pope, with whom I am well acquainted, to grant his blessing for this victory."[48] At this point, Toller checked out Lipp's credentials, only to discover that his foreign minister had recently been released from an insane asylum.

Berlin mobilized the Freikorps, which had grown to more than four hundred thousand men, to move against the Bavarian Communists. Toller's attempt to mobilize his own so-called Red Army proved disastrous. Officers joining this Red Army were offered free liquor and prostitutes, and soldiers were allowed to rob banks to supplement their wages, but the ill-disciplined, corrupt Communist army was routed by the well-trained, well-armed, well-disciplined Freikorps. Shortly before Freikorps troops entered Munich, the revolutionary government began executing prisoners. Twenty of Munich's leading citizens were executed before Toller stopped the executions. This provided an excuse, if any was needed, for the retribution that followed when the Freikorps troops entered Munich. Revolutionaries were hunted down and shot.

Béla Kun's Hungarian Soviet Republic did not last long either. After seizing power in late March, Kun undertook a campaign of terror directed largely at the peasants. Faced with an invasion by Romania, Kun pleaded with Moscow officials, with whom he kept in close contact, to invade Romania, but the Soviet Red Army was bogged down in the Russian civil war. On August 1, 1919, Kun fled to the Soviet Union. He became an important figure in the Comintern, but in Stalin's Great Purge in the late 1930s he was arrested as a foreign agent and sent to a gulag camp, where he died.

Lenin's hopes for spreading the October Revolution, however, remained undiminished. He found another opportunity when Poland's commander in chief, Josef Pilsudski, joined forces with the Ukrainian army to fight the Russians, capturing Kiev in May 1920. The Red Army regrouped to drive Pilsudski's Polish-Ukrainian force back to Warsaw. Lenin ordered the capture of Warsaw, which he saw as the beginning of a campaign to Sovietize all of Europe, predicting pro-Communist worker uprisings among Poles, Germans, and Italians. Lenin ignored Stalin's warning that Polish nationalism was deep and would resist a Russian invasion.

As the Second Comintern Congress convened in Petrograd, a huge map of Europe was hung so that delegates could follow the advance of the Red Army from Ukraine into Poland from red flags pinned on the map. Lenin strutted up and down the platform, assuring the delegates that the world revolution had begun. Meanwhile, Lenin directed Trotsky to work with Cheka to hang all kulaks, priests, and landed gentry along the path of the Red Army advance. He offered a hundred thousand rubles for "each one of them that [was] hanged."[49]

The Poles inflicted a crushing defeat to the Red Army at the Battle of Warsaw in August 1920, and the invasion of Poland became a Communist disaster. In March 1921, the Polish-Soviet War ended with Lenin's having no choice but to agree to a negotiated settlement recognizing the independence of Poland.

Lenin's Last Years

Faced with massive resistance from the peasantry and growing discontent from workers, Lenin had to retreat not only in foreign affairs but in domestic ones. The government was broke, and Soviet money was nearly worthless, because of the government's irresponsible printing of money and the resulting astronomical inflation. In 1921, Lenin announced the New Economic Policy (NEP), allowing peasants to sell food in village markets, a dramatic step back from the failed Soviet attempt at collectivizing agriculture. In 1921–22 an estimated twenty-five million people were starving in Russia, even as the party sent vast sums of money, gold, and silver to foreign Communist parties to fund a world revolution. Lenin's embrace of market socialism was a tactical shift he believed necessary to maintain power. But while he liberalized the economy, he also called for increasing executions and deportations of the regime's enemies. In 1922, as the Russian penal code was being revised, Lenin wrote, "The law should not abolish terror; to promise that would be self-delusion or deception; it should be substantiated and legalized in principle, clearly, without evasion or embellishment."[50]

Lenin faced opposition within his own party over the New Economic Plan. The so-called Left Opposition within the party denounced the policy as a retreat from the advancement of socialism. But Lenin framed the argument within Marxist terms and brooked no opposition. Lenin had spent a lifetime in factional combat, and he was adroit at political maneuvering, but there was no denying that the Communist movement seemed to be devolving. The Workers' Opposition, led by Trotsky, called for harsher measures, including the conscription of industrial workers. Sailors at the naval garrison at Kronstadt, thirty-five miles from Petrograd, who had been among the Bolsheviks greatest supporters in 1917, revolted. They demanded "all power to the soviets and not to the parties." They called for free elections, restoration of a free press, and an end to terror and one-party rule.

Faced with a mutiny that threatened the regime, Communist factions united, and Lenin ordered Trotsky to organize an assault on Kronstadt. Red Army troops were rushed from Moscow to suppress the mutiny. They did so with fierce brutality.

Lenin's health had never been good. He had long suffered from headaches and insomnia. These symptoms worsened after a failed assassination attempt in August 1918, which left bullets in his neck and chest, and after what might have been several minor heart attacks. He grew increasingly irritable, moody, and abusive. He insisted that his office be made soundproof. In mid-1921, the party ordered Lenin to take a rest.

Extraction of the bullet from his neck failed to restore his health. In the spring of 1922, scarcely a month after the operation, Lenin suffered his first stroke. His right side was paralyzed. His speech was impaired. German doctors diagnosed a severe disorder of the blood vessels in the brain, perhaps the result of syphilitic inflation of the artery linings.

In December 1922, Lenin suffered another major stroke. He told his doctors that he wished to dictate a letter for the next party conference. From December 23 through December 29, 1922, Lenin dictated, in 4-minute spans, what became known as his "Last Will and Testament." Some scholars maintain that Lenin in his last days intended to disavow his regime's dictatorship, class war, and terror, but there is little evidence for this view. He lived and died a Leninist.

Lenin knew the end was nearing. He took careful estimation of the character and qualities of his potential successors. In March 1922, Lenin had created a new post, general secretary, expressly for Stalin. Stalin had then used this position to expand his power within the party, at Lenin's expense, and Lenin now regarded him as an enemy. Lenin declared, "Comrade Stalin, having become General Secretary, has concentrated unlimited power in his hands, and I am not convinced that he will always manage to use this power with sufficient care." He then turned to his evaluation of Trotsky, a sometime foe. He described Trotsky as a man of "outstanding talents"—only to add, "To be sure, he is personally the most capable person in the present Central Committee, but he also over-brims with self-confidence and with excessive preoccupation with the purely administrative side of things."[51] When Lenin finished dictating the letter, he ordered six copies made. The letters were to be sealed, and then opened only upon his death. In January 1923, an addendum was attached, declaring, "Stalin is too crude, and this defect which is entirely acceptable in our milieu and in relationship among us as [C]ommunists, becomes unacceptable in the position of General Secretary." In March 1923, Lenin experienced a third stroke that left him mute. On January 23, 1924, Lenin fell into a coma and died.

Six days after his death, Lenin's funeral was held. Stalin made the funeral arrangements and misled Trotsky about the date to ensure his absence. On orders from the Politburo, Lenin's corpse was kept on ice until it was embalmed for public display. The cult of Lenin was essential to the regime; he was to be venerated as a Communist saint.

Trotsky, anxious to avoid party division, joined with Stalin in suppressing Lenin's "Last Will and Testament." Expelled from the Party Central Committee in 1927, ordered into exile, and hounded by Stalin's agents, Trotsky fled from one country to another, finally ending up in Mexico, where a Soviet assassin murdered him in 1940. Trotsky had thought of himself as Lenin's true heir, calling for "permanent revolution" and world socialism. He had dismissed Stalin's slogan of "socialism in one state" as the recourse of bureaucratic mediocrity. But Stalin proved far more adroit than Trotsky at removing his enemies. Of the 139 senior Communist Party members attending the party congress in 1934, only 31 would die natural deaths. In 1937–38, Stalin purged many of the old Bolsheviks, forcing them into show trials that extracted "confessions" of being foreign agents or counterrevolutionaries. They were then sentenced to execution or imprisonment in the gulag camps.

Stalin used the mechanisms created by Lenin to consolidate his power. Lenin had taught that the party was essential to the advent of a perfect society on earth.[52] The regime that Lenin and Stalin created lasted until 1991, when the Soviet Union finally collapsed after decades of oppression, terror, and suffering and the forced deaths of millions.

CHAPTER 2

Mao:
Revolutionary Destroyer

Mao Zedong came to power in China in 1949 and ruled until his death in 1976. In the 27 years of his leadership, he held absolute power, governing over a quarter of the world's population. His tenure was catastrophic. His leadership led to the death of at least 42.5 million of his own people from famine and violence. Some estimates place the number of deaths higher. Without official Chinese figures, we cannot know the exact number. The best estimates attribute 35 to 45 million to the famine during the Great Leap Forward policy (1959–1962), 2 to 3 million during the Cultural Revolution (1966–1976), and another 1 million during other campaigns. Given such carnage, "Mao the Monster" remains an apt moniker for this revolutionary whose policies caused the deaths of those very people he promised to liberate.

Independent scholar Ian Johnson observes that Mao did not "order people to their deaths in the same way that Hitler did," but that Mao's obstinate pursuit of the Great Leap Forward and the Cultural Revolution nonetheless "sealed the fate of millions."[1] The Great Leap Forward was a great leap forward to the grave for millions of Chinese, and his Great Proletarian Cultural Revolution is more aptly described as "cultural destruction." Mao's apologists in China and the American academy claim that the famine was a result of natural causes, not a consequence of his policies. Indeed, one academic scholar even claims that Mao's agricultural policies paid off by the 1970s and set the stage for the Chinese economic miracle today. The Cultural Revolution, this scholar argues, was an attempt to "secure the accountability of the Party bureaucracy" to establish more democratic institutions.[2] Mao showed profound indifference to reports of mass starvation, which led villagers to cannibalism, infanticide, and eating tree bark. In his drive to make China into a militarized superpower, Mao accepted, indeed encouraged, a massive number of deaths. In the Cultural Revolution launched at his call in 1966, Chinese people suffered as fanatic young Red Guards, many of them adolescents, beat, imprisoned, and killed hundreds of thousands of people denounced as "rightist." Teachers, musicians, writers, artists, and intellectuals were the targets. Party elites were sent to prison, tortured, or sent to villages and factories to work. All went through "struggle" sessions in which they were forced by mobs to make public confessions of crimes they never committed.

From his earliest revolutionary days leading a Red Army in the mountains, Mao crafted a careful image of himself as a humble peasant seeking to create a "New China." Western journalists presented this image to the world uncritically. American presidents, including Franklin Roosevelt and Harry Truman, also bought in to Mao's propaganda—perhaps seeing in him a man who shared some of their political ambitions for China. The portrait of Mao as a reformer would stick, but it could not be further from the truth. Under his regime a totalitarian state was erected that would terrorize its own populace. In the final tabulation, the "reformer" Mao killed more people than Lenin, Stalin, or Hitler in their brutal regimes.

Mao ruled by terror and viewed the humane treatment of people as an obstacle to the creation of a new society. He welcomed world apocalypse if it could create the New Socialist Man, speaking openly with his comrades about cleansing the world through nuclear holocaust. He declared that China could afford losing millions of people.

Unlike Lenin or Stalin, Mao was not well-versed in Marxist theory, even though he shared in the Communist faith that destruction was necessary to bring about a new world. His contributions to Marxist-Leninist theory consisted in simplistic aphorisms found in his "Little Red Book," which were repeated by his followers in China and worldwide. Given wide distribution in the West in the 1960s, Mao's "Little Red Book" became a kind of bible in some revolutionary circles. In the United States, Black Panther leaders sold the book and loved the quotation "Political power grows out of the barrel of a gun." Soon young American leftists were wearing buttons with the quotation. In France, intellectuals such as Jean-Paul Sartre, best known for his existentialist philosophy, and his wife, feminist author Simone de Beauvoir, declared themselves Maoist in the 1960s.

Mao shared with Lenin a narcissistic personality with a millenarian vision. As a young man, he declared himself a revolutionary, which eventually brought him to the then small Chinese Communist Party (CCP), later becoming leader of the Red Army. His outlook was shaped earlier however. In papers written for his teacher in 1917, as a twenty-four-year-old returning student, he revealed the moral vision that shaped his later revolutionary outlook. In an extensive commentary on an assigned book, by Fredrich Paulsen, *A System of Ethics*, recently translated into Chinese, Mao wrote, "I do not agree with the view that to be moral, the motive of one's action . . . has to be benefitting others. Morality does not have to be defined in relation to others." He posited that all morality must "be purely calculation for oneself, and absolutely not for obeying external ethical codes, or for so-called responsibility."[3] His callousness ran deeply in his soul even as a young man. Mao's declarations might be dismissed as the hubris of a young man, but later actions show that absolute selfishness lay at the heart of Mao's lifelong outlook. His sincerity as a revolutionary should not be doubted, though revolution for Mao was also a means of self-advancement and self-preservation. He envisioned himself as a new emperor.

The Young Mao

Mao was born in a sprawling courtyard house on December 26, 1893, to a relatively better-off peasant family in Shaoshan, a valley of six hundred people, in the province of Hunan. Mao's mother was born to the Wen clan and did not have a name, like many peasants. She was called the Seventh Sister Wen. She was a devout Buddhist who tried to inculcate her oldest son Mao with these religious principles. She hoped that Mao might become a Buddhist priest, reminiscent of Stalin's mother's hoping her son would join the Orthodox priesthood. His father Yichang was a hard, thrifty man and one of the wealthier peasants in the valley. It did not take much wealth to be wealthy in Chinese peasant society: he owned three acres and hired other peasants to work his rice fields. Later two more brothers were born, one of whom would grow up to become a close political ally of Mao.

Mao began his modest education at the age of eight. He showed remarkable ability and an excellent memory. But at a young age, he also revealed a strong stubborn streak. He was asked to leave three schools before he was ten because he was headstrong and disobedient. His anger was apparent. He later recalled that he hated the Confucian principles taught at the school. He would tell a friend, "There was a Confucian temple in the village, and I wanted nothing more than to burn it to the ground. At first it was because I hated the teacher, and because my father quoted Confucius against me."[4] At the age of fourteen, Mao entered an arranged marriage. When his young wife died two years later, the sixteen-year-old Mao insisted on leaving home to attend a modern school in the trading port of Changsha, a city just fifteen miles down the road, but a world away from rural Shaoshan.

He arrived in Changsha in the spring of 1911, shortly before the collapse of the Qing dynasty and the Republican Revolution led by Sun

Yat-sen. Caught up in the revolution, Mao briefly joined the army in 1911, and he remained on garrison duty during his six months in the army. "Thinking the revolution was over, I resigned from the army and decided to return to my books."[5]

The Qing dynasty's collapse caused China to spin into chaos. While Sun Yat-sen became provisional president of the new Chinese republic on January 1, 1912, the revolution that had brought him to power remained anarchic. Sun was soon ousted by a warlord, and his vision for a new China remained vague. In 1924, a year before his death, Sun articulated his vision of government in *The Three Principles of the People*, in which he declared that the binding principles of the revolution should be Liberty, Equality, and Universal Love. Yet he declared that members of his revolutionary Nationalist Party, the Kuomintang (KMT), should be united spiritually. "In order that all members may be united spiritually, the first thing is to sacrifice freedom."[6] Mao echoed these sentiments when he came to power twenty-five years later.

Mao attended a teacher-training college that offered cheap board and lodging. This school, like others of its sort, was a result of efforts by the Qing dynasty to undertake educational reform. These new schools rejected the goal of turning out Confucian scholar-officials, aiming instead to educate a cadre of modernizers well-read in Western thought. They became hot beds of revolution and graduated scores of revolutionaries. While at his school, Mao developed a strange mix of hero-worship and Social Darwinism. Devouring Western books translated into Chinese, he was especially attracted to stories about Alexander the Great and Napoleon. He was introduced to Social Darwinist theory. He was especially attracted to a Chinese translation of *Principles of Western Civilization*, authored by Benjamin Kidd, a British Social Darwinist. Kidd's central argument, taken to heart by Mao, is that progress comes through struggle, often at the sacrifice of the individual.[7]

Social Darwinism—the application of Charles Darwin's biological notion of "survival of the fittest" to human society—had a lasting influence on Chinese intellectuals in this period, as Western books were translated into Chinese. More significant, however, was the influence of Marxist thought. Following the First Sino-Japanese War in 1895, a major turning point in the fall of the Qing dynasty, Marxist thought came to dominate Chinese intellectual life. Marx, Engels, and Lenin were all translated into Chinese to great acclaim. Their works became an important part of the training the newly Westernized youth received.

Mao read Karl Marx's *Communist Manifesto* for the first time in school. Shortly thereafter, he declared himself a socialist. Mao was not a theorist, but a young revolutionary adjusting theory to reality. While being introduced to Social Darwinism, Marxism, and the role of heroes in shaping history, Mao's inner resentments grew. He was derided by other students in the school as "the dirty little peasant from [Shaoshan]." The experience hardened Mao's personality and sharpened his world outlook, and through his studies nurtured the resentments he had formed at an early age. He excelled in classwork, standing above his classmates in intellectual ability. His inner arrogance abounded. He saw himself above the others, a man of destiny.

After graduation in 1918, Mao found it difficult to get a job. Some of Mao's friends decided to go to France as students, but Mao did not want to join them. He was bad at languages and spoke only his local dialect—and later when he learned "common" Chinese speech, he spoke with a heavy provincial accent. Instead, he borrowed money and set off for Beijing, the nation's capital.

Life was hard in Beijing. Mao lived with seven friends splitting three rooms. Four of them slept in the same bed. They shared two coats and had to take turns going out. He found work at the university library delivering newspapers to professors and students. They treated him as a peasant, even though Mao was anxious to engage with them about politics. Mao recalled, "Most of them [library readers] did not treat me like a human being." Here Mao developed his profound hatred of intellectuals that he would carry throughout his life.

In Beijing, Mao was influenced by Chen Duxiu, dean of the faculty of Chinese letters at Peking University and editor of the radical magazine

New Youth. Mao was an avid reader of the magazine from the publication of its first issue, struck by an editorial in which Chen declared, "The task of the new generation is to fight Confucianism to the death, all the old traditions of virtue and ritual, all the old philosophies and all the old political subtleties."[8] Chen Duxiu emerged as one of the founding members of the Chinese Communist Party. Many years later, when the Communist Party's alliance with the Kuomintang had failed, Chen was expelled from the party. Relations between Mao and his former mentor Chen had already deteriorated by then, so much so that Mao voted for his expulsion.

In 1919, though, Mao considered himself a student of Chen. Although inspired, Mao was financially broke. He returned to Changsha in April 1919 to take a job as a part-time history teacher in a primary school. He joined a small group editing the *Xiang River Review*, a shoestring operation that was ultimately closed by a local warlord. He wrote most of the weekly issues himself. On July 14, 1919, Mao issued a manifesto through the magazine that summarized his political views, declaring that for the time being a "revolution of bombs or a revolution of blood" was not called for. But a revolution in ideas was needed as China faced the new age. "Those who ride with the current will live; those who go against it will die,"[9] Mao exclaimed.

Through these articles, Mao emerged as a leading radical voice in Hunan politics. His voice resounded through the region, and he even led an effort among students and teachers to oust the warlord governing the Hunan province. In 1920, he joined a delegation to Beijing in the effort. On his way back from the capital, he traveled to Shanghai, where he met with Chen Duxiu, who was organizing the new Chinese Communist Party with the active involvement of Soviet agents. Mao was not a founding member of the party, but he was recruited early into party ranks. Chen offered Mao the responsibility to return to Changsha to open a bookstore called the "Cultural Book Society," selling Communist literature—an endeavor that proved remarkably successful. Mao became a contributor to Chen's *New Youth* and helped organize the Hunanese Socialist Youth

League, a Communist front organization. By the age of twenty-seven, Mao was a leading Communist in the province.

He began living with a professor's daughter, Yang Kaihui, eight years Mao's younger. She was European-educated and "liberated." They refused to marry at first. Mao had denounced marriage as little more than a "rape league."[10] Mao, though, was philandering with other women—only to be discovered by Yang. She forgave him, and in 1920 they married, having three children together before Mao eventually left her. She was later executed by the Nationalists.

Nationalism and Communism in China

By 1921, the Comintern in Moscow had decided on making an all-out effort to build the Communist Party in China. The party's first congress opened in Shanghai in July 1923 and was attended by just thirteen people, consisting of mostly journalists, students, and teachers. The Soviet delegate to the congress, Pavel Mif, reported that the congregation was composed of "anarchists, biblical socialists, legal Marxists, and camp-followers."[11] Despite these inauspicious beginnings, Moscow poured money into the new party, eager to grow the movement by flushing the party with resources.

Mao was one of the thirteen in attendance, though he said little at the meeting. He was eventually put on the party payroll in Hunan, leaving his job to devote himself to party work. After ousting a potential rival, he became the Communist boss of Hunan.

In those early days, the Chinese Communist Party remained totally reliant on the Soviet Union. In 1922, 94 percent of party funding came from Russia. Despite their investment in the upstart group, Moscow's party line dictated that China was not ready to lead a Communist revolution. Therefore, the CCP was directed to make an alliance with Sun Yat-sen's Kuomintang party, which also received backing from Moscow in the form of money and advisors. Though some of the Communist Party members were reticent to ally themselves with Sun, Mao followed his directions and ordered party followers in Hunan to enter the Nationalist Party. He would soon become an enthusiastic Kuomintang member, attending their party meetings more often than those of the Communists.

By the time Sun Yat-sen died in 1925, Mao had ingratiated himself with high Kuomintang leadership. The alliance between the Nationalists (Kuomintang) and the Communists appeared tight. Russian agents flooded into Canton, where the Kuomintang was headquartered and held political power. Mao arrived in Canton in September 1925, securing a top position in the Nationalist Party as head of the propaganda department and editor of the Nationalists' new journal, *Politics Weekly*. He sat on the 5-man committee checking credentials for delegates to the Nationalists' second congress. At the same time, he was a member of the Central Committee of the Chinese Communist Party. He walked a political tightrope.

Mao declared himself a Communist, but his activity on behalf of the Nationalist Party showed he was an opportunist advancing himself. He combined his support for revolution and allegiance to the party with a strong instinct for self-advancement. Whatever Mao did, he placed his own career prospects first. He was hardly well versed in Marxist theory, though he would soon show a willingness to use violence that placed him firmly in the Leninist camp.

When a peasant revolution broke out in his home province of Hunan, Mao returned to give guidance to the uprising. The peasant revolt predictably led to the torture and killing of landowners. By the time Mao arrived, the peasant leaders were eager to quell the violence. But Mao had different plans. When Mao was informed that landowners were being beaten to death and being hanged, he replied, "One or two beaten to death, no big deal." He accepted atrocities as necessary to revolution. When locals voiced reservations about the atrocities, Mao would reply that a revolution was not like a dinner party. More violence was necessary, and so he told peasants that stubborn landowners should have their "ankle tendons" cut and their ears chopped off.[12]

The Communists within the Kuomintang operated as a parasite in the larger body, and they made huge gains as the Kuomintang grew. By 1927 Communist Party membership reached fifty-eight thousand members. The newfound popularity of the Communist Party put a strain on relations between the Communists and the Kuomintang. The alliance was bound to deteriorate. In 1927, Kuomintang general Chiang Kai-shek ordered the complete extermination of Communists and socialists in Shanghai, a Communist stronghold. Thousands were slaughtered. At this point, Chiang announced the formation of a new government in Nanjing under the Nationalist Party. Arrest warrants were issued for all Russian agents and CCP leaders, including Mao. As a result, the Chinese Communist Party was driven underground.

Moscow ordered their Chinese comrades to respond by undertaking military action. Obeying orders, Mao launched a military attack in Hunan. This uprising, later known as the Autumn Uprising, gave birth to a legend of Mao's military prowess, thanks in no small part to American journalist Edgar Snow's *Red Star Over China* (1938). In reality, the revolt was a military disaster for Mao and the Communists. In hiding, Mao ordered his troops to abort their attack. On hearing the news of the retreat, the secretary of the Soviet consulate called it "despicable treachery and cowardice" and "a joke of an uprising."[13] When word reached party leadership in Shanghai, Mao was expelled from the party. He withdrew his troops to the Jinggang mountains.

Mao, the Long March

By the time Mao's army reached the Jinggang mountains he had only about six hundred troops. While his troops were poorly fed and clothed, Mao dressed in the garb of a general, fashioning a purple cloak for himself with a collar of rabbit fur—much like the one worn by Chiang Kai-shek. During his fifteen months in the mountains, Mao lived in a two-story mansion. He acquired a personal staff, complete with a cook, horse groom, errand boys, and secretaries. He spent much time reading books looted from rich landlords' homes. At the same time, Mao amassed a personal fortune of looted gold, silver, and jewels, shipped to him by the army in crates marked "To be delivered to Mao [Zedong] personally."[14]

In the spring of 1928, Mao gained more troops when he was joined by Zhu De, a Moscow-trained military officer who had remained in Hunan. When a peasant uprising in Hunan forced him to withdraw, Zhu brought his army to Mao in his mountain base. Now boasting a massive army behind him, Mao was welcomed back into the Chinese Communist Party. He immediately went on the offensive, capturing the provincial capital of Ruijin. When he faced opposition from local Communists, Mao ordered their executions as "counter-revolutionaries." When peasants revolted against Mao's merciless policies, he ordered more arrests and executions. At the same time, Mao continued his purge of party members in the regions he controlled. Mao wrote Shanghai party headquarters that thousands of counterrevolutionaries had been discovered in the Red Army. When party leaders raised questions about confessions made under torture, Mao responded rhetorically: "How could loyal revolutionaries possibly make confessions to incriminate other comrades?"[15] By the time the purge was over an estimated ten thousand soldiers had been killed, a quarter of the Red Army. This was the first large-scale purge in a Communist Party, occurring well before Stalin's better-known Great Purge.

Later, Mao told his biographer Edgar Snow that he improved the health and education of the peasants. In reality, Mao's reign in Jiangxi was one of Red Terror. Peasants were forced to pay a heavy grain tax, while young males were forcibly conscripted into the army. A missionary hospital that had once been used to treat ordinary peasants was reserved only for the Communist elite. Primary schools were reduced to Lenin schools where students were taught only enough to read party propaganda. Secondary schools were mostly closed.

As leader, Mao developed new techniques for propaganda. He gave long lectures to party cadres, declaring, "the Party's General Line is correct and unquestionable." He denigrated intellectuals, observing that "a great many so-called intellectuals [were] actually exceedingly unlearned" and understanding that "the knowledge of the workers and peasants [was] sometimes greater than theirs."[16] That he was the leader who articulated the knowledge of the workers and peasants was assumed. The cult of Mao was beginning to be formed in the mountains.

In the meantime, Chiang Kai-shek had consolidated power in the rest of China. He launched an "annihilation expedition," his fourth, against Mao. Chiang mobilized a half-million troops for the campaign. Then, in January 1932, Japan attacked Shanghai. The League of Nations brokered a cease-fire with Japan, but Chiang was faced with Mao's revolutionary forces in the mountains and Japanese imperialism on another front. By the spring of 1933, Chiang's annihilation expedition had been defeated at the hands of the Red Army's commander, Bo Gu. Mao later took credit for the victory, but in fact he had been pushed aside as military commander by Shanghai Communist leadership in favor of the experienced military commander Bo. In September 1933, Chiang mobilized another 500,000-man expeditionary force after securing a truce with Japan. Using a different military strategy and better-trained troops, Chiang's forces successfully put an end to Mao's brutal regime. Mao had no other choice but to retreat further or face total annihilation. Before the Red Army departed, Mao ordered another massive purge in his ranks. Those considered "unreliable" were hacked to death with knives. The victims totaled in the thousands.

Mao's retreat, the "Long March," took the Red Army on a westward then northward trek of six thousand miles to Shaanxi. During the Long March, elite party members were carried on litters by porters press-ganged into service. Mao's treasure was carried by porters using shoulder poles. Decades later after the march, Mao recalled, "I was lying in a litter. So what did I do? I read. I read a lot." He noted that "when climbing mountains, the litter-bearers could only move forward on their knees, and the skin and flesh on their knees were rubbed raw before they got to the top. Each mountain climbed left a trail of sweat and blood."[17] Thousands died on the march from exhaustion, cold, starvation, and attacks by local warlords and tribesmen. Mao began the Long March with eighty thousand troops; when he arrived at Shaanxi fifteen months later, he only mustered between seven and eight thousand. At this point, the Communists and Mao appeared to have been defeated by the Nationalists.

Shaanxi, in northwest China, was in the Yellow Earth Plateau formed by the Yellow River. It was the cradle of Chinese civilization. Here was to be Mao's home for the next decade. By 1935, he and his supporters had assumed complete control of the Central Committee, although Moscow did not at first fully acknowledge Mao's position. Relations between Moscow and Mao had been uneasy for a long time. Mao had been expelled from the Central Committee in late 1923 or early 1924, a second time in 1927, and a third time in 1934, often for disobedience involving his harsh land reform policies and his failure to achieve military goals. Furthermore, many Chinese Communists raised questions about his understanding of Marxist theory. Few saw Mao as a precocious Marxist or Leninist. Ideology for Mao was a tool for his advancement to power. He dismissed Soviet advisors as fools and blunderers and the chairman of the CCP aligned with them, his old teacher Chen Duxiu, as an "unconscious traitor."[18] He played a key role in the expulsion of Chen Duxiu following the disastrous collapse of the Kuomintang-Communist alliance.

In July 1937 Japan launched a full-scale invasion of China. The Japanese invasion saved Mao. In the ten years before the Japanese invasion, Chiang's Nationalists had essentially reunified the country. Mao had been isolated in a far-away province. With the invasion, Chiang was forced to direct resources to the war against the Japanese. Any possibility of modernization under Chiang came to a halt with the war. It was during the Second World War, declared historian Lucien Bianco, that "the Kuomintang *lost* [original italics] the civil war."[19] With the outbreak of war with Japan, the Chinese Communist Party transformed itself into a party of patriotic nationalism. Before the invasion, Stalin had ordered Mao to form an alliance with Chiang. Mao was instructed by Moscow to cooperate in the war against fascism. This, in effect, entailed recognizing the legitimacy of the Nationalist government. Promised Soviet military aide, Chiang agreed to assign territory to the Red Army, but neither Chiang nor Mao accepted the alliance. Mao continued to preserve his forces, although some Red units organized guerrilla action in the northern provinces.

The Myth of Mao

In the late 1930s, Mao undertook a campaign to create an image of himself as a benign revolutionary. Public opinion in China, as well as the West, remained deeply anti-Communist. Mao asked the Shanghai Communist underground to find a foreign journalist who might be sympathetic to his cause. They found such a person in Edgar Snow, an American journalist who had come to China in 1931. He had developed a close friendship with journalist Agnes Smedley, a suspected Comintern spy and a known lover of Soviet spymaster Richard Sorge. Smedley vouched for Snow's leftist sympathies.

Before Snow's arrival, Mao instructed his comrades to show Snow "security, secrecy, warmth, and red carpet."[20] Snow had to submit his interview questions beforehand and accepted Mao's narrative at face value. Real facts fell on the sympathetic journalist like snowflakes: they just melted away. Mao and his comrades did a real job on the journalist. Over the course of the next three months, Snow spent hours interviewing Mao and his well-rehearsed comrades. Mao shared for the first time with the press his early boyhood experiences, his early activism, and his claim to heroic military exploits, including the Long March. He presented the Chinese Communist People's Party as an agrarian reform movement intent on bringing education and betterment to the peasants while downplaying his Moscow connections. He insisted that comrades read everything Snow wrote, amending and rewriting parts of the book. Snow's *Red Star Over China* appeared in English in 1937–38. It remained a major source of information on Mao for years to come.

Red Star Over China cemented Mao's image in the international press as an agrarian reformer. Dozens of other reporters flocked to meet Mao, many of whom shared left-wing sympathies, including Agnes Smedley, Anna Louis Strong, James Bertram, and T. A. Bisson.[21] Their sympathetic portrayals of Mao encouraged American and European policymakers to see him as a different kind of Communist. For example, General Patrick Hurley, appointed by Franklin Roosevelt as a special envoy to China in 1944, returned to the United States to tell the National Press Club in Washington in November 1945, "The only difference between Chinese Communists and Oklahoma Republicans is that the Oklahoma Republicans are not armed."[22]

Behind the image of the simple peasant rebel, Mao lived in comfort. He kept large houses, including secret retreats in the hills and a mansion in Shaanxi. During this time, he took another wife—now his fourth—a twenty-six-year-old actress, Jiang Qing. She was a devout Communist involved in the Shanghai underground prior to coming to Mao. The daughter of a concubine, Jiang Qing was a tough, beautiful woman with a hard past. She brought with her a notorious reputation, which appears to have rubbed many comrades the wrong way. In Shanghai she had lived with at least four separate men, her stormy relations with her lovers often becoming tabloid news. Many did not like Mao's flagrant affair with this actress of notorious reputation. After the marriage, Jiang Qing became known as Madame Mao. She would later play a major role in the Cultural Revolution.

Mao Comes to Power

The brunt of repelling the Japanese invasion fell on Chiang's forces. By late summer 1937, Japanese troops had taken Beijing, Shanghai, and Nanjing, the capital of the Chinese Republic. Chiang was forced to move his capital to Chongqing (Chungking) in the interior and later further inland to Wuhan. What had started with the Japanese occupation of Manchuria had become a full-scale war of conquest. In trying to defend Shanghai, Nationalist troops lost 73 of their 180 divisions—over 400,000 men. Japanese casualties were estimated at about 40,000 losses. The Japanese military campaign in China had been vicious, plumbing the depths of human depravity. The occupation of the capital Nanjing in 1937 anticipated what was to come. December 1937 saw a six-week orgy of death, as thousands of civilians were rounded up to be machine-gunned down, blown up with land minds, or beheaded. Females, including children and the elderly, were gang-raped and killed. In Manchuria and northern China, Japanese doctors used living captured Chinese peasants for human experimentation. "Autopsies" were performed on live patients. In the last days of the war, Japanese troops undertook a systematic scorched-earth policy of retaliation against guerrilla attacks. Villages were burned, women were raped, and peasants were shot in mass executions.

Mao's game of holding back his forces raised Stalin's suspicions. Mao ordered army commanders to "focus on creating base areas . . . [n]ot fighting battles."[23] Privately, Stalin wondered whether Mao was a Japanese agent. And some Comintern agents who had direct dealings with Mao gave Stalin reason to believe that when, under torture in 1938, they accused Mao of being part of the Bukharin conspiracy. Bukharin, former head of the Comintern and part of the ineffective Right Opposition, an anti-Stalin faction, fell under Stalin's knife in the Great Purge and show trials of 1938.

The relationship between Mao and Stalin remained tense throughout the war, but both understood the importance of purging party ranks to maintain power. During the war against Japan, Mao initiated more purge campaigns to extract confessions from army or party members accused of having Japanese or Nationalist sympathies. Party officials were instructed to conduct "thought examinations" of peasants and army personnel, with Mao commanding them, "Get everybody to write the thought examination and write it three times, five times and again and again. . . . Tell everyone to spill out everything they have ever harbored that is not so good for the Party."[24]

By 1940, the Red Army controlled huge tracts of land in Northern China. There, they imposed heavy taxes on the peasants under their rule. To raise further funds, Mao ordered the growing and production of opium, all carefully hidden from outsiders, especially the Americans. President Franklin Roosevelt was well disposed to Mao. In late 1940, before America entered the war, Roosevelt sent one of his top White House aides, Lauchlin Currie, to meet with Mao personally. Currie reported to the White House, "It appears at ten thousand miles away the Chinese Communists are what in our country we would call socialists. We like their attitude toward the peasants, toward women and Japan." He told Roosevelt, "The Communists have been the only party which has been able to attract mass support."[25] In 1995, the release of American intercepts of Russian embassy telegrams (known as the Venona files) revealed that Currie had been acting as a spy for the Soviet Union.[26]

At the Yalta Conference in February 1945, Roosevelt, Churchill, and Stalin, agreed to create a new postwar world. Stalin was well-prepared for the meeting, because American spies had shared key documents with him beforehand. At Yalta, the three Allied powers agreed that Stalin would declare war on Japan as soon as the European war ended and that the Soviet Union would be allowed to keep Outer Mongolia. Following the conference, Stalin kept true to his word, declaring war on Japan and breaking the Neutrality Pact he had agreed on with the Japanese earlier. Three days after the dropping of the atomic bomb on Hiroshima on August 9, 1945, Soviet troops swept into Japanese-occupied northern China. Stalin arranged secretly to surrender Soviet-occupied territory and tons of Japanese arms to Mao. The seized territory was fewer than one hundred miles from Beijing. Soviet aid was in clear violation of an earlier treaty Stalin had signed with Chiang.

Chiang sought American aid for the civil war that he knew was coming. Harry Truman, who had assumed the presidency following Roosevelt's death in April 1945, continued his predecessor's Chinese policy. Americans insisted that Mao and Chiang meet in person. Mao was reluctant, but Stalin also demanded a meeting. In August, Mao flew on an American plane to meet with Chiang in Chongqing. After forty-five days of discussions, a peace agreement was reached between the two leaders. Publicly Mao proclaimed, "We must stop [the] civil war and all parties must unite under the leadership of Chairman Chiang to build a modern China." When he returned home, though, Mao told his comrades that the peace agreement was a "mere scrap of paper."[27] It was theater presented to the gullible Americans.

Though Japan was defeated in August 1945, the Japanese occupation left China in rubble. Chiang faced the tasks of restoring order, rebuilding a devastated nation, and facing a well-armed adversary in the Red Army. He confronted two major problems: the military task of defeating Mao's well-trained army and the political task of winning popular support. Chiang's Nationalist army appeared to have the advantage. His troops were U.S.-trained, better armed, and battle-hardened. But the need to restore order to a war-torn country created an additional obstacle that he had to navigate. Chiang faced a discouraged populace that had lost confidence in the Nationalist commitment to social reform, as rampant postwar inflation hamstrung Chiang's ability to govern effectively.

Chiang's other problem was that he was not well liked by the Americans. They saw him as corrupt; though he personally was not, the Nationalist party was plagued by widespread corruption. While Chiang was egocentric, Mao had become a kind of mythic figure in American eyes. This became apparent when America's top general, George Marshall, arrived in China in December 1945 bearing a mandate to stop the civil war. Marshall had no idea of Mao's relationship with Stalin. Upon arriving in China, he told Chiang, "It is very important to determine whether or not the Russian Government was in contact and was advising the Chinese Communist party." (Later, in 1948, Marshall was still wondering about this relationship when he told Congress, "In China we have no concrete evidence that [the Red Chinese army] is supported by Communists from the outside."[28])Mao assured Marshall that he did not want a civil war. Under pressure from Marshall, who said that the United States would stop all aid to Chiang unless a truce was called, the Nationalist army stopped its pursuit of Mao in Manchuria and northern China, and Chiang pledged himself to social reform. Mao could not believe his good fortune.

The truce did not last long, however. In the summer of 1946, the Communists announced the creation of the People's Liberation Army. In mid-1947 the Communists launched a full offensive. Lin Biao masterminded the Red Army campaign that began with the seizure of Changchun, the strategic city located in Manchuria north of the Great Wall. Surrounding the city with well-positioned troops, Biao ordered that Changchun be turned into a "city of death."[29] At least 160,000 people died of hunger and disease during the five-month siege.

Communists seized villages and cities, and work teams undertook to liquidate "landowners." Close to two million so-called landowners were killed in this campaign. As the year drew to a close, the Red Army won a major victory outside the city of Suzhou, a city about a hundred miles northwest of Nanjing. The battle turned out to be Chiang's Waterloo. In the four months from September 1948 to January 1949, the Nationalist army lost almost a million men. The heavy defeats forced Chiang to resign as president of the Republic of China on January 21. Just a few days later, Beijing fell. The Red Army entered the city blaring, "Welcome the People's Army on Its Arrival in Beijing! Congratulations to the People of Beijing upon Their Liberation!"[30] Soldiers led the procession, followed by students carrying two huge portraits of Mao. On October 1, Mao declared the founding of the People's Republic of China (PRC). Just thirty-two years after the Russian Revolution, the largest Communist country in the world had been established.

The ruling classes stepped aside in Mao's ascent to power. The bourgeoisie, small shop keepers, and the peasantry welcomed the arrival of Communism. Mao's promise to build the "New China" appealed to a people humiliated by Western colonialism, Japanese atrocities, and domestic corruption. Many young Chinese students believed, as one later Red Guard activist wrote of her mother, that "only the Chinese Communist Party could save China. It would provide secure jobs for intellectuals and liberate workers and peasants from slavery. It would root out corruption that had plagued all previous governments and revive China's economy that had collapsed in the 1940s."[31] Many expats returned to China to help rebuild the nation.

Such was the case of Robert Loh, a Chinese student who had been educated in the United States at the University of California, Los Angeles. Upon hearing the news of Mao's coming to power, he decided to return to China because, as he later wrote, "They [the Chinese Communist Party] were working to build a new Chinese social order." He confessed, "I was dedicated to the same endeavor. If they were really reformers, my training would be valuable to them, and my future possibilities were limitless." He returned to mainland China against the express wishes of his father living in Hong Kong, who warned him, "My son, I beg of you, don't leave us. If you go there, it will be as though you fell into a bottomless well. I shall never see you again."[32]

Loh returned to China, taking an administrative position at a Shanghai flour mill. He discovered oppression, not liberation, and soon found himself living in fear. After work at the mill, he was required to attend Communist discussion groups. The physical effort of work and incessant meetings was exhausting. Worse, though, was the mental strain of the meetings. "The smallest error—a mistaken response, a wrong gesture, a slip of the tongue—could mean catastrophe," he later wrote. "What bothered me most was the constant fatigue. . . . I perceived how much I had been deluding myself about the communist intentions, for when I saw myself clearly as they had remolded me, I was filled with loathing and horror."[33] Loh was one of the fortunate ones. With his father's help, he escaped to Hong Kong to reveal his experiences in Mao's China to the world.

Creating a Totalitarian State

Mao was fifty-six years old when he came to power in 1949. Over the next three decades he constructed the largest totalitarian state in the world, completely remaking China's system of government in accord with what he deemed necessary to maintain his own power. Mao ordered that every household member register with the central authorities, giving each individual a class label. He ordered law courts to be replaced by party judiciary committees and suppressed the free press. In the first few months, the new regime avoided mass executions. Within the year, however, purges began. Collectivization of farms was initiated as peasants were herded into large communes. In this campaign to collectivize agriculture, landlords became the target. Their land was expropriated, and millions were killed. Historian Frank Dikötter estimates that between 1.5 and 2 million people were killed in this early campaign. As Dikötter observes, "Mao's regime was born in chains. These chains tightened during Mao's years in power. All to create what he called 'The New People.'"[34]

In October 1950, Mao began a "campaign to suppress counter-revolutionaries." He called for "massive arrests, massive killings." Exact quotas were set about how many "bandits," "spies," and "little capitalists" should be executed. As the campaign intensified, Mao warned that cadres were "being too lenient" and not killing enough. Local cadres, he instructed, should "kill counter-revolutionaries on a grand scale with big publicity." Local cadres responded by raising execution quotas. In most provinces, Mao set the quota at around one person per thousand. Dikötter found provincial party reports showing that deaths ran as high as four per thousand in Guizhou, Sichuan, and Yannan. In Beijing, some thirty thousand sentencing and execution rallies were attended by over three million people. To ensure that the entire workforce was not killed off, Mao created labor camps, where many were worked to death. One estimate placed one million people in labor camps during any given year.

In the summer of 1951, Mao's minister of culture initiated a cultural campaign against history and the old culture. Antiques, old books (including rare ones), Buddhist temples, and statues were destroyed. Even graves of noted ancient artists were dug up. The culture war targeted Christians, as Catholic schools, hospitals, and orphanages were taken over by the state. Catholic priests were accused of murder, cannibalism, and medical experiments on babies. Chinese Catholic laymen (3.3 million) were terrorized, tortured, and beaten to death. In 1953, the campaign came to an end—for the time being.

Mao enjoyed power and the lifestyle it brought him. Over the course of his 27-year rule, Mao built over 50 villas for himself. Five were in Beijing alone. He had a special train outfitted for him and a plane always on call. While he traveled, the nation's rail service was halted; when he flew, no other plane could be in the air. He lived like a tyrant and initiated monstrous policies on the people he claimed to liberate.

While consolidating his regime, his relations with Stalin remained tense. Stalin feared creating a rival monster. Eventually Stalin agreed to loan Mao funds to purchase Russian-made weapons and establish fifty industrial plants. Mao wanted more, but at that point he had to defer to Stalin. Their relationship remained strained while Stalin lived, but Mao and Stalin shared a vision of spreading the Communist revolution.

In this goal, Mao encouraged North Korean Communist dictator Kim Il-sung to invade South Korea by promising him help: "If necessary, we can stealthily put in Chinese soldiers for you."[35] He told Kim that the Americans would not be able to tell the difference between North Korean and Chinese soldiers. Stalin was at first hesitant to give the go-ahead to Kim, but in the spring of 1950, he told Kim that the Soviet Union was prepared to assist the invasion of the South. Stalin believed that a Korean war would provide a chance to test new Soviet jets in action, view American military technology, and expand Communism in Asia. Stalin also thought war between the Soviet Union and the United States was inevitable, so it was better to start it now than to wait. Stalin wrote of a possible Third World War: "Should we fear this? In my opinion, we should not."[36]

Mao did not fear a Third World War either, even if it meant nuclear holocaust. He believed China could lose half its population and still come out ahead. Mao was equally enthusiastic about war in Korea. He wired Stalin, "With or without air cover from the Soviet

Union, we go in."[37] He was convinced that Americans were too tied to military codes and regulations, and U.S. soldiers were too "afraid of dying." Chinese troops, he believed, were tactically flexible, politically conscious, and good at "close combat, night battles, mountain assaults, and bayonet charges."[38]

North Korea's invasion caught South Korea off guard. By August, North Korean troops occupied most of South Korea. President Truman responded quickly. In September 1950, General Douglas MacArthur, general of the UN coalition forces, in a brilliant military move, landed north of the North Korean forces, cutting off many of the troops from their supply lines. MacArthur drove north, crossing the border at the 38th parallel. Mao responded by unleashing 450,000 troops. The fighting was bloody on both sides, eventually forcing the combatants to the negotiating table. And though Stalin decided that the war must end, Mao refused to agree to a peace. When Stalin died in March 1953, the Kremlin sent a direct message to Mao: end the war. Mao was forced to bow out; at this point he was still too reliant on the Soviet Union to strike out on his own. In August 1953, a truce was signed ending the Korean War. In return for Mao's capitulation, the Kremlin sold China 91 large industrial enterprises.

Mao used the Korean War as an opportunity to further propagandize his people through a massive "Aid Korea, Resist America" campaign. The population was asked to sacrifice more and root out spies in their ranks. Intense and unrelenting "struggle" sessions were conducted in schools, factories, and communes. He accelerated the drive for agricultural collectivization in which peasants were assigned work units, which met with some resistance among the party's senior leadership. Despite their Communist ideology, many thought that the campaign against so-called "landowners" was eliminating the ablest and most hardworking peasants. In a major speech, Mao countered, "Some of our comrades, tottering along like a woman with bound feet, are complaining all the time, 'You're going too fast, much too fast.'"[39] Such "rightist" deviation was to be crushed. By 1957, seven hundred thousand communes had been consolidated into twenty thousand giant communes with all the land owned by the state and worked in common.

After Stalin's death in 1953, the Kremlin sought to repair relations with China. Nikita Khrushchev, the new leader of the Soviet Union, offered to provide factories, military arms, and technical advice to China. In a secret agreement, Khrushchev promised the delivery of a Soviet atomic bomb. In 1957, Mao flew to Moscow to meet with Khrushchev and to attend a summit with Communist leaders from throughout the world. At the summit, Mao shocked his comrades when he declared that a nuclear holocaust might further the Communist cause. Speaking from his chair, he declared, "Let's contemplate this, how many people would die if war breaks out. . . . One-third could be lost; or a little more, it could be half." But so what? "I say that taking the extreme situation, half dies, half lives, but imperialism would be razed to the ground and the whole world would become socialist." Mao was not just content to leave it there, going out of his way to defend mass suffering as beneficial to the Communist cause: "People say that poverty is bad, but in fact poverty is good. The poorer people are, the more revolutionary they are. It is dreadful to imagine a time when everyone will be rich. . . . From surplus of calories people will have two heads and four legs."[40]

Statements like that only managed to alienate members of the Soviet Comintern. So while Mao's visit to Moscow was a sign of renewed friendship between the Soviet Union and the Chinese Communist Party, it also revealed the tensions that would persist. Unsurprisingly, Khrushchev, in his meetings with Mao, concluded that Mao was a megalomaniac—hardly the impression one hoping to curry good favor with an important ally would want to leave.

Forced Industrialization at the Expense of the People

Mao sought to transform China into a military and industrial superpower. In 1958, he would announce the Great Leap Forward (also known as the Second Five-Year Plan), with the goal that China might overtake Britain economically in the next fifteen years. In order to accomplish this, Mao needed to rely on exporting food for cash payments to invest in a military and industrial buildup. While this may have been a good development plan for an agricultural powerhouse, in China it meant depriving Chinese people of food, as the Chinese landmass has little arable land for farming.

Mao was aware of food scarcity problems well before launching the Superpower Program (the First Five-Year Plan) in 1953, yet he decided to go forward with the mass export of agricultural goods anyway. He understood that his industrialization program would cause his people to suffer. As early as 1951, he told party officials, "The only way available for us to raise money is by depriving our people." He believed that through suffering a new society would be created. As his industrialization program proceeded, Mao began to hear reports of starvation. His reply was heartless: "Educate peasants to eat less and have more thin gruel. The State should try its . . . hardest to prevent peasants['] eating too much."[41]

Instead of relenting, Mao intensified the campaign to collectivize farms. Under collectivization, party officials took control of the food supply. Work hours on collective farms were increased. To suppress resistance Mao ordered more arrests. He set quotas for arresting alleged counterrevolutionaries, instructing cadres, "We must arrest 1.5 million counter-revolutionaries in five years. . . . I am for more arrests."[42] He cracked down further on state employees, intellectuals, and university professors by calling for "struggle" sessions and public confessions. At the same time, Mao declared that the nation should worship its leader. Party cadres followed suit. As one cadre member proclaimed, "We must have blind faith in the Chairman! We must obey the Chairman with total abandon!"[43]

Khrushchev's speech denouncing Stalin in 1956 began to have its effects in China. Mao publicly denounced Soviet revisionism and proclaimed himself Stalin's true heir. Yet, as he watched Communist parties throughout the world, Mao worried that Chinese comrades might see him as another Stalin, having created his own personality cult. To defuse criticism, in the winter of 1956–7, he called for public criticism of the party. At a high party meeting in February 1957, Mao declared, "Let a hundred flowers bloom[;] let a hundred schools contend."[44] The party, he concluded, should welcome criticism.

The outpouring of disapproval against the regime caught Mao by surprise. His personal physician Li Zhisui recalled that Mao stayed in bed depressed and apparently immobilized: "[He was] sick with the cold that called me back, as the attacks grew even more intense. He was rethinking his strategy, plotting his revenge."[45] Whether Mao's "Hundred Flowers Bloom" speech was a clever guise to out critics or whether he was trying to defuse criticism remains beside the point. Mao issued a crackdown on the "rightists," calling party critics bandits and whores. A half million were sent to a gulag-style camp system Mao erected after the Soviet model. Afterwards, Mao stepped up his personality cult.

In May 1958, Mao finally announced his Great Leap Forward campaign to "overtake all capitalist countries in a fairly short time, and become one of the richest, most advanced and powerful countries in the world."[46] The campaign called for making more harvests, increasing workloads, clearing new fields, clearing forests, increasing steel production through backyard steel furnaces, constructing new buildings, and exporting more food. Massive irrigation projects were initiated across the country. Communes were organized along military lines.

The program created one of the worst disasters in modern Chinese history. Exhausted peasants, overworked and underfed as food rations were cut, simply could not produce enough food. Mao urged local cadres to order the people to eat less so they would not develop big stomachs like foreign capitalists. He ordered the further collectivization of agriculture into larger units to facilitate tighter control by local cadres, who became little more than slave drivers. Famine came in 1958 and worsened the following year. It lasted four years. Experts estimate that the number of deaths it caused ranges from twenty-five to forty-two million. Reports flowed into Beijing of mass starvation and epidemics facilitated by mal-nutrition. Livestock, pigs, and cattle died due to neglect. Over half of the pigs and half of the cattle stock died in the following five years. Mao responded that errors were inevitable, telling party leaders, "Deaths have benefits. They can fertilize the ground."[47]

Mao faced little opposition within the top echelon of the party. Lower-level cadres who did not meet their quotas were replaced by even more hardened cadres. During the famine, purges were conducted periodically. Competition for higher party posts intensified. Local cadre leaders with access to food feasted while those under them starved. Corruption spread throughout society. A black market for agricultural goods and consumer products developed in every region, while theft became commonplace. Without a formal justice system, many criminals were sent to local reeducation and labor camps. In any given year during the famine, the prison population was between eight to nine million people.

A few higher-ranking party members brought Mao reports of starva-tion in the countryside, sharing that peasants were turning to cannibal-ism to survive. Mao ignored it all. The only dissenter in the upper reaches of the party was Marshal Peng Dehuai. He had complained to associates about Mao's cult of personality and the luxurious lifestyle Mao pursued while people starved. Peng described Mao's procurement of pretty girls as "selecting imperial concubines."[48] Mao retaliated by labeling Peng and those close to him as an anti-party clique. Peng was replaced by defense minister Lin Biao, who purged the army of Peng sympathizers. At the same time, Mao ordered a global campaign to propagate his thought.

Many in the West refused to recognize mass starvation in China or the totalitarian state that had been erected, still enamored by the myth of Mao. The American Central Intelligence Agency reported in 1959 that there was no famine in China. Western China-watchers agreed with this assessment. Britain's famous Field Marshal Bernard Montgomery con-cluded after several visits to China that there were only food shortages in certain areas.

Mao's cult of personality attracted Western defenders. Simone de Beauvoir and her husband, French philosopher Jean-Paul Sartre, declared that Mao exercised no more power than Franklin Roosevelt had during the New Deal and that the new Chinese constitution prevented authority's resting in a single person's hands. To promote the cult of Mao, the Foreign Ministry and Foreign Economic Liaison Bureau began extending foreign loans—even amid mass starvation in their country. Cash and arms were extended to the Algerians, the North Vietnamese, several African countries, and others. Fidel Castro's new government in Cuba received a $60 million dollar loan, which Mao said did not have to be repaid. Mao's money was used to buy influence within the Communist movement and to launch Maoism. In late 1964 Mao's reputation in the world was enhanced when China detonated a nuclear weapon. China had become a nuclear power on the world stage, even as its own people starved. In some twisted way, Mao had gotten what he had wanted all along.

The Cultural Revolution that Destroyed Culture

Despite the lack of open criticism, the failure of the Great Leap Forward was readily apparent to many within the top echelon of the party. Mao, recognizing signs of dissension in the ranks, prepared to take further steps to secure his power—a "Cultural Revolution" from the masses against elites. In 1962, before a party audience, Mao declared acerbically, "The more books you read, the more stupid you become." He condemned reading even a little. Party leaders hearing this must have wondered how their leader, well-known for laying in his bed surrounded by books, could possibly mean this. He revealed to his inner circle exactly what he meant: "We need a policy of 'keep the people stupid.'"[49]

Mao undertook a full purge of the Communist Party starting in 1962. More than five million party members were punished as class enemies and revisionists in the following three years. It was just the beginning. In spring 1964, Mao set the stage for the Cultural Revolution that would convulse Chinese society by openly criticizing traditional Chinese opera, a popular form of entertainment. Mao was a devoted fan of the opera, but that didn't seem to matter. He mandated that singers, poets, balladists, playwrights, and writers be sent to the villages to learn from the peasant masses. And so, Mao established the blueprint that would be used to launch a Cultural Revolution, a violent throwing-out of the old and traditional forms of Chinese life. What followed was unimaginable horror for average Chinese people—teachers, professors, artists, and eventually even party leaders. Unlike Stalin's public show trials, Mao used enraged masses of the young as his weapon.

His wife Jiang Qing, a paranoid, resentful zealot ambitious for power, was also unleashed. Appointed to the Ministry of Culture, she began denouncing critics of Mao's thought and party leadership. She formed a clique of three other hard-liners around her who became known as the Gang of Four, and so the cult of Mao was promulgated as never before. Beijing's newspaper, the *People's Daily*, ran front-page photos of Mao with his quotations daily. Buttons with Mao's portrait began to appear, and over 4.8 billion badges would be manufactured in the coming years, while his "Little Red Book" was distributed widely.

Mao's greatest weapon in all of this was, again, the Chinese youth. He had a talent for mobilizing the young, calling on students of all levels to condemn teachers who were poisoning their heads with counterrevolutionary thoughts. Mao understood that the young could be easily excited. And after years of propaganda and studying heroes of the revolution and the wisdom of Mao, students provided him with a natural street army. They were full of idealism and deep adolescent anger. He understood it thus: "We have to depend on them [the young] to start a rebellion, a revolution. Otherwise, we may not be able to overthrow those demons and monsters."[50]

In June 1965, Mao suspended school so that students could mobilize politically. In mid-June, university students at Beijing University began hauling out scores of professors in front of crowds to denounce them as reactionaries. Students blackened the faces of their victims and forced them to wear dunce caps (which was, ironically, a cultural accommodation from the West) and kneel before hysterical crowds. Frenzied youths formed Red Guard units in their campaign of terror, and the adolescents proved especially vicious. At the girls' school administered by Beijing Normal University, the female vice-principal was tortured to death and placed in a garbage cart. In August, dressed in a military uniform, the smiling Mao reviewed thousands of Red Guard youths in Tiananmen Square. His appearance threw the tens of thousands of Red Guards who had gathered into a frenzy. Mao told them to smash the "four olds: old ideas, old culture, old customs, and old habits."

Red Guards were unleashed in Beijing to destroy shop signs and street names. Antique merchants and clothing stores were destroyed by crazed revolutionary guards. Women with long hair were sheared by crazed young gangs. Throughout China, uniform-like Mao suits became the only acceptable dress. This was still not enough for Mao. He declared, "Beijing is not chaotic enough. . . . Beijing is too civilized."[51] The Red Guards became unrestrained in their violence. One adolescent later recalled, "When I first started beating people, I did not quite know how to go about it. I was weak. But soon enough I could hit harder than any other student: no matter how hard you hit, I will hit harder, like a wild animal, till my fists hurt."[52] Other young Red Guard members grew to love violence too. The sight of blood as their victims begged for mercy became a powerful drug that had them hooked. By August, Red Guard movements had sprung up throughout China.

Chaos spread across the entire country as everything "old" came under attack. Even saying "Good Morning" was considered politically incorrect. Students looked for signs of counterrevolutionary thought everywhere. In one middle school, a Red Guard student alerted his comrades to the back cover of an issue of *China Youth*, a photo of a wheat field, that he believed showed, upon closer examination, four Chinese characters reading "Long live Kai-shek!" Like witch-hunters of old, his classmates immediately perceived the veiled message of counterrevolution. Students in the school began to "scrutinize textbooks, teaching methods, and even teachers themselves."[53] Pet cats and dogs were killed, flower shops were destroyed as wasteful, cemeteries were trashed, and headstones were overturned. The mobs destroyed ancient pagodas, sacked libraries, and burned books. Red Guard units began to search people's homes unannounced, seizing jewelry, luxury items, and signs of a perceived decadent lifestyle. In nearly every city across China, trucks loaded with confiscated art, jewelry, furniture, and books clogged the streets as they headed to central depots with their loot to be inventoried. Bands roamed train stations, public centers, and main streets looking for class enemies. The elderly were easy targets.

The Red Guard exploded with the vicious emotion of young, true believers. After years of Communist indoctrination in their schools, the Chinese students had been given the charge of saving China from counterrevolutionary "demons and ghosts." These young revolutionaries expressed the frenzy of the mob, the idealism of revolutionaries, and natural adolescent resentment toward their elders. As one Red Guard activist, Rae Yang, later recalled in her gripping memoir, *Spider Eaters* (1997), her education had instilled in her a conviction that her duty was to continue the revolution at all costs. Her duty was such: "Climb a mountain of knives. Jump into an ocean of raging fire. Face a forest of rifles and charge forward into a shower of bullets. I would do it for his sake. Proudly and gladly. Let my body be pierced a hundred times and my bones shattered. My heart would remain true to him. With my last breath I would cry, 'Long Live Chairman Mao!'" In joining the Red Guard at her middle school, she found herself exhilarated by the violence as never before: "I had never felt so good about myself before, nor have I ever since."[54]

Rae Yang found herself denouncing her teachers. She watched her comrades force a middle-aged male teacher to crawl in a circle in the school's fountain as they threw bricks at him. "He crawled in the fountain," she recalled, "round and round, like an animal in the zoo." Such violence became acceptable, even welcome. As Yang wrote, "The future of China and the fate of mankind [is] depending on us. . . . We must purify China and make it a shining example. Someday the whole world would follow us onto this new path." [55]

In September 1966, Mao revealed his true intention: he wanted to destroy opposition within the party. The Red Guard was to shift its attention to "capitalist roaders" inside the party. Warning of Nationalist agents within the party, Mao called for the investigation of thousands of party cadres. In 1967, the campaign escalated to the top ranks of the party when a report claimed to have discovered hundreds of "renegades" within the party. Top leaders were singled out, and Mao even forced out his second-in-command Liu Shaoqi and placed him under house arrest. Red Guards put Liu on public display, dressing him in a dunce cap and a placard, before placing him in solitary confinement. Prison officials refused to treat his diabetes. He died suffering a year later. Such was the fate of a comrade who had joined the party in 1925, had fought with Mao in the mountains, and was once considered Mao's successor. Mao had no regard for past loyalty, no regard for the nation, and no regard for human life. Mao's sole concern was maintaining power.

In villages and cities, thousands of people were brought before enraged crowds. Many were beaten to death as "class enemies." In the southern province of Guangxi in 1968, an estimated one hundred thousand were beaten to death. As the Red Guard became more frenzied, it began fighting among itself. Red Guard groups grew into competing factions and attacked one another for not being politically correct—or over food, living quarters, or space on railroads. Having seized weapons, some Red Guard units were in open warfare. Finally, in early January 1967, the People's Liberation Army (PLA), under Mao's orders, stepped in to restore order. PLA troops took over schools, factories, and government offices. Some Red Guard members fought back. In response, in December 1968, Mao ordered students to go to the countryside and factories to learn from the masses. Millions of students were sent to communes, where they were resented by villagers. Many of the female students were raped and forced into marriage. Soon other so-called class enemies were sent to the countryside. Journalists, professors, artists, actors, and office workers found themselves working on pig farms, rice fields, or factories. Leading party members were not immune. They too were sent to agricultural communes or factories. Among them was Deng Xiaoping, who was sent with his family to work in a steel plant until much later, when he was restored by Mao to prominence in the party. Millions of party officials had been replaced mostly by army personnel from the PLA. The PLA became integral to party structure and businesses. This was to have long-term consequences after Mao's death.

In the ten years from the Great Purge to Mao's death in 1976, no fewer than three million Chinese people died violent deaths. In this way, the Cultural Revolution achieved what Mao sought—an assurance of absolute power.

Mao's Sharp Turn: Opening China to the West

Although relations with the Soviet Union improved when Soviet premier Nikita Khrushchev was forced out of power in 1964, tensions along the Sino-Soviet border remained. In the spring of 1969, as the Cultural Revolution was hitting its peak, Mao ordered an elite army unit to launch a tightly controlled attack on Russian units on the far northeast of the Russian-Chinese border. The ambush left 32 Russian soldiers dead. The Soviet Union retaliated with heavy artillery, tanks, and missiles. Later, in August, Soviet tanks launched attacks across the 7,000-mile border. The massive response stunned Mao. He feared a nuclear attack by the Soviets. U.S.-USSR détente further alarmed him. Mao sued for peace with the Soviet Union, but the prospect that the Soviet Union and the United States might gang up on China terrified him.

Soon after Richard Nixon stepped into the White House, he sent a signal to Mao that he was open to repairing relations between the two nations. Nixon and his secretary of state, Henry Kissinger, sought to create a new world order through a balance of power with rival nations. This entailed détente with the Soviet Union through trade and arms control and opening relations with China—a natural balance to the Soviet Union.

Through diplomatic intermediaries, secret talks were arranged between Kissinger and Zhou Enlai. In 1971, Kissinger made his first secret visit to China. In the meeting, Kissinger offered to drop U.S. support for Taiwan in return for recognizing China in 1975. This presumed Nixon's reelection in 1972. In the meantime, the United States would support China's entrance into the United Nations. Perhaps even more shocking, Kissinger offered to reveal the details of current negotiations with the Soviet Union for the Strategic Arms Limitation Talks and to share American intelligence about Soviet nuclear and military strength. To make good on his promises, in October 1971, mainland China was admitted to the United Nations and replaced Taiwan on the Security Council.

Nixon travelled to Beijing in February 1972. His meeting with Mao would be brief. Mao was too ill to meet long with the president. He had been put on a regime of antibiotics and digitalis prior to the meeting. He began practicing getting up and down. His hair was cut for the first time in five months. The meeting lasted an hour. Nixon had opened diplomatic and trade relations with Communist China. He was convinced that he had outfoxed the aging Mao, who by this point was gravely ill. From Mao's own point of view, he achieved what he had wanted. He had gotten Nixon, the president of the United States, to come to China for an audience with him. The propaganda value itself for Mao was immense. In addition, he secured high-level American intelligence about the Soviet Union. Behind the scenes, Kissinger encouraged Britain and France to sell China nuclear reactor technology. Mao was delighted when Nixon returned to the United States to declare, "Under Mao the lives of the Chinese masses have greatly improved."[56]

Mao had been seriously ill when he met Nixon. In 1974, doctors diagnosed him with a degenerative disease that eventually paralyzed his arms, legs, throat, and tongue. Mao was never told of his disease, even as his muscles deteriorated. His speech became indecipherable. Mao died on September 9, 1976, shortly after midnight.

In 1977, Deng Xiaoping came to power. Mao's death allowed party officials now to openly attack Madame Mao and her three comrades, who were the face of the Cultural Revolution. These were arrested and placed on trial. At the trial, Jiang Qing—Madam Mao—remained defiant to the end. She told the court, "I was Chairman Mao's dog. I bit whomever he asked me to bite."[57]

Even under new leadership, the party continued to maintain the personality cult of Mao. He brought order to China, but at a high cost. He left behind a legacy of death, untold suffering, and a repressive regime. He, like Lenin and Stalin before him, had failed to create the New Socialist Man. His poisonous dream of creating a New Society led to a toxic reality from which China has still not recovered.

CHAPTER 3

Castro: Megalomania Empowered

"For us, principles are above other considerations[,] and we do not struggle because of ambition." So proclaimed Fidel Castro on January 8, 1959, upon his arrival in Havana following the fall of dictator Fulgencio Batista. Early in the day, Fidel Castro entered Havana to the cheers of tens of thousands yelling "Viva Fidel!" and showering the rebels with confetti. His ten-year-old son from his first marriage, Fidelito, rode beside him dressed in military fatigues. The Havana crowds who cheered Castro had taken him at his word when he had declared earlier in the week, "My task is to guarantee . . . the rights of the people."[1] He promised free elections once order was restored.

When the 90-year-old Castro died in 2016, 8 years after turning the regime over to his brother Raúl, Cuba still had not had a free election. During Castro's 57-year rule, he created a one-party police state under the tight control of the Cuban Communist Party and erected a surveillance system more extensive than in Stalin's Russia. Castro's economic experiments had left the Cuban market tottering on the brink of collapse as meat, dairy products, and other consumer goods were rationed. Castro proclaimed that the people had free healthcare and free education, but average Cubans knew that while privileged party and government leaders received better and more accessible healthcare, average Cubans could not find basic over-the-counter medicines. As for free education, Cuban cities were full of high school dropouts who saw no future. For the more than one million Cubans who fled Cuba during the Castro years, "liberation" meant exile.

Two years after Fidel died, Fidelito committed suicide. Educated as a nuclear physicist in the Soviet Union, Fidelito had spearheaded the development of a Cuban nuclear plant from 1980 to 1992, when it failed for lack of funding. Fidel fired his son after the failure. As a child, Fidelito had been subject to a dramatic custody fight following the divorce of his parents, until his mother, Mirta Díaz-Balart, finally relented in 1959 and let Fidel take custody of their son. Fidelito was sent to school in the Soviet Union. When he returned, he became estranged from his father. Their relationship was so strained that Fidelito had to make an appointment to see him. He soon discovered that his father had used him as a pawn. Others who thought themselves close to Fidel came to the same realization. Former revolutionaries who had fought in the Sierra Maestra mountains were imprisoned or shot on orders from Castro when they became threats. Fidel sent Che Guevara to Bolivia to a certain death.

But it would be a long time before the world saw Castro for a cruel dictator. For years, Castro cultivated the impression that he was a well-read intellectual and a simple man only concerned about his people. The international press ignored that Castro sent thousands of Cuban soldiers to their deaths in wars in Africa and Latin America. In 1962, when the world stood on the brink of nuclear holocaust during the Cuban missile crisis, the press tended to portray Castro as a man caught between two superpowers, not as an intentional actor urging the Soviet Union to launch a first-strike nuclear attack on the United States—a strike that would have led to the deaths of millions.

Did Castro seek to make himself a dictator from the outset? Did he ever really believe his promise to bring democracy to his country? Or did he become intoxicated by his power once he suddenly found himself the leader of Cuba, adulated by the Cuban people and much of the world?

Perhaps answers to these questions do not lay in the man himself, but in his dream—a dream he shared with the Cuban nation. The Cuban people were not the first in modern history to discover that the dream of revolution, equality, and liberation and the creation of the "New Man" lead to unscaled human tragedy. But Castro the man certainly did his best to turn that dream into a nightmare.

A Young, Narcissistic Thug

Castro grew up in a wealthy family, born out of wedlock to a major landowner, Ángel Castro. Ángel Castro had come to Cuba as a conscripted Spanish soldier sent to crush the Cuban revolution in 1895. After Spanish rule ended, Ángel stayed in Cuba and through hard work acquired enough money to buy land in the eastern Oriente Province in the majestic mountain ranges of Sierra Maestra and Nipe-Sagua-Baracoa. Over time he expanded his landholdings, where he grew sugar cane and corn, harvested timber, and bred cattle and poultry. Working closely with the United Fruit Company, he became a man of wealth, employing dozens of laborers, including many Haitian immigrants.

In 1911, he married María Luisa, a local schoolteacher. He expanded his landholdings to reach forty-two square miles. Eventually the couple drifted apart after the births of five children. In 1920, forty-five-year-old Ángel began an affair with a young peasant, seventeen-year-old Lina Ruz, whom he had hired as a house servant. Ángel would have three sons and four daughters with Lina. The third child, Fidel, was born August 13, 1926. Ángel was fifty-two years old when Fidel was born. Because Fidel was born out of wedlock, he was not baptized until he was eight. By that time, Ángel's first wife, María, had moved to the city, and Lina was running the household. In 1940, Ángel and María officially divorced; two years later Lina and Ángel married in a church ceremony.

Fidel grew up an indulged child, the son of the big boss. The plantation house was large, staffed with two maids and a cook, and it housed its own dairy, bakery, and store. Fidel rode horses, hunted, hiked in the nearby mountains, swam in the river, and got what he wanted. He was not close to his father, who ran his properties in the typical macho-style, tempered by a paternalistic bent. The Castro household was not religious, and Fidel as a young child did not receive formal religious instruction. Though his mother Lina prayed daily to various saints to grant her wishes, it was not clear that his father had any religious convictions. At the time of Fidel's birth, Cuba had the highest literacy rate in Latin America, although fewer than half of eligible children were enrolled in school. Fidel was taught some reading, writing, and arithmetic in a one-room school hut by a teacher sent by the state from Santiago. He proved to be an unruly student, even at the age of three, when he first began attending the school. He quarreled with the teacher and his classmates.

When he was six, he was sent along with his younger sister to live with a teacher in Santiago. The teacher lived in a dilapidated, crowded house with six other people, including her father and sister. There was never enough to eat. Fidel's education consisted of memorizing multiplication tables and practicing handwriting. Conditions were so bad that his mother insisted that Fidel and his siblings return home. Ángel was persuaded by the teacher, however, to return Fidel and his sister to Santiago. Finally, Castro was placed with his brothers Ramón and Raúl in the LaSalle Catholic school run by the Marian Christian Brothers.

Within a year, Fidel was asked to leave the school. Teachers found him arrogant, spoiled, and willful. After a year at home, he was enrolled in the Dolores School in Santiago. His classmates were sons of the island's wealthiest businessmen and landowners. He went to the school at first on a trial basis, living in the house of one of his father's business acquaintances. He fought with his new guardian over bad grades and his belligerent behavior. Things improved when the young Castro became a full-time boarder at Dolores. In tenth grade, he transferred to the Colegio de Belén in Havana, the most prestigious private prep school in Cuba. He was joined by his brother Raúl, who did not last long in the rigorous academic environment. Raúl was described by one of the priests as "intellectually limited."[2] This ended Raúl's formal education, which had not gone beyond primary school. Later, when the Castro brothers came into power, Raúl oversaw the closing of Belén.

Belén had been founded in 1854 by the Jesuits and had soon become the school of choice for the island's elite. The campus included an indoor swimming pool, a gymnasium, a billiard hall, an observatory, and a library to rival most Latin American universities'. The tall, handsome, athletic Castro made an immediate impression on his fellow students. He began getting good grades, and he had an impressive memory. One fellow student recalled, "We'd ask him, 'Fidel, what does such and such a book say on such and such page?' and he'd answer exactly."[3] Although boastful and aggressive, Fidel emerged as a natural leader. He excelled at sports and debate. He became fascinated by wars and battles, especially those of Alexander the Great, Mark Antony, and Caesar Augustus. Although later he declared himself a Marxist, he remained attached to a view that heroic individuals could change the course of history. Historical transformation came through the will to power, which is more a Nietzschean than a Marxist idea. He left Belén shortly before his nineteenth birthday in 1945 to study law at Havana University. There he became politically active. Havana University had long been a hotbed of left-wing politics, going back to the 1930s when dictator General Gerardo Machado had sent hired thugs to terrorize and assassinate student opposition leaders. Machado's government was overthrown in 1933 in a military coup lead by army sergeant Fulgencio Batista. The coup became known as the Sergeants' Revolt.

Batista, handsome, charming, and intelligent, proved to be an adroit politician. He made a tactical alliance with the Cuban Communist Party, called the Popular Socialist Party, to control organized labor. Communists placed ministers and senators in the Batista government. Under Batista, a new and truly democratic constitution was adopted in 1940. That same year, Batista won election to the presidency. The economy boomed under his presidency, but in 1944, much to his utter surprise, Batista lost reelection to Dr. Ramón Grau, a Havana University law professor who had organized a new party, the Authentic Cuban Revolutionary Party. Once elected, however, Grau proved not to be an idealist professor, but another corrupt politician who gave money and jobs to his supporters while unleashing violence against his political enemies.

This was the political environment Castro found when he arrived at Havana University, driving a new, shiny black Ford V-8 car given to him by his father. In school, Castro got by through last-minute cramming for final exams, taking advantage of his remarkable memory. The young Castro was self-centered and pretentious. He made himself the center of attention at any gathering. On his first day of law school, one of his classmates remarked, "I hope this guy is for good, because if he is for ill, he will be impossible to resist."[4]

Castro remained friendly with the Communists, but the party saw him as a hothead and a wild card. Castro formed an alliance with the Socialist Revolutionary Movement (MSR), closely aligned with Grau's political grouping. The Socialist Revolutionary Movement's major rival on campus and the streets was the Insurrectional Revolutionary Union (UIR), opposed to Grau. Members of both gangs carried guns and fought one another in the streets. There were few ideological differences between the two groups, however.

The hot-tempered Castro began carrying a pistol. There was an air of violence on campus. On December 10, 1946, Castro joined a group of MSR members who attempted to assassinate rival UIR members entering a sporting event at the university stadium. Two UIR members were shot, one in the back. Castro later claimed that he was one of the shooters. Following this, Castro drifted away to join a breakaway group from Grau's Auténticos. The new party called itself the Ortodoxos. Both parties believed in the ballot box. Castro, though, considered himself a revolutionary.

In the summer of 1947, Castro heard about an international expedition to overthrow General Rafael Trujillo, the dictator of Cuba's Caribbean neighbor the Dominican Republic. Since his first days at the university, Castro had been involved in activities supporting revolution in the Dominican Republic. He personally became acquainted with Juan Bosch, a well-known Dominican intellectual. The revolutionaries gathered in late July in the Oriente Province to launch an invasion of the Dominican Republic. The band was mostly made up of Dominicans and Cubans, with unofficial representatives of a few other Latin American countries thrown into the mix. The men were given uniforms and weapons. Castro was placed in charge of the mixed-nationality platoon. A few days later, this revolutionary brigade was transported to the small, uninhabited island of Cayo Confites. They stayed on the speck of an island for fifty-nine days waiting for orders to launch the invasion, but the commands never came.

In late September the expedition was canceled, but Castro refused to let the adventure go. Instead, he joined a scaled-down operation under Juan Bosch. Before landing in Santo Domingo, however, the expedition was intercepted. Castro escaped arrest. He returned to Havana to continue work as a political agitator.

As a student leader often quoted by the press, Castro was invited to join a delegation to meet in Havana with a visiting Argentine senator, a supporter of populist president Juan Perón. The senator had come to Havana to promote Perón's demand that Great Britain turn over the Falkland Islands, which lay off Argentina's coast. At the meeting, Castro stood out when he endorsed Perón's call for a conference of anti-imperialist Latin American students to be held in Buenos Aires. Castro suggested that a preliminary conference be held first in Bogotá, Colombia. Castro's meeting with a representative of the Argentine government drew heavy criticism from the Left, who saw Juan Perón as a fascist. Castro replied bluntly to these critics: anti-imperialists, whether Left or Right, needed to stand united against the United States. Castro's clear and bold stance against American imperialism attracted attention. Many began to see in the young Castro a new political visionary, the voice for the future. Even the staid leadership of the Cuban Communist Party liked Castro's rhetoric. Castro, however, continued to keep his distance from the party. Castro declared privately and publicly that he abhorred the party's servile obedience to the Soviet Union. He told one high-ranking party official with tongue in cheek, "I would be a Communist if I could be Stalin."[5]

Castro and his friend Rafael del Pino arrived in Bogotá in early April 1948. Although Castro claimed that the trip was financed by his own money, it's more likely that the Argentinian embassy paid for the flight. Castro could not have arrived at a more propitious moment for a young revolutionary in the making. While Castro and del Pino were on their way to meet with Colombian Liberal Party presidential candidate Jorge Eliécer Gaitán, the great hope for reform in the country, they caught word that Gaitán had been assassinated. Riots broke out across Bogotá. Three thousand people would die in the ensuing two days of chaos. Castro and del Pino joined the mobs. Castro secured a rifle and urged an attack on the presidential palace. In the end, the Cuban embassy located the two young men and returned them to Havana.

Castro drew two lessons from the Bogotá events. First, he grew convinced that only armed revolution could bring change to Latin America. The murder of Gaitán proved in his mind that peaceful change through the electoral process was impossible. The second conclusion was of more importance: he saw that revolutions needed to be led from above. The spontaneous uprising of the masses alone would not lead to revolutionary change. The masses needed to be directed by a disciplined revolutionary vanguard—the same lesson taught by Lenin and Mao.

Castro the Revolutionary

Castro returned to Havana in April 1948. He married Mirta Díaz-Balart, who came from a politically influential conservative family. His father gave him a new Pontiac as a graduation gift and after the marriage sent the couple on an extended honeymoon in the United States. Castro played with the idea of taking an advanced degree at Harvard, Columbia, or Princeton only to learn that, even with a doctoral law degree from the

University of Havana, he might only be admitted as a freshman at one of these schools. For a while, Mirta and Fidel were happy. They settled into a nice apartment in Havana and soon rejoiced at the birth of a boy, whom they named Fidelito. Castro undertook a serious study of Marxism for the first time, reading Marx's *Das Kapital*. He paid special attention to Lenin's *What Is To Be Done?*, which confirmed his views of the need for a disciplined, centralized revolutionary vanguard. After graduating from law school in 1950, he set up a small legal practice in Havana. He took on a few small cases, but his real occupation was that of a political agitator.

In the autumn of 1951, Castro declared himself a delegate for the Ortodoxo Party representing central Havana. Castro campaigned feverishly. He sent personal notes to thousands of party members in the district. When he won, he put his name up for nomination to the Cuban House of Representatives in 1952. He began a half-hour radio program on a local station and became consumed with campaigning. When his wife, Mirta, complained that he had promised her, her parents, and his parents that he would go to Paris to study at the Sorbonne for a master's degree, he replied, "I will fight in Congress, and one day I will seize power."[6]

Political life in Cuba changed forever on March 10, 1952, when General Fulgencio Batista, realizing his chances for election to the presidency were minimal, undertook a military coup ousting President Carlos Prío, who had been elected four years early. The coup confirmed Castro's view that the only recourse was revolutionary action. He later recalled, "When the coup took place, everything changed."[7] Castro began organizing what was called "the Movement," a revolutionary organization. Fidel was joined by his younger brother Raúl, who had early joined the Communist Party. Raúl's true loyalties, though, were to his brother, not the party. Castro demanded complete secrecy from the Movement's members and absolute obedience to him as the leader. He broke members into cells, comprised of ten each, that had no knowledge of the others. All communication was directed through Castro himself. Within a year, over twelve hundred people had joined the Movement, organized into more than a hundred cells. In January 1953, Castro announced his formal break with the Ortodoxo Party. The Ortodoxo Party had only been an instrument for Castro's own advancement. Now he no longer needed it. He had become a force unto himself.

Members of the Movement were completely enchanted by the young Castro. For many, joining the Movement was akin to a religious experience. As one young lawyer, Melba Hernández, later recalled on joining the revolutionary cause, "Castro spoke in a very low voice . . . came close as if to tell you a secret; and then you suddenly felt you shared the secret."[8]

Castro shared with only his closest comrades a wild-eyed scheme to attack the Moncada army barracks and armory located in the city of Santiago in the Oriente Province, on the easternmost part of the island. The plan was bold, reminiscent of John Brown's raid on Harper's Ferry in 1859. The goal was to seize the armory, establish a revolutionary force in the region, and spark a general revolution across the country. Eight years after the failed raid, Raúl Castro described the goal of the Moncada attack as a small engine that would "trigger the big engine, the people fighting" with weapons they had seized.[9] Much like Brown's raid, the Moncada attack was ill conceived militarily—the plot not of a military strategist, but of a revolutionary dreamer.

In preparation for the attack, a select group of approximately a hundred revolutionaries were enlisted to seize barracks normally occupied by over a thousand soldiers. Castro decided that the attack should come on July 26 during the festival of St. James, when many officers and soldiers were on leave or returning from all-night revelry in town. Fidel told no one outside the group of his plan—with one extraordinary exception: one of his former professors, Herminio Portell Vilá. As he began to organize for the attack, Castro met with his old teacher. A conversation followed in which Castro asked the professor about the state of the barracks. When Castro asked about weapons and other logistics, the professor got the gist of his plans. After Castro confirmed that he intended to attack the outpost, the professor replied, "You don't have a chance in the world. You don't know the life in the barracks. It would be a slaughter."

"Yes, but I'm going to do it," Castro retorted.[10]

The attack began early in the morning on July 26, 1953. Beforehand, Castro gave a speech to his small force. "In a few hours," he told the nervous group, "you will be victorious or defeated, but regardless of the outcome—listen well, friends—this Movement will Triumph."[11] With these words, the small caravan of 16 cars filled with revolutionaries approached the base gate. Castro jumped from the lead car and began to shoot in all directions, forfeiting any element of surprise the rebels may have had. Fidel jumped back into his car, but the car would not start. While he took cover behind his car, five other rebels entered the barracks. They were lightly armed with .22-caliber rifles and old shotguns. They were gunned down. Fidel ordered a retreat. The rebels lost six men and had fifteen wounded, while killing nineteen soldiers. Within days Fidel, his brother, and their comrades were rounded up and placed on trial.

On the opening day of his trial on September 21, 1953, fewer than two months after the Moncada attack, Castro revealed that his goal was to place the Batista government in the defendant's box. Declaring that he would serve as his own lawyer, he transformed the courtroom into a political theater. He told the court that he had "no interest in making politics," saying, "I only aspire to open the path to truth." The truth was that he had not needed to persuade his comrades to undertake the attack. "They showed me the way," he said in a chilly voice, "convinced that the road we ought to take was the one of armed struggle, once we had exhausted all the other possible roads, so that this generation would not face the danger of losing itself."[12] In this way, Castro portrayed himself as only the instrument of the people. The trial ended with the sentencing of Raúl Castro and another leader to thirteen years in prison. Twenty others were given ten years, and three others received three-year jail terms. The court decided that Fidel was to be sentenced by a separate court. He was given permission once again to serve as his own lawyer.

In October, Fidel appeared in court to offer a speech that became known as the "History Will Absolve Me" speech. Fidel would revise the speech many times while he was in prison, adding the titular line to it. The speech opened with Castro's declaring, "Honorable Judges, never has a lawyer had to practice his profession under such difficult conditions." He continued, "He who speaks to you hates vanity with all his being, nor are his temperament or frame of mind inclined towards courtroom poses or sensationalism of any kind." He proceeded to outline the rationale and legitimacy of the Moncada attack and the need for revolution in the face of "the cruelest and most inhuman oppression in all their [Cubans'] history." He called for the restoration of the constitution of 1940, a return to democracy, land reform, and the right of workers "to share [30] percent of the profits of all large industrial, mercantile, and mining enterprises, as well as sugar mills." Sugar workers should share 55 percent of the value of the crops they produced. He looked to the future by predicting that Cuba could support a population three times larger, with markets flooded with produce, pantries full, and everyone employed. He spoke on the behalf of the downtrodden and with eloquence on the rule of law because, as he pointed out, "The [c]onstitution is understood to be the basic and supreme law of the nation, to define the country's political structure, regulate the functioning of government agencies, and determine the limits of their activities."

His speech ended with dramatic flourish: "I do not fear the fury of the miserable tyrant who snuffed out the life of these brothers of mine." The line that gave the speech its name he wrote in prison later: "¡Condenádme, no importa! ¡La historia me absolverá!" ("Condemn me, it does not matter! History will absolve me").

Castro Makes a Revolution

In the Isle of Pines prison, called the Presidio, built in 1931 by dictator Gerardo Machado to house five thousand inmates, Castro undertook to build a revolutionary vanguard well-versed in Marxist theory and practice. He read Hewlett Johnson's *The Secret of Soviet Strength*. Johnson, the head of the Anglican Church in England, was known as the "Red Dean of Canterbury" for his unwavering support of the Soviet Union. Jean-Jacques Rousseau's *Discourse on Inequality* confirmed Castro's belief that the rule of law was only an instrument of class oppression. He wrote to friends, "The prison is a terrific classroom. I can shape my view of the world in here and figure out the meaning of life."[13] Castro imposed a strict regime and discipline on his prisoner comrades. Comrades were instructed to rise a half hour before other prisoners. The day was followed by classes taught by Castro on history, philosophy, Spanish grammar, and revolutionary thought. He smuggled letters to outside supporters and began conducting a "love" affair through correspondence with a married woman from the upper class, Natalia "Naty" Revuelta, who had grown infatuated with the young revolutionary. He persuaded his wife Mirta to smuggle letters out of prison and encouraged her to make public statements denouncing the Batista government. Her public statements embarrassed her family. She was finally convinced by her brother Rafael Díaz-Balart to sue for divorce.

Castro's speech "History Will Absolve Me" became a major propaganda tool for the movement. Over one hundred thousand copies of the speech were printed and distributed throughout Cuba. The public began to demand Castro's release. Batista, having won reelection in a prospering Cuba, granted amnesty to the Moncada prisoners. On Mother's Day, May 15, 1955, Fidel, Raúl, and the other prisoners were released. Castro returned to Havana to begin organizing the 26th of July Movement (M-26-7). Fidel only remained in Cuba seven weeks; fearing arrest after staging a series of terrorist bombing attacks, Castro fled into exile in Mexico City. Close comrades soon followed. Before leaving he spent time with Revuelta, who had separated from her husband. A year later, after Castro had gone into exile, Naty gave birth to a baby girl. It was Fidel's.

In Mexico, Castro began preparing an armed expedition to overthrow the Batista regime. Castro arranged to have members of his small force housed in separate apartments. He insisted on tight discipline. Members were instructed not to talk to outside people or to maintain contact with relatives in Cuba. While his comrades trained in Mexico, Castro sent instructions to M-26-7 members in Cuba to prepare for revolution by infiltrating political clubs, trade unions, and government institutions.

Among those who joined Castro in Mexico was a young revolutionary, an Argentine physician called Che Guevara. The two dreamers hit it off immediately. In their first meeting in the summer of 1955, they spent the night sharing their revolutionary visions into the early hours of the morning. Both believed in armed revolution. Castro understood, though, that for the revolution to succeed it needed money. With this in mind, in the fall of 1955 he undertook a 6-week fundraising trip to the United States, where he tapped into Cuban exile communities, who turned out in the hundreds to hear Castro exclaim, "I can inform you with complete reliability that in 1956, we will be free or we will be martyrs!"[14]

Castro raised thousands of dollars from these exile communities. His greatest fundraising coup came when he met with former Cuban president Carlos Prío in a small Texas town across the U.S.-Mexican border. Castro abhorred Prío, a millionaire many times over. The meeting lasted for two hours. As they talked, Castro audaciously jabbed Prío with his finger. In the end, Prío gave him $100,000 on the condition that they form a united front against Batista and that Castro inform him when he left for Cuba. Castro took the money and bought more arms but never informed Prío that he was on his way to Cuba.

Castro had a single, audacious plan: land a guerrilla army in the northern province of Oriente and spread the revolution. Oriente was where the great revolutionary hero José Martí had landed in 1895, only to be killed in battle. Where Martí had failed, Castro was confident he would succeed. He arranged to have his small force trained by General Alberto Bayo, a veteran of the Spanish Civil War. Bayo trained the troops in night fighting, weapons, and explosives. Castro kept in contact with revolutionary opposition inside Cuba. He arranged to meet in Mexico with the young leader of the anti-Batista Student Revolutionary

Directorate, José Antonio Echevarría, who was instructed to launch attacks in the cities to coincide with Castro's landing.

On November 25, Fidel and his small group of revolutionaries boarded a small, formerly American-owned yacht named *Granma*. Overloaded and overcrowded, the small craft chugged along, traveling a 1,200-mile voyage from Mexico to the east of Cuba. On December 2, 1956, the *Granma* touched Cuban soil in more of a shipwreck than a landing. The boat got stuck in the mud about a mile from its designated landing spot. Castro's troops had to wade through the water and were separated from one another. The day before, the expected urban uprising had occurred and had been quickly crushed by the police. Castro's revolution had gotten off to a bad start.

Scattered in the landing, under attack by Batista's soldiers, and unfamiliar with the Sierra Maestra mountains, Castro's troops finally regrouped. Castro announced to a local peasant, "I am Fidel Castro. My companions and I have come to liberate Cuba."[15] From the beginning, Castro was confident of ultimate victory. After days of wandering in the forests of the Sierra Maestra, Castro reunited with Raúl. Upon meeting, Fidel asked his brother, "How many rifles did you bring?" Raúl answered five. Fidel was ecstatic. "And with the two I have, this makes seven. Now, yes, we have won the war!"[16] They began recruiting local peasants and were later joined by young revolutionaries from the cities.

In the beginning, military clashes were infrequent and constituted little more than skirmishes. Castro's small band of marauders would ambush Batista's troops in the mountains. Late in the campaign, Batista sent in special forces, but they proved ineffective in the unfamiliar Sierra Maestra mountains. Instead of trying to win over the peasants in the area, government troops tried to intimidate the peasants through arrests and executions, which further turned the peasants against the government.

Castro understood the importance of political warfare. Only two weeks after *Granma*'s landing, the thirty-year-old Castro reached out to a contact in Havana to bring a foreign journalist to the Sierras for an interview. The contact arranged to fetch fifty-seven-year-old vacationing *New York Times* foreign correspondent Herbert Matthews to interview the young revolutionary. The meeting took place on February 16, 1957, in a clearing that Fidel had built to give the appearance of a busy command post. The post was only twenty-five miles from the city of Manzanillo, but Matthews was given the impression that it was deep within the jungles of the Sierras as Fidel's soldiers marched him around for days to get to the meeting. At the command post, Fidel ordered his men to give the appearance of great activity. One of his aides was instructed to rush forward, while Castro met with Matthews, to report, "Comandante, the liaison from Column Number 2 has arrived."

"Wait until I am finished," Fidel ordered.

The easily beguiled Matthews published the first of three long articles on February 24, 1957. He exclaimed in that article, "From the look of things, General Batista cannot possibly hope to suppress the Castro revolt." He described Castro as having a political mind, not a military one, with "strong ideas of liberty, democracy, social justice, and the need to restore the [c]onstitution and to hold elections." Castro, Matthews assured the public, held no animosity toward the United States and the American people. Indeed, Castro noted, "Above all, we are fighting for a democratic Cuba and an end to dictatorship."[17]

Just as Mao had charmed Edgar Snow in the Chinese mountains thirty years earlier, Castro had fooled the fifty-seven-year-old, supposedly worldly *New York Times* reporter. Matthews's three-part series became international news and was widely distributed in Havana with the help of Castro's allies. This would not be the last time that Castro mesmerized international journalists or young leftists throughout the world, who came to see in him a symbol of liberation, freedom, and—if not at that moment, then later—genuine democracy.

Castro adroitly formed alliances with other opposition groups, many of them anti-Communist. One of his greatest coups was winning over key members of Cuba's elite. In July 1957, he met with Raúl Chibás, president of the Ortodoxo Party, and Felipe Pazos, former president of the National Bank of Cuba. Castro convinced them of the need for a united front against Batista. The parties agreed to sign a document, later known as the Sierra Manifesto, that pledged the formation of a provincial government that would include representatives from all opposition parties. This provisional government would appoint provisional mayors throughout the country "after consultation with local civic institutions." The new provisional government was pledged to accelerate the industrialization process, to distribute "unused land," and to compensate large-scale sugar growers for land turned over to "sharecroppers, tenant farmers, and squatters."

Most importantly, the manifesto guaranteed that the provincial government was to hold general elections for "all national, provincial[,] and municipal posts within the year" in keeping with the "norms of the 1940 constitution." Following the elections, the provisional government would "immediately turn over power" to victorious candidates.[18] This was not the first time in the history of revolution that the "bourgeois" elite, opposition groups, and the masses were misled by the promises of revolution.

Throughout early 1957, Castro continued to organize and recruit young men in the cities to join the rebels in the hills. Ignoring signs of a growing revolutionary movement, Batista remained confident that he had nothing to fear. Batista saw tourism booming, national income and output rising, and relative political tranquility. Rulers are often deceived that all is well—until their final fall.

It was not until the summer of 1958 that Batista finally ventured a direct military attack on Castro's base in the Sierra Maestra. Castro's guerrilla detachments caught Batista's troops in the mountains and forced the surrender of over six hundred government troops. The battle—relatively small, with a loss of fewer than a hundred government troops—was a major political victory for the rebels. By the end of December 1958, entire provinces were under rebel control, including rail and bus transportation in Oriente. Town after town fell to Castro's forces. Batista's army of forty-six thousand troops began to melt away to Castro's small force of just a couple thousand.

On January 1, 1959, Batista and his family fled the country after the United States withdrew its support from the regime. Many within the American embassy in Havana and within the CIA in Washington were pro-Castro. As one CIA agent, Robert Wiecha, told journalist Georgie Ann Geyer, "They [the CIA leadership] were all pro-Castro. All. And so was everybody in State except Earl Smith [the U.S. Ambassador to Cuba]."[19] Two days later, Che Guevara and a few hundred other bearded fighters marched into Havana to restore order. Throughout Havana mobs tore down the hated street meters, sacked the homes of Batista relatives and supporters, and rampaged through the gaming rooms of the Deauville, El Morocco, Plaza, and St. John's hotels. The only casino that was spared was at the Capri Hotel, when an American actor famous for his gangster roles, George Raft, who operated the casino at the hotel, confronted the crowd, snarling, "Yer not comin' in my casino."[20]

Castro Takes Power (and Democracy Never Comes)

Castro entered Havana with Fidelito beside him on January 8, 1959, only two years after having landed in Cuba. He was greeted by more than a million people cheering the liberator, who promised, "Now, we are going to purify the country."[21] Castro quickly disarmed the Student Revolutionary Directorate in Havana, which had seized arms from an armory.

Castro set up headquarters at the Havana Hilton, where he settled into the top three penthouse floors. He had arranged the appointment of a moderate, Manuel Urrutia Lleó, to serve as interim president of a transitional government until free elections could be held. The new slogan "Revolution first, elections afterwards" was heard.[22] In January, though, all political parties were banned in Cuba. Castro explained that his revolution was erasing "the views of the past, all old political games." He said, "Party politicians should not be allowed to undermine the Revolution with their opportunism and hypocrisy."[23] All congressmen elected under Batista were banned from future political life. Thirty-six out of forty supreme court judges were newly appointed. National and local administrations were purged, replaced often by illiterate Castro supporters. Miró Cardona, a law dean, served as prime minister, but Castro soon forced his resignation. Feigning great reluctance, Fidel assumed the post of prime minister.

The first signs of the regime's sheer brutality came swiftly as Castro consolidated power. He told several hundred thousand Cubans who gathered outside the Presidential Palace in Havana on January 21 that Batista henchmen should be tried and executed as "war criminals."[24] Left as military governor in Santiago when Fidel began his triumphant march to Havana, his brother Raúl ordered the trial of some seventy Batista soldiers. All were tried and executed in a single day. When the foreign press began to talk of a bloodbath in Santiago, Raúl asked them why they were worried. "After all there's always a priest to hear their confessions."[25]

In late January 1959, Castro, who had promised to outlaw capital punishment, launched trials of so-called *Batistiano* war criminals. He exclaimed, "What is legal right now is what the people say is legal."[26] Castro asked the crowds whether *Batistianos* should get a pardon or go to the wall. Excited mobs replied, "To the wall." The first trial, that of Batista major Jesús Sosa Blanco, was held in the Havana sports stadium, where seventeen thousand gathered to pronounce a death sentence. Others followed. By the end of March, the number executed stood at around five hundred men.

In February, forty-three pilots, aircrewmen, and mechanics who partook in bombings against rebel forces were placed on trial in a military court in Santiago. When the court acquitted these men, Castro went on television to appeal the decision. He declared, "Revolutionary justice is not based on legal precepts, but on moral conviction."[27] The presiding judge and comandante of the first trial committed suicide. In the second trial, the defendants were sentenced to thirty years in prison. After the showcase trials, other prosecutions went on. Most were of ordinary citizens from all walks of life. They included Catholic priests, Jehovah's Witnesses, and Seventh Day Adventists. They were intellectuals and students, taxi drivers, farmers, and peasants. Some were shot, and many were sent to prison.

Access to Fidel was controlled by Celia Sánchez, a devout Fidelista who had served as quartermaster in the Sierra Maestra. Eventually Castro acquired other residences, boasting the suite at the Hilton Hotel, an apartment in the wealthy Vedado section of Havana, a penthouse on twenty-second street, a small house in the Miramar area, and "retreats" throughout Cuba. Rebel commanders took over palatial residences and began to live like aristocrats. Guevara moved with his mistress into a beach house near the capital, declaring that it was on doctor's orders. Sánchez paid the bills as Castro and his cronies rang up huge charges at hotels and restaurants, sometimes as much as $150,000 at a time.

In his first year of power, Castro's council of ministers enacted thousands of laws. United Fruit lands and Texaco and Shell refineries were expropriated. Many of the laws were ill conceived. The Educational Reform Law, for example, abolished kindergartens because they were a "privilege of the wealthy class."[28] The Rent Reduction Law imposed rent reductions up to 50 percent on all houses in Cuba. As a result, construction fell off. The Urban Reform Law followed, which established a flat top tax rate of four dollars per yard regardless of location.

Raúl Castro began forming a secret police force modeled on the Soviet Union's. Working with East German and Soviet security experts, Raúl Castro and Che Guevara established an extensive surveillance system. On Castro's orders a separate internal surveillance system for party officials was created.

United States officials were repulsed by Castro's nationalization of industry at the expense of American interests in Cuba and the regime's repression of political opponents. American leaders soon abandoned hope that Castro might prove to be a democratic leader in Cuba. From the outset of his reign, Castro was intent on severing relations with the United States. Within two years of taking power, he had aligned himself with the Soviet Union. This alignment with the Soviet Union came out of economic necessity more than ideological agreement with Soviet leadership.

As the alliance with the Soviet Union was being forged, Castro gave the go-ahead for guerrilla attacks on neighboring countries. In April 1959, a small Cuban-led guerrilla force sought to "liberate" Panama, only to be captured by the Panamanian National Guard. In June, Cuba launched guerrilla attacks on the Trujillo dictatorship in the Dominican Republic. These too failed. The attacks on Panama and the Dominican Republic were harebrained from a military standpoint. Still, to extend the revolution, Castro established a highly secretive training camp, Punto Cero de Guanabo, fifteen files east of Havana, where guerrilla fighters from all over the world were trained. In 1975, he created Departamento América, an intelligence agency intended to train spies. This enterprise paid dividends. One spy recruited was Adina Bastidas, an advisor to the Sandinista government and the later vice president of Venezuela under Hugo Chávez.

Castro was consumed with anti-imperialist fervor. Already in April 1959, he privately told Cuban comrades that U.S. aid was unacceptable. Yet when he flew to Washington, D.C., later that month at the invitation of the State Department, he tried to assure his hosts that the Cuban revolutionary government would protect foreign private industry in his country and that he expected to uphold the hemispheric mutual defense treaty (Inter-American Treaty of Reciprocal Assistance). He met with State Department officials, as well as Vice President Nixon, and gave a speech at a luncheon sponsored by the American Society of Newspaper Editors. Huge crowds turned out to cheer Fidel in Washington, D.C., and New York. The day of his return to Cuba, Castro announced his new agrarian reform measure.

The Agrarian Reform Bill, although moderately worded, stripped American and Cuban sugar mills of their sugar fields. All sugarcane lands (and others) were placed in the hands of the state. As a result, Cuba's 65,000 sugarcane growers—50,000 of whom had only two workers or fewer—had, as Teresa Casuso observed, "found themselves with fewer rights than before."[29] Sugarcane workers had their wages cut and hours increased. The centralized National Agrarian Reform Institute (INRA) determined for each farmer which crops were to be planted and also set crop prices. Agrarian "cooperatives" were to be established. These cooperatives were turned into state farms. In 1960, an American University field staff investigator, Irving Pflaum, concluded after a 6-month investigation of every field office of INRA that political chicanery and complete incompetence was evident in the appointment of zone officials overseeing the program. He concluded that he could not find any administrator who knew what "he was responsible for or what he was supposed to do."[30] The egg program was a fiasco, corn was sown where it could not grow, peanuts were planted at the wrong time of year, and the cattle program was a complete disaster. INRA created its own 100,000-person army to be headed by Raúl Castro. It was charged with seizing private lands, constructing roads, and building tourist resorts. The institute became a power within the government.

By the summer of 1959, Castro had accumulated enough power to take the next steps in creating one-man, one-party rule. Castro began meeting with members of the old Cuban Communist Party to erect a new centralized party. Later, American journalist Tad Szulc in his biography of Castro claimed that, from the time Castro marched into Havana, a "hidden" government plan had already been drafted. Regardless of whether Szulc's disputed claims are true, Castro used the old Cuban Communist Party to organize his own Fidelista Party. The old Cuban Communist Party, the Popular Socialist Party, provided a disciplined tool in establishing his power. As Castro later explained, the Cuban Communists had "men who were truly revolutionary, loyal, honest, and trained." "I needed them," he said.[31]

In the summer of 1959, Castro ousted Manuel Urrutia Lleó, who had remained prodemocracy and anti-Communist. In preparing the attack on Urrutia, Castro instructed Carlos Franqui, editor of the official 26th of July newspaper, *Revolución*, to run a bold headline: "Fidel

Resigns." Castro told Franqui, "I'm not going to resort to the usual Latin American style coup. I'm going directly to the people, because the people will know what to do."[32] Immediately upon publication, pro-Castro demonstrations broke out across the country. Castro then went on television to announce that the reason he was resigning was because of his difficulties with President Urrutia. He accused Urrutia of treason. Urrutia was stunned by the charge. He quickly resigned from the presidency to take political refuge in the Venezuelan embassy. Later he went into exile in the United States, finding work as a Spanish teacher at Queens College in New York. For his part, Castro bowed to the "wishes" of the people and returned as prime minister. He appointed Osvaldo Dorticós as president. Dorticós served as president until 1976, when a new constitution imposed by Castro merged the posts of president and prime minister. (Castro assumed the title of president.)

Castro turned next to remove former comrade in arms Comandante Huber Matos, a popular military commander assigned to a base in Camagüey. When Castro discovered that Matos was criticizing the implementation of agrarian reforms, Castro traveled to Camagüey to rally the masses. Castro told the mob that gathered in the city square that Matos was a foreign agent who was preparing a barracks revolt. Returning the next day to Havana, Castro called his ministers to a meeting. At the meeting, always dependable Raúl declared, "Huber Matos is a traitor to the revolution and should be shot."[33] When Fidel was accused in the meeting of pursuing *Batistiano* terror, he responded, "No, this is revolutionary terror."[34] Matos and thirty-eight other officers were tried in an ugly show trial with Castro acting as prosecutor. In a televised trial, Castro appeared on the witness stand to denounce Matos for the next seven hours. Matos was sentenced to twenty years in prison. He was removed from the official photograph of the guerrilla fighters entering Havana in January 1959.

In the fall of 1960, Castro announced the formation of the Committees for the Defense of the Revolution (CDR), to be organized on every level to ensure "collective vigilance" to protect the revolution. Under direct supervision of the Department of the Interior and the G-2 intelligence service, committees were formed in every block, neighborhood, and village to report antirevolutionary remarks and activities.

In 1961, members of the old Communist Party, the Popular Socialist Party (PSP), began to move into key positions in the government: first cultural institutions, then publications, the university, and then local political and administrative positions. The PSP was merged with the 26th of July Movement into a new United Party of the Socialist. In building the new party, Castro gave PSP leader Aníbal Escalante free reign in setting up cells throughout the civil administration. Castro found an opportunity to thwart the growing Escalante on March 22, 1962, in a televised address to students at Havana University. In a rambling speech, he called for the creation of the New Socialist Man, which would begin with the young, the most obedient, the most studious, and the most self-sacrificing. Castro then denounced the "privilege and miserable sectarianism" that was creating economic disorder. He announced a "War against Sectarianism," which soon turned to attacking Escalante. Castro warned that being a Communist should not guarantee a "title of nobility."

Escalante agreed to forced exile in Czechoslovakia. He returned later but in 1967 was convicted of being part of a "micro-faction" conspiring with Eastern European governments to overthrow the Cuban government. "Micro-factions" presented Castro with another opportunity to purge another forty-two members of the party. He also used the occasion to close more than fifty-five thousand private enterprises from pushcart stands to small family businesses. The black market for consumer goods grew by the day.

In October 1965, Castro announced the formation of the Communist Party of Cuba, a centralized organization based on Leninist principles under the control of the Politburo that ran the day-to-day affairs of the nation. The Central Committee met twice a year, and a party congress convened every five years, although the first party congress was not convened until ten years later. Fidel served as the first secretary of the Central Committee until he was replaced in 2011 by Raúl Castro.

State propaganda was pervasive. Children in school were taught that their first loyalty was to the party, not to their parents. During Christmas 1960, government propaganda displayed a nativity scene with the Three Wise Men as Fidel Castro, Che Guevara, and Camilo Cienfuegos. Party propagandists described Castro as "Jesus Christ incarnate, who came to put the affairs of Cuba—and other places—in order." [35] Movie-going Cubans watched crude propaganda films touting "heroic" industrial and agricultural workers or films imported from the Soviet Union and Eastern Europe, well known for their heavy-handed propaganda.

On the Brink: The Bay of Pigs and a Missile Crisis

In response to the expropriation of American-owned sugar mills and lands in Cuba, Dwight D. Eisenhower placed a ban on further imports of Cuban sugar. Castro turned to the Soviet Union for help. As relations between Cuba and the Soviet Union drew closer, relations with the United States deteriorated, making Castro more reliant on the Soviet Union. This posed a huge problem to the incoming John F. Kennedy administration. Kennedy understood the threat Castro posed to Latin America. The new Kennedy administration sought to combat the growing Communist threat by developing a Peace Corps, as well as military counterinsurgency programs. Kennedy entered the White House after planning for a U.S.-supported invasion of Cuba by a CIA-trained guerrilla force made up of Cuban exiles had already begun. Whether his predecessor, Eisenhower, approved the specific plans for the Bay of Pigs invasion remains unclear. Eisenhower, as former Allied commander of the Normandy invasion during the Second World War, understood the difficulties of an amphibious invasion and might have disapproved of the CIA plan if he had been fully informed about the invasion. President Kennedy was told in a special cabinet meeting that the plan could not succeed without strong American air support. The attack proved a fiasco from the beginning, and when Kennedy withdrew full U.S. air support, the mission failed. The outcome was an embarrassment to the Kennedy administration and a coup for Castro, allowing him to brag that he had defeated the imperialists, while giving him an opportunity to further crack down on dissidents at home.

Clearly the CIA officials did not understand Castro's popular support nor that he was prepared for such an invasion. On April 15, the Bay of Pigs invasion began with bombing attacks by planes piloted by Cuban exiles. Castro responded by rallying the Cuban people. He had the coffins of Cubans killed in the bombing attacks paraded through the streets of Havana. He went on national television to declare that the American imperialists could not forgive the Cuban people for "making a socialist revolution in the very nostrils of the [United States]."[36]

Within a day and a half, the landing force had been routed. The captured troops, numbering over a thousand, were held captive and later ransomed by Cuba to the United States at a cost of $53 million worth of medicine and equipment. On May 1, 1961, a million people gathered in the Plaza of the Revolution in Havana to hear Castro declare that the Cuban people had defeated U.S. imperialism. The failed Bay of Pigs invasion bolstered popular support for the Castro regime. This support came even as the Cuban economy was collapsing.

That same year, on December 1, 1961, Castro appeared on the television show *Popular University* to announce, "I am a Marxist-Leninist and shall remain a Marxist-Leninist till the day I die."[37] Even before Castro's official announcement, Marxist-Leninist ideology had been imposed on popular and high culture. In June 1961, leading writers, intellectuals, artists, and filmmakers were summoned to the José Martí National Library, where the thirty-four-year-old Castro, with his gun laid on the table, lectured them on the need for revolution in art, film, and literature. Castro's hostility to intellectuals was well-known. He was given to disparaging intellectuals as *maricones*, homosexuals. The ostensible reason for the meeting was to discuss the Film Institute's refusal to support an avant-garde film portraying Cuban lower-class life. As typical, Castro packed the meeting with supporters.

The two-day meeting began as Alfredo Guevara, a Stalinist and former fellow student with Castro from Havana University, berated writers, artists, and film directors producing decadent, elitist, and subversive works. On the second day, Castro appeared. In a long tirade, he declared that cultural production needed to reflect the values of the revolutionary masses, the peasants, and the workers. Cultural experimentation was denounced as reactionary. "Within the Revolution, everything," Castro exhorted. "Against the Revolution, nothing."

The Bay of Pigs attack revealed the island's vulnerability to a full-scale invasion. Defensive measures needed to be taken. Cuba's new ally Nikita Khrushchev stepped forward in July 1962 with a military proposal to the Cuban government to place nuclear missiles in Cuba. After meeting with Kennedy in Berlin in the summer of 1961, Khrushchev had concluded that Kennedy was weak and nothing more than a playboy. In late August, Russian ships began carrying missiles to Cuba. CIA agents in Cuba reported the building of missile sites, but reports were initially ignored. When American U-2 spy planes confirmed in October that ballistic missile sites were being built, President Kennedy could no longer ignore the threat of Soviet missiles located only ninety miles from American shores. Kennedy ordered a blockade in late October 1962. The world stood on the brink of nuclear war. The crisis reached an apocalyptic point when on October 27 a Soviet missile took down an American U-2 spy plane flying over Cuba. Later it was claimed that Castro had personally launched the rocket.

While the United States and the Soviet Union were engaged in frantic negotiations, Castro recommended that Russian officials launch a nuclear first strike on the United States if Americans tried to invade Cuba. Such a strike, he argued, "however harsh and terrible," would be legitimate.[38] On October 28, Radio Moscow announced the withdrawal of the missiles in exchange for the United States' withdrawing its missiles from Turkey. The crisis had passed, thanks to American and Soviet diplomacy.

Castro went ballistic when he heard the news. He yelled slanders against Khrushchev to his Cuban comrades, pulling out every name in the book for the Soviet premier, including calling him a homosexual. Cuba, however, was too dependent economically and militarily on the Soviet Union for Castro to allow a breakdown in diplomatic relations. And so, he had to acquiesce to Khrushchev's wise decision for peace.

Castro's Failed Economy

By 1961, Castro had imposed a centrally planned economy on the country. This was not what most Cubans had expected in supporting Castro's coming to power. Leading party official Osvaldo Dorticós declared with bravado in a June 14, 1961, speech, "A large part of our population—let us mention this with complete frankness—even a large part of our workers were frightened by the very word [socialism]. Now, he declared, they are applauding the Socialist Revolution."[39]

Castro avoided day-to-day management of the government or economic affairs. He hoped to industrialize the economy and change its reliance on sugar exports for a manufacturing economy. He failed. Castro relied on Czech, Hungarian, Polish, and Soviet technicians to set up individual projects, but the content of the planning was determined by Cubans, amateurs lacking rudimentary statistical or accounting skills or economic training. Some of Castro's efforts were downright loony. He tried to introduce a new breed of dairy cow to the island, much against the advice of husbandry experts. He had read scientific literature on husbandry and thought he knew better than the experts. The crossbred dairy cows died in the heat. He ordered new types of crops, once again refusing to heed the advice of agricultural experts. The crops failed, just as the experts had predicted. He ordered coffee to be planted on the outskirts of Havana. The soil proved too swampy to grow coffee plants, and within a year they were dead. He ordered the draining of a huge swamp, the Ciénaga de Zapata, which stretched from the Bay of Pigs to central Cuba, in order to plant rice. That project also failed.

The real problem was not just Castro's experimental antics, but the regime's centralized economic planning. Castro saw unplanned market forces as creating social inequalities, so he touted centralized planning on the Soviet model. Castro was dazzled by Soviet space and missile technology—and knew little of the poor quality of Russian-produced goods.

Che was appointed to head the industrialization project. Che, a committed Communist, imposed centralized planning based on the Soviet model. Soviet industrial products and entire factories were introduced into the economy. The Soviet products were inferior. Centralized planning excluded the advice of managers of state-owned industries. These managers saw firsthand why production quotas were failing.

On top of these doomed forays into centralized industrialization, Castro entered into a trade agreement with the Soviet Union in 1960 to export an unrealistic quota of sugar annually. The Soviets provided a $100 million loan to buy machinery and factory buildings and sent technical assistance for industrial and agricultural projects. Khrushchev promised Castro that the Soviets would develop new cane-harvesting technology to allow increased production. Castro told the masses that Khrushchev had told him personally that if the Soviets had solved the problems of space travel, they could surely develop a machine to harvest sugarcane. The sugar combine, finally developed in Russia and shipped to Cuba, proved useless to work the uneven cane fields. Other Soviet goods were equally shoddy.

Making a World Revolution

While the Cuban economy collapsed, Castro diverted Cuban resources towards building his military and supporting revolutions abroad. By the close of the 1960s, Castro was supporting twenty-seven active guerrilla organizations abroad. In Angola, Castro deployed at least four hundred thousand troops. He made Cuba into a major compound for training foreign guerrillas. Guerrilla activities were supported in Argentina, Peru, Venezuela, Chile, Colombia, Guatemala, El Salvador, Honduras, Costa Rica, and many Caribbean islands. In Colombia, Cuban-trained guerrillas allied with drug cartels.

Che Guevara remained a thorn in Castro's side. His efforts to centralize the Cuban economy proved a disaster. Gradually, Castro began to strip powers from Che, who remained a true believer that moral incentives, not economic ones, could create the New Cuban Man. In 1965, his *Man and Socialism* appeared, in which he wrote, "One of the fundamental ideological tasks is to find the way to perpetuate heroic attitudes in everyday life. . . . To build [C]ommunism it is necessary to change man at the same time as one changes the economic base."[40] That same year, Castro found a way to remove his former comrade from affairs in Havana. In 1965, Che was sent to Africa to command two hundred Cuban troops in the Congo Crisis of 1960–65. They found in the Congo a maniacal madness full of vicious fighting, often with racial overtones. Even leftist Congolese guerrillas distrusted the light-skinned Che. After six months, Che returned to Cuba a defeated man. Castro and Che met for over forty hours in private meetings. Whatever was discussed in these secret meetings has never been revealed, but after the meeting Che declared, "My only serious failing was not having trusted more in you from the first . . . and not having understood quickly enough your qualities as a leader and a revolutionary." He continued, "Other nations of the world call for my modest efforts. I can do that which is denied you because of your responsibility as head of Cuba[,] and the time has come for us to part."[41]

In what proved to be a quixotic adventure, Che traveled to Bolivia, disguised as a balding businessman, where he joined seventeen comrades in the high, forested eastern slopes of the Andes. Here they hoped to organize local Indians and peasants and spread the revolution to Argentina and other Latin American countries. Little preparation had been undertaken. Little was known about the peasants or the Indians. Che did not speak their language. Che himself was overweight, and the high altitude affected his asthma. Often his force had to stop moving until Che recovered. The Bolivian peasants were uncooperative and often hostile. Moreover, the Bolivian Communist Party refused to support the action. The Secretary-General of the Bolivian Communist Party, Mario Monje, after meeting with Che in the Bolivian Andes, asked for a private meeting with the fifteen Bolivians who had joined Che. He told them, "I am sure you will fail because [you are] under the direction of a foreigner. You are going to die very heroically because you have a no chance for victory."[42]

Neither Che nor his band died heroically. As the U.S.-trained Bolivian army moved in on the guerrillas, Che pleaded with Fidel for more supplies and troops. Fidel remained silent. Che wrote in his diary that his men were hallucinating for lack of food and that he was so sick he soiled himself. In October, surrounded by Bolivian troops, Che and his small band surrendered. Under orders from the capital, Che was executed. The effort had proven to be a suicide mission. Fidel seems to have known it. He had wanted Che removed from Havana. The death of Che shocked the world. Fidel proclaimed him a martyr, a hero of the revolution. He had removed another rival, in this case a revolutionary romantic.

Cuba in the 1970s

Castro continued to remain a firm ally of the Soviet Union. In 1968, when Soviet troops invaded Czechoslovakia to crush a popular uprising, Castro condoned the invasion. He declared that the idealistic youth of Prague had been manipulated by fascists. He used the opportunity to unleash the Committees of Defense and the state police to attack the "hippie infestation" in Havana, arresting more than five hundred "ideologically confused" youths in a single evening. Those wearing blue jeans became special targets.

Havana itself began to look more and more like an Eastern-bloc capital as the city's beautiful buildings deteriorated. Broken streets remained unrepaired. Even Soviet-imported Ladas, cars once prized by party leaders, fell apart. In March 1968, Castro, mimicking the Chinese Cultural Revolution, announced the Great Revolutionary Offensive, nationalizing all 58,012 remaining small businesses. Castro denounced many: "Those who do not work, the loafers, the parasites, the privileged, and a certain kind of exploiter that still remains in our country."[43] As Cubans celebrated the tenth anniversary of the Triumph of the Revolution, they found few goods on the shelves of state stores. Even on the streets, Cubans found that hot dogs could not be bought because vendors had been driven out and accused of being profiteers. Restaurants had little to offer, and workers had little incentive to serve their few clients. Rations were cut to meet the food shortage. Castro explained that the shortages were due to bad weather.

In 1969–70, Castro called on the people of Cuba to join the sugar harvest to fulfill the 10-ton quota promised to Russia. The entire country was mobilized to meet the quota. Urban and factory workers were drafted to work in the fields and mills. Students were sent to work. Approximately 80,000 Cubans—soldiers, students, factory workers, and others—were mobilized to meet the quota. By July 1970, however, Castro announced defeat. The harvest fell 1.5 million tons short. Even Christmas had been abolished to try to meet the harvest. In mobilizing the failed effort, the economy fell 20 to 40 percent as men and machinery had been directed to the sugar effort.

Castro went on television. His mood was unusually somber as he announced shortfalls in not only sugar, but also dairy and a range of other products. Over one hundred thousand people had dropped out of the workforce entirely. He told the crowd that party leadership was to blame. He was to blame. He offered to resign. When a few handpicked voices shouted no, Castro grew more animated. He offered to resign right then and there, if that was the people's will. The crowd knew that Castro's offer was their cue: they began chanting in unison, "No, No, No!" and, "Fidel! Fidel! Fidel!"

The people had spoken, and Castro listened. That did not mean that he supported "bourgeois democracy." Instead, hundreds of mass meetings were called to allow the grass roots to voice their criticisms and to offer suggestions on how things could run more smoothly.

As in Communist China, the decision to let a hundred flowers bloom did not last long. In April 1971, Castro ordered the arrest of internationally known poet Heberto Padilla, who like other writers and artists had tested the limits of artistic freedom. In 1962, Padilla published a poem called "Instruction for Joining the New Society." It was clearly sardonic reading:

First be an optimist.
Second, be tidy, obliging, and obedient.
(Have completed all the fitness tests.)
And lastly walk
Like every other member:
One step forward, and
Two or three back,
But always applauding.[44]

The arrest drew international criticism. Even friends of the revolution Jean-Paul Sartre, Octavio Paz, and Mario Vargas Llosa protested. The interrogation of Padilla proceeded. Tapes of Padilla making disparaging remarks about Castro in private conversation were played. Tapes of his wife were played. Padilla collapsed. In the hospital, Fidel came to visit. The guards were dismissed. Castro told Padilla that his criticisms were playing into the hands of counterrevolutionaries abroad. Faced with a long prison sentence, Padilla prepared a long, groveling public confession. Abroad many found Padilla's confession cowardly, reminiscent of the Moscow show-trials. A few found in the confession subtle parody. Castro, for his part, denounced those "false intellectuals" and pseudo-leftists living abroad who converted "snobbery, extravagance, homosexuality[,] and other social aberrations into expressions of revolutionary art."[45] Padilla was finally allowed to leave the country in 1980.

Castro portrayed himself as the beacon of socialism in the Third World and Latin America. His hopes for socialism soared when his friend and ally Salvador Allende was elected president of Chile in 1970. Castro had scorned the belief that revolutionary socialism could come through elections, but Allende came to power by the ballot box. Castro visited

Chile in 1971, a year after the election, to cement relations between the two countries. His visit was supposed to last a week; he ended up staying over three weeks. He encouraged support of Allende's attempt to nationalize major industries.

Castro's prolonged presence aggravated tensions within the country. An anti-Castro demonstration turned violent as protesters shouted for Castro to leave the country. Castro told Allende that he should begin purging the Chilean armed forces. On September 11, 1973, the military, supported by the CIA, moved against Allende. As troops surrounded the presidential palace, Allende committed suicide. A military junta took power and remained until 1990. Castro had lost a critical ally in Latin America.

Castro did not give up his revolutionary hopes. He persuaded Nicaraguan revolutionary groupings to consolidate into the Sandinista National Liberation Front, which in 1979 overthrew dictator Anastasio Somoza. Castro sent doctors, teachers, and security forces to aid the Sandinista government. A Cuban military mission headed by General Arnaldo Ochoa Sánchez reorganized the Nicaraguan army. Castro gained further confidence that he was riding the tide of history when the left-wing New Jewel Movement came to power in the small Caribbean island of Grenada. Castro sent three hundred construction workers to build an enlarged airport on the island, capable of handling large military aircraft. Castro was thus secretly aiding revolutionary movements throughout Central America with training, advisors, and arms.

At the same time, Cuban military presence in Africa was fully evident. Cuban troops were engaged in combat in Angola, Ethiopia, and other African countries. Castro had a godlike stature to revolutionaries around the world.

The tide began to turn against Castro in the 1990s. In 1989, U.S. Marines invaded Grenada and overthrew the revolutionary government. In Nicaragua, U.S.-backed counterrevolutionaries, the Contras, launched a vicious campaign against the Sandinista government. The Sandinistas returned in kind.

Things started to go bad in Angola, where Soviet, Cuban, and Angolan government troops faced a combined force of South African and opposition troops under the UNITA banner. Fifty thousand Cuban troops took part, under the command of General Arnaldo Ochoa, the general who had fought with Castro in the Sierra Maestra and had been involved in the Cuban interventions in Syria and Nicaragua. He had won a spectacular victory for Ethiopia against Somalia in the Ogaden War in 1977. As Angolan, Soviet, and Cuban troops under Ochoa's direct command sought to prevent a complete military disaster, Castro tried to conduct the war from Havana. He sent orders on the smallest of tactical deployments, rations, and the number of hours troops should sleep. No detail was too small. Reports that Ochoa's officers openly called Castro "crazy" led Castro to reprimand Ochoa—a reprimand with future dire consequences.

The world was changing beneath Castro's feet. In 1985, Mikhail Gorbachev became the head of state of the Soviet Union. He embarked on a series of summits with President Ronald Reagan to end the Cold War. At home he announced a policy of *glasnost'* ("openness") and the opening of markets. In negotiated talks with the United States, the Soviet Union, Cuba, and South Africa agreed that all foreign troops would be withdrawn from Angola. The Cuban adventure in Africa was over.

After a decade-long bloody civil war in Nicaragua, the Sandinista government under Daniel Ortega agreed to hold free and democratic elections. In February 1990, the Sandinistas—indeed, the world—were stunned when the opposition swept to victory with 55 percent of the popular vote. Castro had privately criticized Ortega as unprincipled and opportunistic, but he had lost another ally in Central America.

Matters worsened when Gorbachev announced that he was withdrawing troops and aid from Cuba. Suddenly Eastern European–bloc countries began treating their long-term trade agreements with Cuba as null. They demanded hard currency for goods supplied. In Cuba, an already weak economy went into collapse. Factories closed. Power cuts were made. Bicycle transportation replaced cars and busses due to fuel shortages. Even bread was rationed. Castro urged resistance: "Socialism or Death."

Castro undertook a new purge. He targeted the popular General Arnaldo Ochoa, the same distinguished military general who had commanded troops in Venezuela, Angola, Ethiopia, and Nicaragua. In June 1989, Cuban newspapers announced the arrests of him and three other high-ranking officials for corruption and drug trafficking. An extensive drug-smuggling ring had been established between Colombian drug cartels, the Cuban military, and Miami drug distributors. Ochoa, who lived simply with his wife in a small house owned since the revolution, was not directly charged with drug trafficking. Instead, Raúl Castro accused Ochoa of "unbridled populism" and attempting to convince other military officers to "accept Gorbachev's vision of glasnost."[46] At the trial, Ochoa, fearing for his wife, confessed that he had done "atrocious things," saying, "I despise myself. . . . I deserve to die." He was sentenced to death. Ochoa and the three others were executed in the early morning of July 13, 1989. Before he was shot, Ochoa told his executioners, "I just want you to know that I'm no traitor."[47] Castro later watched the execution on videotape. Raúl undertook further purges within the Interior Ministry, the Ministry of Culture, the Ministry of Agriculture, and the Ministry of Construction, as well as the Tourism Institute and the Movie Industry Institute.

The Failure

Castro promised liberation. True liberation came for those thousands who fled Castro's Cuba. An estimated one million people fled from Cuba from the day of the revolution to the end of the century, approximately 10 to 15 percent of the population.

For those thousands of political prisoners tortured and jailed in Castro's Cuba, liberation never came until their release. Castro's penal institutions came under international condemnation as little more than concentration camps. Many starved and were worked to death. Meals consisted of a piece of bread in the morning and maggoty beans and rice in the evening. Most prisoners suffered from malnutrition, and scurvy, anemia, polyneuritis, beriberi, tuberculosis, and hepatitis were not uncommon. Guards were notoriously brutal. Some prisons were so overpacked that prisoners slept in shifts.

In 1985 Castro launched a new five-year plan to remedy what he saw as the past errors of centralized planning. Unlike Mikhail Gorbachev's *perestroika* ("restructuring") effort to decentralize the economy, Castro called for tighter centralized control of the economy. He cracked down on private farmers and small vendors that had spouted up in the economy. He denounced "all those things—and that there [were] many that strayed from the revolutionary spirit, from revolutionary work, revolutionary virtue, revolutionary effort, and revolutionary responsibility." He revived Che's concept of the New Socialist Man. Che had been dead for thirty years, but Fidel sought to revive his spirit.

In 1992, loans from the Eastern bloc were no longer available—some $1.5 billion a year from the Soviet Union and approximately $160 million from the rest of Eastern Europe. Castro made peace with China, which became Cuba's second-largest trading partner. As petroleum became scarce, Castro ordered that the people should begin riding bikes. The Chinese helped build five factories to produce bicycles. Basic foods and medicines, including aspirin, became scarce. The American Association of World Health reported, "More than [three hundred] medicines and basic medical supplies are unavailable in Cuba, and surgery is performed only on selected cases."[48]

Cuba found new revenue from two major sources: tourism and Venezuela, after 1999 when Hugo Chávez came to power. In October 2000, Castro strengthened ties with the Chávez regime, which was preparing to launch his so-called "Bolivarian Revolution." In the 4-day visit, Castro agreed to a 5-year agreement for economic and technical cooperation, including Venezuela's providing daily 53,000 tons of oil or oil derivatives to Cuba. In return, Cuba agreed to send technicians, teachers, and medical personnel to Venezuela. Cuban security and intelligence officers assisted in creating a police state. By 2006, Venezuela was supplying Cuba with 150,000 barrels of discounted gas a day. Cubans became essential to the Venezuelan regime, providing personnel for Venezuela's military, security apparatus, border security, and computer services. When Chávez was dying from cancer, Cuba helped guarantee Nicolás Maduro's succession. As a young man, Maduro had received political training in Cuba.

Cuba was attracting three hundred thousand foreign visitors a year by 1980. Under Raúl Castro, tourism was expanded as new hotels and resorts were built. Deals were made to bring in Spanish and other European chain hotels. Many of the rooms were specially rigged to listen to conversations and film targets who might prove useful for the regime. Securing jobs at these tourist hotels meant having political connections. Many of the employees were university graduates. The government began to import apples, pears, and grapes for the tourist trade. For many young hotel workers, they had never seen such fruit. Outside the resorts, consumer goods remained scarce for average Cubans. The government launched new genetic and biotechnological centers. Medicines remained in short supply. At the bottom of every prescription in Cuba, a notice reads to this day, "Health Care in Cuba is Free, But It Costs Money."[49]

The Death of a Tyrant

In 2008, the eighty-one-year-old ailing Fidel Castro stepped down as president of Cuba to turn over power to his brother Raúl. Any hopes for real economic or political change soon faded, as the country sagged "under the weight of six decades of grand promises."[50] For many young Cubans, especially in the cities, the 1959 Revolution was a thing of the past. As journalist Anthony DePalma observed, "The mythology of the revolution means little to Cuban youth, who, with their tattoos, smartphones, and seething nihilism, see the old men of the Sierra as impossibly out of touch with their own reality."[51] Castro for them was a relic of the past. Yet, many still held that Fidel was a saint. When Castro announced at the party congress in April 2016 that he was not long for this world, many disbelieved him. One Cuban told a journalist, "It's a lie." Castro could not possibly die. He was literally immortal.

Modest changes came under the new regime. Cubans were allowed to buy cell phones, which were in the past only obtained on the black market. The government lifted its prohibition on Cubans' staying at resort hotels, although few could afford it. Vacant land was distributed to private farmers, and citizens were allowed to buy and sell real estate openly. Some individuals opened small and medium-sized businesses. Still, business licenses were state-controlled, and tax laws were burdensome. In 2018, Raúl stepped down as president, replaced by Miguel Díaz-Canel Bermúdez, a fifty-seven-year-old low-key party functionary (apparatchik) known for his enthusiasm for technology. He was the only candidate to run. In his acceptance speech, Díaz-Canel pledged to maintain the Communist system and to defer to Raúl Castro, who remained head of the Communist Party. He promised moderate growth of private enterprise, while important sectors of the economy would remain in the hands of the state. The general feelings of younger Cubans were summed up as one thirty-five-year-old tour guide observed, "It's going to be the same old thing. I want the old Communism to go away and something new to come. And I want old people to go away . . . because as long as the old people stay, it's going to be the same here."[52]

Before his death on November 25, 2016, Castro lived in luxury. He owned twenty properties throughout Cuba, including a private island he developed, Cayo de Piedra, often visited by Mexican novelist Gabriel García Márquez. He shared his life with Dalia Soto del Valle, with whom he had five children, but he kept many mistresses. His children had to make appointments to see him. Dalia saw her five sons as the sole legitimate heirs. Fidelito, Castro's son with his first wife, was excluded from visiting his father. Each Castro family member had his own cow, so as to satisfy everyone's taste in milk. Castro kept a careful diet, never drinking coffee, and later, as his health deteriorated, he gave up cigars. Castro left a country that remained under one-party rule.

In 1959, the Cuban people welcomed Castro as a liberator. They ignored the lessons of failed revolutions and the betrayal of leaders who make promises of democracy, equality, and the creation of the New Man. Those earlier supporters of Cuba projected onto Castro their dreams for liberation and a new age in their history. They ignored signs of a dictator to come. In prison Castro had proclaimed the virtues of French revolutionary Maximilien Robespierre and his Reign of Terror in 1793–94. Castro wrote of the Terror, "It was necessary to be harsh, inflexible[,] and severe. It is better to sin out of excess than by default. . . . Cuba needs many more Robespierres."[53]

Castro's reign lasted longer than Robespierre's. He had learned the lessons of revolution and how to establish an enduring dictatorship. These were the same lessons learned by Lenin, Stalin, and Mao before him. The repeated lessons of betrayed revolutions went unheeded by the masses mesmerized by the revolutionary call for liberation, justice, and equality. This was the calamity of Castro's Cuba, mirrored in the tragedy of our age.

CHAPTER 4

Robert Mugabe: Monster of Zimbabwe

Robert Mugabe became the first prime minister of the newly created African state of Zimbabwe in 1980, coming to power in an election marred by intimidation, voter fraud, and violence. The next thirty-seven years of Mugabe's rule would follow the precedent set by that first election, as Mugabe quickly became a tyrant who destroyed any semblance of law in Zimbabwe. Mugabe, like his fellow revolutionary monsters, created a one-party state that committed genocide against its people and left them poor and starving—citizens of a failed African state and victims of a Marxist dictatorship.

World leaders and the international press initially refused to see Mugabe for the power-hungry tyrant that he was. By this time, Western luminaries ought to have learned their lesson from Lenin, Mao, or Castro. But instead of condemning Mugabe, world leaders chose to pin their ideological hopes on the barbarous madman. They wrote off Mugabe's Marxist revolutionary and antiwhite rhetoric as populist bombast mouthed by an otherwise reasonable ruler. They were resolved on bringing an end to European colonial, white-minority rule in Africa, and they were convinced that Mugabe would usher in a new era in which Africans controlled their own destiny.

The Making of a Revolutionary

Robert Gabriel Mugabe was born on February 21, 1924, at the Kutama Jesuit Mission hospital, fifty miles west of then Rhodesia's capital, Salisbury. At the time, Rhodesia was a British colony spanning fifty thousand square miles in southern Africa. The colony was composed of a small minority of whites, a little less than 2 percent, and a large population of Africans, mostly Shona-speaking, along with a smaller Ndebele-speaking population. In 1930, the Land Apportionment Act assigned 49 million acres of the most fertile and productive land to the white population of fifty thousand people. The black population of a little over a million people occupied native reserves of 29 million acres.

Following the Second World War, Rhodesia's population grew at a tremendous rate. By 1970 the nation claimed 5.4 million subjects. The population growth was largely thanks to a massive increase in the black African population, which had grown almost 5 times from where it had stood in 1941. The boom would create tensions that eventually led the country to erupt into civil war.

As a young boy, Mugabe showed a cool, self-contained personality, with only his brother and his books for friends. His personality gave no indication of his later pathological behavior, though perhaps the distance he kept from his peers and his sense of superiority reveal incipient narcissism. Mugabe was the educational product of a Christian missionary system. Indeed, much of the black nationalist leadership in Rhodesia was composed of former Christians. The mission that Mugabe grew up around was headed by Father Jerome O'Hea, an Irish Jesuit priest who championed black education in Rhodesia. Father O'Hea invested personally in providing Africans with services, creating a teacher-training college and a technical school at his own expense, as well as building a local hospital.

Both Mugabe's parents were devout Catholics who joined the mission. Mugabe's father, Gabriel, worked as the mission's carpenter, and his mother taught catechism and the Bible. As a young child, Mugabe was secretive and preferred books to friends and school activities. When Mugabe was ten, his father deserted his wife and six children for another woman. The event scarred the boy, who as a young Catholic had been taught the sanctity of marriage and whose family saw Christianity as a religion superior to the traditional African religions. He never forgave his father for deserting the family.

After Mugabe completed the sixth grade, Father O'Hea invited him to enter the teacher-training college. Mugabe had shown promise, and O'Hea thought he could make an educator out of him. At the college, O'Hea instructed his class on church catechism and Western philosophy. In addition to the formal instruction all Jesuit-educated students could expect, Father O'Hea taught his students about his native Ireland and its struggle for independence, imparting his hatred of the British upon his young students and preaching a doctrine of racial equality. Mugabe stood out as an excellent student and soon became Father O'Hea's favorite. In 1941, Mugabe began teaching at the primary school, receiving a salary of two pounds per month to support his mother and siblings. Three years later, his father returned home with three more children born to him by his second wife. He died a short time later, leaving young Robert with the responsibility of supporting his mother and six children.

In 1945, Mugabe left the mission to take a series of teaching posts. At the age of twenty-five, he won a scholarship to the University College of Fort Hare in South Africa, an elite black school where Nelson Mandela had studied ten years prior. Fort Hare was a hotbed of Marxism, and so Mugabe began reading Marx and ordered Marxist tracts from London. He joined revolutionary study groups, but his peers found him, as one teacher later attested, a "cold fish." He neither drank nor smoked; instead, he devoted himself to revolution.

In 1955, Mugabe moved to Zambia, then known as Northern Rhodesia, to assume a post at a teacher-training college in Lusaka. He spent his spare time gaining a third degree by correspondence from University of London. Three years later in 1958, he moved to Ghana, the first African country to have gained independence. Its new leader, Kwame Nkrumah, sought to create a model socialist society and drew international attention from blacks throughout the world. Mugabe, now a committed Marxist, shared Nkrumah's vision of the New Socialist Society. While in Ghana, he met fellow teacher Sally Hayfron, who would become his wife. Politics became, as she recalled, their major source of enjoyment.

Over the course of Mugabe's time away, Rhodesian politics grew more and more tense. The situation changed drastically with the formation in 1957 of the Southern Rhodesian branch of the African National Congress (SRANC), under the leadership of Joshua Nkomo, a railroad union official and a preacher in the British Methodist Church. The SRANC called for the end of racial discrimination, land reform, and extension of franchise to all black Africans. The new formation soon gained a mass following in urban and rural areas. The white Rhodesian government banned the party a year after its establishment. Over five hundred Africans were arrested, and Nkomo fled into exile. Following the banning of the SRANC, nationalists formed a new organization, this time a more radical organization, the National Democratic Party (NDP). When three leaders of the NDP were arrested, forty thousand protesters gathered at a rally in their defense. Mugabe, who had returned to Rhodesia from Ghana a few months earlier, would speak at the rally. In an impassioned, angry speech, he called for a new Zimbabwe to replace white rule. The crowd cheered wildly for him. They had found a new leader; Mugabe's political career was born. Though an obscure teacher just months prior, Mugabe was elected publicity secretary at the first convention of the NDP.

The white Rhodesian government soon imposed harsher measures as the popularity of the black nationalist movement grew. The Law and Order (Maintenance) Act was enacted to provide sweeping powers to the government to curb civil liberties and to arrest and detain anyone without trial. (Later, Mugabe used this same law to arrest and detain opponents when he was in power.) In response to the crisis, British officials convened a meeting of nationalist leaders and government officials to try to resolve the situation. An agreement was reached to replace the 1927 Rhodesian Constitution with a new constitution that allowed for limited black representation in the lower house through a complex voting system clearly intended to limit black enfranchisement. British officials proposed giving Rhodesia virtual autonomy and provided that nationalists could receive fifteen out of sixty-five parliamentary seats under the new voting system. Joshua Nkomo, who had returned recently to Rhodesia from his exile, represented the National Democratic Party at the summit. Following negotiations, Nkomo announced he supported the new constitution, only to face a fierce backlash, led by Mugabe, to the compromise arrangement. Under sizeable pressure from his own supporters, Nkomo was forced to repudiate the agreement he had helped to craft.

The agreement was subject to a referendum in which black Africans were expected to participate. But instead of simply encouraging their followers to vote down the agreement, the nationalists called to boycott the election. Blacks were urged, both with speeches and the force of arms, not to register to vote. Across townships and villages, black nationalists orchestrated terror campaigns to ensure that blacks did not turn out for the election. Gangs of youth roamed the streets and villages looking for blacks who supported the new constitution publicly. Homes, shops, and beer halls were looted and burned. Mugabe declared at antiboycott rallies, "Europeans must realize that unless the legitimate demands of African nationalism are recognized, then racial conflict is inevitable."[1]

White Rhodesians voted overwhelmingly in favor of the new constitution. They saw it as a means of maintaining white-minority rule for decades and a first step toward independence for their country. As a result, the referendum passed by a vote of almost two to one. But with the new constitution's passage, whatever chance there was for peace in Rhodesia soon collapsed. When the NDP was banned, nationalists responded by forming the Zimbabwe African People's Union (ZAPU) under Nkomo's leadership. ZAPU leaders made two important decisions to escalate the mounting strife: they started bringing arms and ammunition into the country, and they began to send young men abroad to receive military training.

When racial violence broke out in Nyasaland, an adjoining British territory, white anxieties escalated. Over thirty-three incidents of violence were reported in the nine months following the referendum. Prime Minister Sir Edgar Whitehead, a fifty-year-old bachelor and leader of the United Federal Party that had backed the referendum, declared white extremism dead. It was not. The formation of ZAPU sent chills down the spines of white Rhodesians. In response to the mounting tensions, the Whitehead government detained nearly four thousand people and banned ZAPU. But it was not enough to keep Whitehead's United Federal Party in power.

In the 1962 elections, Whitehead's party was defeated by the newly formed Rhodesian Front party, headed by Winston Field, a prominent tobacco farmer. In the run-up to the election, attacks on European property grew more frequent, with mobs burning the woodlands and crops and killing and maiming the cattle of white farmers. Black nationalist guerrillas blew up rail lines and attempted to derail trains. In this atmosphere, the Rhodesian Front grew more and more popular. Seeking to reassure white voters, Field promised continued racial integration without black majority rule along with stricter security measures. He ran on a program of stability, not radical change. Yet, he too could not contain the growing reaction within the white minority. Although initially popular among voters, Field faced an intractable problem: African nationalism could neither be reconciled with nor crushed. Diplomacy was not an option, as Nkomo was beholden to radicals in his own party who viewed discussions as compromise; but brutal suppression of the nationalist movements was unacceptable to the British government. The situation appeared certain to deteriorate.

Field stayed in office only eighteen months before a party revolt in April 1964 forced his resignation. In a paradigmatic example of understatement, Field announced, "Serious disagreements have arisen between my party and the House and myself in relation to policy."[2] The exact reasons for Field's dismissal were never made clear, although Field later said that the Rhodesian parliament had rebuked him for his failure to secure independence from the British.[3]

Field's successor was Ian Smith, a white Rhodesian, born in 1919 in a small mining town with a population of nine hundred people, who had served as a Royal Air Force officer in World War II. Despite his obscure origins, Smith would soon establish himself as a force to be reckoned with.

The African nationalist movement faced its own internal difficulties. Militants within ZAPU saw Nkomo as too indecisive and weak. They accused Nkomo of selling out when he had agreed to participate at the early Salisbury negotiations that had created the new 1961 constitution. Rebel dissidents sent a telegraph to their supporters, declaring,"Nkomo must go." A subsequent statement denounced Nkomo's "political treachery, cowardice, tribalism, and nepotism."[4] Nkomo supporters replied by accusing the dissidents of being "quislings" and "saboteurs." Disgusted, the dissident faction broke with ZAPU to form the Zimbabwe African National Union (ZANU) in August 1963, under Nkomo's former close ally, Ndabaningi Sithole, a church minister and author of *African Nationalism* (1950). After the split, Mugabe was selected as general secretary of the new party.

On the surface, there was not a great deal of difference between Nkomo's ZAPU and Sithole's ZANU. Both called for majority rule and the need for armed resistance. Both armies press-ganged young recruits. Violence erupted as the two parties sought hegemony in the revolution. The rivalry spilled into gang warfare, petrol bombings, armed assaults, and killings. The violence provided the pretext for the government to crack down further on the nationalists. In March 1964, Mugabe was arrested and sentenced to prison.

In prison, Mugabe was placed in a large communal cell with Sithole and other ZANU leaders. He enforced tight discipline on his cellmates, organizing daily study classes while he devoured books on his own. Over the course of his time in prison, Mugabe acquired more advanced degrees through correspondence classes sponsored by the University of London. Mugabe saw himself as a professional revolutionary. Prison further tempered his revolutionary steel. He was hardened yet more when prison officials refused to allow him to attend the funeral of his firstborn son. He never forgave the government for its lack of sympathy.

White Minority Rule under Ian Smith

While Mugabe remained in prison for the next eleven years, the Rhodesian Front government tightened its hold on the country. In November 1965, the Smith administration declared its independence from Britain. British leaders threatened military intervention, but it was a hollow threat given Britain's own economic problems at the time. Instead, world leaders, led by the United States, Britain, and the United Nations, condemned the new apartheid Smith government. The coalition placed sanctions on Rhodesia, but given the country's large quantities of crops and minerals, the sanctions had little effect. Indeed, mineral exports rose from 32 million pounds in 1965 to 49.4 million pounds in 1970.

At the same time, the Smith regime instituted strict segregation in the education system. Missionary schools with racially mixed student bodies came under intense pressure to conform to government policy. The Catholic Church in Rhodesia was committed to a multiracial society and had more and more influence as it won more converts. The African Catholic population in Rhodesia had grown from 76,000 in 1950 to 437,000 by 1970.

In 1964, Rhodesia led Africa (with the exception of South Africa) and Latin America, and some Middle Eastern countries, in education, having over 90 percent of its school-age population at school—627,000 African and 35,770 Europeans enrolled. This was to change under the Smith regime, as the federal government began withdrawing federal funding of schools that refused to segregate. Smith began to attack the Jesuits as collaborators with local ZANU forces and as subversives "operating under the guise of religion."[5]

Ironically, before Smith came to power, Rhodesians had looked down on South Africa and its many Dutch settlers. Yet, in seeking to maintain white minority rule, Rhodesian measures were as harsh—and in many ways harsher—than South African apartheid. In Pretoria, South Africa's capital, the ruling Nationalist Party leadership denounced Rhodesia's declaration of independence as a needless and stupid act that allowed black nationalists an opportunity to rally international support. But Smith's government was not going to heed to South African or international complaint. Instead, the new government instituted measures that totally disregarded the rule of law by allowing for detentions of up to two years without trial. The rule of law, the pride of British legal tradition, vanished as hundreds of alleged black terrorists or guerrilla sympathizers were arrested and detained. Many of the measures instituted by the Smith regime were a continuation of previous government policies, but under Smith, countersubversive policies became harsher.

Smith represented the belief among white Rhodesians that white minority rule needed to be maintained to prevent chaos. The aftermath of independence in other African countries instilled profound fear among white Rhodesians. From their perch in southern Africa, these European-descended Rhodesians had seen bloody civil war follow Congo's declaration of independence in 1960. In a period of three months after independence, the new government in Léopoldville had lost total control over half of the country. In Stanleyville, former prime minister Patrice Lumumba's supporters had set up the People's Republic of the Congo and ordered the execution of all "counter-revolutionaries" and "intellectuals." At least twenty thousand Congolese died in the Stanleyville reign of terror. Patrice Lumumba held office sixty-seven days as prime minister before he was murdered and Joseph Mobutu came to power. Mobutu created a single national party, the Mouvement Populaire de la Révolution, with an official ideology of Mobutism. Within a couple of years in power, Mobutu concluded, "Everything is going wrong in the Congo. Nobody works in the Congo anymore. Nobody produces anymore."[6] The country was in ruins.

Similar stories could be heard from other African countries freed from colonial rule. Following independence in Tanzania in 1962, a one-party state was instituted, and when the army mutinied, British troops were called to restore order. After Zanzibar's independence in 1963, thousands of Asians and others were massacred, and a dictatorship was installed. Likewise, Kenya, Uganda, and Ghana all descended into chaos after their liberations.

White Rhodesians knew that colonization in their country had been brutal. Tribes had been cheated and natives had been killed. The repression of an African tribal uprising in 1897 had been savage. Africans called this uprising *Chimurenga*, a Shona word loosely translated as "liberation." The word lived on as folklore in the villages and townships. But most whites had come to Rhodesia after World War II. If white Rhodesians expressed any guilt about this brutal suppression of a native revolt, it was buried under their belief that blacks were incapable of ruling themselves.

The British government continued to pressure the Smith government to accept reforms that would assure majority rule with the promise of eventual universal suffrage. The Smith government's declaration of independence did not stop British officials from exerting more pressure to bring the government and nationalists to the negotiating table. Finally, in 1971, Smith agreed to negotiations. While Smith may not have had the sincere desire to reach an agreement, he did release imprisoned black nationalist leaders, including Mugabe, as a sign of good faith.

Mugabe saw any negotiated deal for what it was—a postponement of black majority rule for decades. As a result, he refused to participate in the discussions. Smith reacted with open hostility towards what he perceived as Mugabe's insolence. As a result, following the breakdown of talks, guerrilla warfare intensified across the northern border in Mozambique and in Zambia, while South Africa sent combat police and special forces into Rhodesia to suppress the guerrillas.

In December 1974, just a month after his release from prison, Mugabe attended a summit called by African nationalist leaders in Lusaka, the city capital of Zambia. The purpose of the summit was to unify the revolutionary forces in Rhodesia, specifically ZANU and ZAPU. Mugabe came to the meeting opposed to any forced consolidation of the two parties. He made his position clear: power must come through revolution and the seizure of power, not through negotiation. Armed struggle was the only true path toward creating his vision of a truly egalitarian society. He came to Lusaka convinced that the African leaders were selling out the revolution. Mugabe portrayed himself as a true revolutionary on the level of Mozambique's Samora Machel, Tanzania's Julius Nyerere, and Zambia's Kenneth Kaunda, all of whom had led successful revolutions in their countries. Mugabe's arrogance in equating himself with these leaders reflected a man who had already concluded that he spoke for the people. ZANU's attacks on rivals, savage destruction of villages, and pressed army recruitments of young men showed that Mugabe and ZANU actually had little faith in the virtue of the people. Like Lenin before him, he believed the will of the people needed to be subjugated to the will of the party, speaking in the name of the people.

Mugabe's resistance to a settlement was also a political calculation. Mugabe represented the hard-line position in his faction-ridden party. ZANU had broken with Nkomo, accusing him of being given too easily to compromise. Mugabe could not backtrack now without looking like he too was a compromiser. The situation was reminiscent of the Bolshevik-Menshevik divide on the eve of the Russian Revolution.

At the meeting, though, African leaders demanded that ZANU and ZAPU unite. Mugabe continued to resist until African leaders demanded that Mugabe agree to a merger or face expulsion from their countries. "Nyerere," Mugabe recalled, "attacked both ZANU and ZAPU. He scolded us, and then Kaunda spoke and attacked us still more viciously, calling us treacherous, criminal, selfish, and not taking the interests of our people to heart."[7] Kaunda threatened to expel all ZANU and ZAPU military presence. (He later arrested over three hundred ZANU fighters in Zambia following the conference.)

Mugabe had no other recourse than to capitulate to the demand for a united military front. In the integration of the two military forces, Mugabe and ZANU party members carefully placed their man as the new chief commander, and key posts in the army were controlled by ZANU personnel. A ZANU party directive to the rank-and-file assured them that the party held on to key posts in this united front, commanding members and party cadres to "highlight ZANU and never allow the name of the party to fade away."[8] This ploy to express solidarity while in fact preventing unified command proved critical when Mugabe came to power a few years later.

In 1974, ZANU was a party riven by factions. Internal fighting was commonplace, especially among the party's top brass. Sithole, the founder and leader of the party, would be an early victim to Mugabe's quest for leadership. Known for his vanity, Sithole had renounced armed struggle—setting the stage for Mugabe to dispose of his former ally. Before Sithole knew what hit him, he was displaced by the ascendant Mugabe, who was hell-bent on using violence to advance his revolution.

After the conference in Zambia, Mugabe intensified his recruitment for ZANU's guerrilla army. Mugabe was assigned Salisbury. He frequently attended meetings at the Silveira House, a Jesuit training center for black leaders, where he was given an office and a telephone. He also lectured on Christianity and Socialism, which he saw as one doctrine. Anxious to gain control of the guerrilla campaign in Mozambique, he enlisted the help of Catholic clergymen to escape from security police to Mozambique. He arrived in Mozambique in early April 1975. Within two years, Mugabe had consolidated his power. By 1977 he was head of ZANU.

Upon taking leadership of the party, Mugabe dedicated the group to spreading armed insurrection across Rhodesia. This commitment to violence caused the collapse of the united military and political front

ZAPU had agreed to with ZANU in Zambia—an agreement Mugabe had never liked. Instead, Mugabe sent ZANU forces based in Mozambique to fight in eastern Rhodesia with the support of Chinese funds and advisors. Meanwhile Nkomo's forces, based in Zambia and supported by the Soviet Union, conducted a separate campaign in western Rhodesia. Over the course of the conflict, Mugabe would send five groups of ZANU guerrillas to China to learn mass mobilization, strategy, weapons use, and tactics. Later, Chinese and Soviet military advisors were sent to guerrilla training camps in Tanzania. Witnessing Soviet and Chinese involvement in Africa, U.S. secretary of state Henry Kissinger began pressing for a political settlement in Rhodesia.

The War

By the late 1970s, no place was safe for a white Rhodesian. The so-called "Bush War" would claim the lives of over twenty thousand Rhodesians, and by 1977 even Smith had to admit that the counterinsurgency was not going well. The head of Rhodesian intelligence told him Rhodesia was in a no-win war. In an act of desperate counterinsurgency, Smith organized the Selous Scouts, a group of crack fighters who became notorious for their own brutality. Every part of Rhodesia was under attack. Hundreds of guerrilla forces were ensconced in tribal lands, following directives from Chinese advisors to live among villagers and to educate them on socialism and the war of liberation.

As the security situation deteriorated, the country's defense budget spiraled out of control. In 1979, Smith sought to preserve white control by offering moderate African leader Abel Muzorewa a position as prime minister. Still, however, the United Nations, Britain, and the United States refused to recognize the new regime. Mugabe denounced Muzorewa as "treacherous."[9] Smith continued to resist more meaningful reforms, such as free elections or much-needed land reform. By September 1979, time had run out for the Smith regime. Under pressure from South Africa, which threatened to cut off all support to Rhodesia, and pressure from the United States and Britain, the Smith government agreed to take a seat at the negotiating table.

In September 1979, Britain called a conference in London at Lancaster House. The conference brought together the leaders of competing Rhodesian factions—Joshua Nkomo, Abel Muzorewa, and Ian Smith— with British representatives, who included newly elected Prime Minister Margaret Thatcher. Once again Mugabe resisted attending. Victory, he declared, should come at the barrel of a gun, not sitting around a table. While in Mozambique, Mugabe had declared repeatedly that Smith and his "criminal gang" should be tried and shot and that white land should be expropriated. He insisted on the need for a one-party Marxist state. He opposed negotiation, asking, "Why should we be denied the ultimate joy of having a military overthrow [of] the regime here?"[10] And once again the leaders of neighboring African countries (that Mugabe still relied on for support) replied bluntly: either negotiate or we will close down the war of liberation.

Mugabe had no choice but to attend negotiations. Arriving in London, he displayed a cold, austere personality. He did not hide his dislike of the British. "I never trusted the British," he later wrote. At the outset of the negotiations, he told the British foreign secretary, Lord Peter Carrington, "It is we who have liberated Rhodesia—you are simply intervening now to take advantage of our victory."[11] Thatcher, a staunch conservative, surprised the world by declaring her support for black majority rule. Her only condition was that white Rhodesians receive a permanent representation in parliament. Thatcher's position hastened a final agreement, known as the Lancaster House Agreement. The new government would be elected by members of the parliament for a term of six years with a limit of two terms. The Senate would consist of forty members, with ten white and the rest most likely black, while blacks were to be allotted eighty seats and whites twenty seats in the House of Representatives. Furthermore, the United Kingdom, the United States, and other nations were to participate in a multinational donor effort to provide economic aid. Free elections were to be held under a general cease-fire. A British-appointed governor was to assure a fair election.

Land reform was critical to cinching the deal. Rhodesia was the breadbasket of Africa, exporting maize, sugarcane, coffee, cotton, and tobacco, as well as beef, to countries across the continent. Agricultural production consisted of white commercial farming and large-scale black subsistence farming. The Lancaster House Agreement sought to provide equitable land redistribution without destroying the vital contribution made by white landowners. The new government was charged with developing land reform based on the principle that land was bought and sold on a willing basis. Britain pledged to create a fund to finance half the costs of land bought by the new government for redistribution. (In the 1990s, Britain terminated this part of the agreement after years of abuse, fraud, and outright embezzlement by the Mugabe government administering the funds.)

Mugabe agreed to the terms. When he returned to Salisbury on January 27, 1980, after five years in exile, he was welcomed as a hero. Before Mugabe left Mozambique, his host and fellow Communist, President Samora Machel, offered simple advice: "Don't play make-believe Marxist games when you get home." Machel had witnessed the collapse of his country's economy and infrastructure when whites fled Mozambique following independence in 1975, leaving only two engineers, three agronomists, five veterinary surgeons, and thirty-six doctors. "You will face ruin if you force the whites there into a precipitate flight," Machel told Mugabe.[12]

Mugabe seemed to take Machel's advice to heart, at least for appearance's sake. During the election campaign, in which Mugabe decided against forming a unity ticket with former ally Nkomo, Mugabe reassured whites that they need not worry if ZANU came to power. Practical realities needed to be faced, he said; the capitalist system could not be changed overnight. "Racism, whether practiced by whites or blacks," he declared, "is anathema to the humanitarian philosophy of ZANU."[13]

Meanwhile, ZANU party thugs conducted a campaign of violence against Mugabe's rivals. In eastern Rhodesia, Nkomo supporters were beaten and killed. Supporters of Muzorewa's United African National

Council did not fare much better. Across the county, blacks were forced to attend ZANU rallies and join the party. Nkomo protested to little avail. "The word intimidation is mild," Nkomo warned. "People are being terrorized. It is terror. There is fear in people's eyes."[14]

Nkomo's protests carried little credibility, because his followers had also attacked Mugabe's supporters. But Mugabe's party was bigger and better organized, able to carry out intimidation schemes on a larger scale. Instead of addressing the messy corruption charges and opening themselves up to the accusation that they had put their thumbs on the scale, the British officials overseeing the election turned a blind eye. On March 4, Mugabe scored an overwhelming victory at the polls, winning 63 percent of the vote. Such a wide margin of victory rendered impossible any intervention by British officials. They could not control the violence demonstrated throughout the campaign, though it would serve as a foreboding sign of what was to come.

Mugabe in Power

Mugabe's first order of business was to rename the country as well as its cities and landmarks. The country's name was changed from Rhodesia to Zimbabwe, the nation's capital of Salisbury became Harare, colonial streets were renamed for revolutionary heroes, and some monuments of the past were torn down.

But Mugabe was not keen to change everything all at once. He moved into the governor's mansion, keeping the furniture and art the same. He left the civil servants in place, which included forty thousand people, twenty-nine thousand of whom were black, although senior positions were mostly held by whites. He invited Ian Smith, who had led the few white members in the parliament, to meet with him regularly. After his first meeting with Mugabe, Smith recorded in his diary, "I hoped it was not a hallucination. He behaved like a civilized Westerner, the antithesis of the [C]ommunist gangster I had expected."[15] Mugabe invited Ken Flower, head of the Central Intelligence Organisation since

1964, to stay on. When they met, Mugabe and Flower joked about how they had tried to kill each another just a short time earlier. He offered Nkomo a position in the government, which the friend-turned-rival accepted. On the opening day of parliament, Mugabe entered the chamber with Ian Smith. In his speech, Mugabe again reassured the approximately six thousand white farmers, who owned three-quarters of the best land, that their land was safe under the conditions of the Lancaster House Agreement.

For a brief moment, many white Zimbabweans were reassured. But there were reasons to have doubts, and those who did fled the country. For one thing, Mugabe reneged on his promise to dismantle the repressive security apparatus established by the old regime. The Emergency Powers Act, the Law and Order (Maintenance) Act, and the formidable police and intelligence services were all kept in place. As time would reveal, Mugabe saw that he could use these institutions to build a one-party state.

Mugabe was not an original thinker, either as a guerrilla fighter or leader of a new country. His revolutionary writings echoed the rhetoric of other African nationalists. It borrowed from Karl Marx, Mao, and the anticolonial writer Frantz Fanon. As a revolutionary he praised Lenin as "the brain and the hero behind the application of Marxist-Leninist principles," and he spoke warmly of Stalin and Fidel Castro.[16] He shared a belief in the necessity of a one-party state with these revolutionary minds; like them, he thought that he alone could be the leader. Mugabe did impart a twist on the Leninist argument for a one-party state by describing dictatorial rule as uniquely African.

Mugabe would soon take more actions that showed he was eager to build a one-party state built on a corrupt crony-patronage system and the repression of opponents and critics. Early when in office, Mugabe used funds donated by Nigeria to buy a South African company that owned most of Zimbabwe's newspapers. White editors were fired and replaced by government appointees. In the first years of the Mugabe regime, violence escalated against political rivals, while a patronage system for political allies extended into more domains of Zimbabwean life. National radio and television, as well as newspapers, were turned into propaganda instruments for Mugabe's party. Attacks on "racist" whites became a common theme in state-controlled newspapers, radio, and television, even though Mugabe continued to speak in conciliatory tones.

A new black elite replaced the old white elite as property, farms, and businesses were seized. As one Mugabe protégé, Phillip Chiyangwa, candidly put it, "I am rich because I belong to ZANU–Patriotic Front. If you want to be rich you must join ZANU–PF."[17] Plundering state agencies became the norm. And ZANU cronies had a lot of funds to loot, as international aid flowed into Zimbabwe state coffers from around the world. The United States provided a three-year aid package of $225 million. International donors pledged another one-year aid package of £636 million. Some of the funds were used by Mugabe to extend education and health services. However, massive amounts of funds went to party loyalists.

To deflect opposition, party officials organized gangs to seize hundreds of white-owned farms. The national economy tumbled as average wages dropped, unemployment tripled, and inflation skyrocketed. The rule of law was replaced by the whims of Mugabe and party officials. To deflect from these economic problems, Mugabe accused Britain, the United States, and South Africa of trying to sabotage his revolution. He urged his followers, "[Strike] fear in the heart of the white man, our real enemy."[18]

As the attacks on white farmers increased, Smith denounced Mugabe. Mugabe responded that Smith and other white farmers were abetting South Africa in a campaign to undermine his government. There were grounds for Mugabe's accusations against South Africa, and some white farmers were involved in this effort. Following Mugabe's rise to power, the South African government had organized a 5000-member force of former Rhodesian military personnel to conduct sabotage missions inside Zimbabwe. This destabilization campaign played directly into Mugabe's hands. Though denouncing South Africa, Mugabe's main target was

Nkomo. When a massive bomb blew apart ZANU party headquarters in the nation's capital, Mugabe called the "honeymoon" with Nkomo and his followers over. He warned, "My government is bound to revise its policy of national reconciliation and take definite steps to mete out hard punishment to this clan of unrepentant and criminal savages."[19] At the same time, Mugabe attacked white bourgeois capitalists for sucking the blood of black workers like "vampires." Within three years of taking power, half the white population had fled Zimbabwe, leaving a rump of a hundred thousand whites.

Violence against white farmers was rampant, but Mugabe's black enemies would also become targets as the new president waged a genocidal war against the Ndebele and Kalanga tribal peoples. This campaign, conducted by special forces trained in North Korea, revealed Mugabe the monster in full. Mugabe wanted to crush his rival Nkomo's base of support and had prepared his for war against the Ndebele many years before his rise to prominence.

Mugabe waited for the right opportunity to crush the Ndebele and Kalanga peoples. After the terrorist attack on his party's headquarters, Mugabe saw his chance. He would blame his rival Nkomo for the attacks; Mugabe-directed party officials began to denounce Nkomo as a "self-appointed Ndebele king." Unfortunately, Nkomo would not be the only victim of Mugabe's lust for power. He would use the attack as a justification for rooting out Nkomo's Ndebele support.

Mugabe set the stage for the campaign against the Ndebele by sacking Nkomo from the government, denouncing him as a "cobra in the house." The only way to deal with a snake, Mugabe declared, was to "strike and destroy its head."[20] ZAPU's businesses, farms, and property were seized. In late 1982, Mugabe unleashed his Korean-trained "Fifth Brigade," composed of Shona-speaking ex-ZANU guerrillas. They operated outside of the regular army structure and even sported their own uniforms. Once deployed in Matabeleland in January 1985, the brigade undertook a campaign of mass murder. The terror campaign was as vile an act against humanity as anything Lenin, Stalin, or Mao did.

Within the first few weeks of the campaign, at least two thousand civilians were slaughtered. Tens of thousands were tortured, raped, or imprisoned. A 1997 Catholic Commission of Justice recorded some of the worst atrocities. In March 1983, five children between ages seven and twelve eating maize outside their village home were gunned down; in July 1983, twenty-two villagers in one village were herded into a hut and burnt to death; in March 1983, sixty-two villagers were lined up on the banks of the Cewale River and executed. Rape of Ndebele women was prescribed policy to create "Shona babies." By the end of four years, an estimated ten thousand civilians had been killed. Entire villages had been rounded up and placed into camps where villagers were beaten and harangued for hours with political indoctrination. The Fifth Brigade imposed curfews, shooting anyone trying to escape. Transportation was banned, shops were closed, and tens of thousands were tortured. Hundreds disappeared. A drought had left the region dependent on international aid for nourishment, but the government ordered the stores dispensing food to close. One officer in the Fifth Brigade told starving villagers, "First you will eat your chickens, then your goats, then your cattle, then your donkeys. Then you will eat your children[,] and finally you will eat your dissidents."[21] When Catholic bishops complained, Mugabe called the bishops "sanctimonious prelates" playing to an international audience and being manipulated by external masters.

One Party, One Leader, and Tragedy

As the election of 1985 approached, Mugabe undertook the next phase of his campaign. Youth gangs modeled on China's Red Guards were organized across the country to attack villagers and townspeople. Average black Zimbabweans were attacked, beaten, and forced to buy party cards and attend ZANU party rallies. ZAPU party officials were abducted, never to be seen again. Nkomo's home was raided, and his aides and bodyguards were arrested. All ZAPU rallies and meetings were ordered closed. Step by step, Nkomo's political base was ground to dust.

In late 1987, Nkomo had no other choice than to merge his broken party into Mugabe's ZANU.

As part of the so-called "unity" accord, Mugabe's party controlled ninety-nine seats in the hundred-member parliament. He strengthened his hold on government by declaring himself executive president of the parliament with the power to dissolve parliament and the right to run for unlimited terms in office. He controlled appointments to all senior civil service, police, and military posts. Parliament became irrelevant.

In the 1985 election, Ian Smith's party, now named the Conservative Alliance, won fifteen of the twenty white seats guaranteed in the Lancaster House Agreement. A visibly angry Mugabe declared, "We will kill those snakes among us; we will smash them completely."[22] Mugabe's forces undertook a campaign of intimidation against Smith, attempting to seize his farm while declaring him a public enemy. Smith continued to resist to his dying day, but he had been reduced to an annoying gnat by the all-powerful Mugabe.

By 1987, Mugabe's power was nearly absolute. That did not mean his position was safe: mass dissatisfaction with his regime grew under conditions of mass unemployment, rampant inflation, and abject rural and urban poverty. Once the breadbasket of Africa, Zimbabwe now was an importer of food. An estimated thirty thousand ex-combatants were unemployed, many living in the streets of Harare begging for food. In the weeks before the 1990 elections, Mugabe increased his power by increasing the number of seats in parliament and giving himself the right to appoint twenty of the new seats directly. Parties holding more than fifteen seats were provided public funds, allowing ZANU to be publicly funded. Mugabe escalated the government's expropriation of white land, despite the protests of the United States, the World Bank, and the International Monetary Fund.

In the 1990 elections, Mugabe's former ally Edgar Tekere stepped forward to challenge him. Tekere had served eleven years in prison with Mugabe and after his release had fled to Mozambique, where he had played a critical role in organizing the guerrilla campaign. For his loyalty,

Mugabe had awarded him a cabinet post in his new government. Tekere was no angel; he was as brutal as Mugabe. In 1980, Tekere and his seven bodyguards were arrested in the killing of a white farm manager, Gerald Adams. The court ruled that Tekere was not guilty, for he had acted on a conviction that was protecting state security. In 1988, he was elected to ZANU's Central Committee. In this position he began to criticize Mugabe, declaring that a one-party state was not part of ZANU's principles and that one-party states lead to corruption.

Tekere's challenge was doomed from the outset, as he was known as a hothead and alcoholic. His anti-Mugabe coalition included white nationalists and corrupt former ZANU party officials, such as Patrick Kombayi, the mayor of Zimbabwe's third-largest city of Gweru. Kombayi ruled Gweru as a dictator, putting his supporters on the public payroll while increasing residents' taxes by 50 percent. He funneled city contracts into his own private business and was so bad that ZANU had expelled him from the party and removed him from his position. So though Kombayi had a grudge to bear against Mugabe, he did not represent a force for reform.

Initially, Mugabe dealt with the internal challenge by following his usual pattern of intimidation. But this time, he would go a step farther: he would plan to assassinate a major rival. On March 24, 1990, a gang of ZANU youth broke into Kombayi's mini-mart shop, broke open the safe, and set fire to the building. They then fired shots at his surrounding supporters. Kombayi was on the scene and organized an effort to take the wounded to the hospital. On the way to the hospital, the truck transporting the wounded was stopped, and the driver was shot in the stomach. The vigilantes then set fire to the truck. Following in his car, Kombayi stopped, but before he could get out of his car he was hit by a volley of shots. Uniformed police watched the violence. The wounded Kombayi rolled down his car window and shouted, "Okay, stop[;] you have killed me."[23] He survived, though, but crippled for life. During the campaign five opposition candidates other than Kombayi were assassinated. The culprits were arrested but later pardoned by Mugabe. Mugabe's party won 116 of 119 seats. Following the election, Tekere went into hiding, emerging only occasionally to criticize corruption and Mugabe's rule of terror.

Following the election, Mugabe continued his campaign to further appropriate white land without compensation. Land seizure became a political weapon to be used against his opponents. Mugabe's former ally, Ndabaningi Sithole, fell into the crosshairs of the government. Sithole had bought an 830-acre farm and subdivided it for members of his own tribe. The settlement was called Churu. The government ordered 4000 families to vacate the land. One Mugabe official, in defense of the removal, declared, "So let the Churu Farm settlers join their homeless colleagues, and we will deal with them there."[24]

As unemployment continued to soar, with at least a third of the workforce out of work, Mugabe unleashed once again a torrent of anti-white rhetoric. Large antiwhite advertisements appeared in newspapers. Homosexuals also came under attack. When human rights activists protested and seventy members of a conference on AIDs released a public statement calling for the protection of gay rights, Mugabe responded by describing homosexuals as "guilty of sub-human behavior." He told the gay activists, "Let the Americans keep their sodomy, bestiality, stupid and foolish ways to themselves, out of Zimbabwe."[25]

Seven years later, in 1997, Mugabe's government faced another challenge when Morgan Tsvangirai, the forty-seven-year-old vice president of the National Mine Workers' Union of Zimbabwe, organized a general strike to protest rising taxes. Tsvangirai was brutally attacked and severely beaten, saved by his security guards at the last minute from being thrown out of his tenth-floor office window. Mugabe the Marxist was now at war with the working class. Faced with massive demonstrations, Mugabe was forced to withdraw the tax hike, choosing instead to print more money. Further troubles came with food riots in Harare, which were suppressed by army soldiers, who left several protesters dead and hundreds injured.

The ever-cunning Mugabe was not finished, however. In 2000, he proposed a national referendum on a new constitution that lifted any limit to his term in office. This was brought before the electorate in the parliamentary elections. In response, Tsvangirai organized the Movement for Democratic Change (MDC), running candidates and calling for a "No" vote on the proposed constitution. Faced with his most serious challenge in a decade, Mugabe undertook a campaign of violence not seen since the Matabeleland campaign. Party thug Chenjerai "Hitler" Hunzvi, head of the War Veterans Association, was assigned the job of crushing the opposition. Hunzvi had taken the name "Hitler" because he admired Nazi ruthlessness. In the course of the repression, over 37 suspected supporters of MDC are known to have been murdered. Thousands more were assaulted, raped, abducted, and tortured. Photos of sickening attacks became international news, leading to sanctions that would prevent Mugabe and his cronies from traveling to Europe and America. In two days of voting, March 9 and 10, 5.6 million voters went to the polls. The 78-year-old Mugabe announced victory, claiming 56 percent of the vote over rival Morgan Tsvangirai.

By 2002, inflation had reached 120 percent, and unemployment was at 60 percent. Medicine, toothpaste, toilet paper, and other essential items were expensive and scarce. Ground maize and sugar could not be found in the markets. Riot police were assigned to every supermarket to prevent looting. Mugabe blamed the West, telling the press,"The West enjoys seeing people suffer."[26]

Mugabe's audacious accusations against the West were accompanied by his banning Western food charities Oxfam and the Save the Children Fund from distributing food aid in the country. Villagers who were suspected of supporting the opposition party were specifically targeted. Withholding food became a weapon for the Mugabe regime.

As dictators before him, Mugabe tried to distract from economic turmoil by creating a cult centered on himself. He required that his photograph be hung on every government office wall. Party newspapers declared him their "Consistent and Authentic Leader." Mugabe continued to declare himself a Marxist and a believer in "scientific socialism," even as other African leaders declared socialism a failure.

In creating this cult of personality, Mugabe refrained from publicizing details of his private life. He did so for obvious reasons. In 1987, Mugabe entered into an affair with a secretary in his office, Grace Marufu. She was a married woman with one child. He was sixty-seven years old, and she was twenty-three years old. He wanted children. The affair was kept from the public, although Mugabe later said, "I knew what I was doing, and my wife knew. She might not have liked it, but she knew."[27] A year after the romance began, Grace gave birth to a daughter. Two years later, she bore Mugabe a son. In early January 1992, five years after the affair began, Sally Mugabe died.

In 1995, an independent monthly announced the affair. Outraged that his private life had been revealed, he ordered the publisher of Zimbabwe's *Financial Times* and two of its editors arrested. All were subsequently prosecuted and fined. In a widely publicized event, he forced Roman Catholic archbishop Patrick Chakaipa to perform an official marriage in August 1996. Their affair had begun before the death of Sally. Grace was now pregnant with her third child. Over 12,000 people attended the marriage celebration. The couple soon moved into a grand family mansion in a 25-acre site in Harare. No expense was spared in building the compound. As first lady of the nation, Grace took little interest in charity and spent her time shopping for clothes, jewelry, cars, and going on luxurious vacations.

The End

Under Mugabe's reign, corruption permeated Zimbabwean society. In 1997, it was revealed that the head of the war veterans' compensation fund had awarded himself $500,000 (ZWD) for "impaired hearing" and "sciatic pains of the thigh." Mugabe's brother-in-law received $800,000 (ZWD) for "a scar on his left" knee. Other party officials were awarded large amounts for fabricated ailments. In 1999, the Zimbabwe Electricity Supply Authority became insolvent because of corruption. The state oil company ran out of money for oil imports because its managers had defrauded the company of $150 million over five years. Airport construction, telephone communications, banks, the biggest tobacco auction house, and oil concessions went to Mugabe cronies at the expense of the Zimbabwean people. The seizure of the means of production by the state soon turned out to mean the ownership of Zimbabwe's greatest resources by ZANU crooks.

While the party elite lived in luxury, taking lavish European vacations, hosting grand social parties on their private estates and yachts, and sending their children to expensive private schools, the people suffered under unemployment, runaway inflation, and the lack of land. The socialist utopia promised by Mugabe had turned into another kleptocracy—the common pattern shown by dictators like Lenin, Mao, and Castro. Among those who suffered were the ex-soldiers who had fought for liberation. Mugabe refused to undertake land reform, fearing that it was against the party's interest, because if rural people were not dependent on government, they would never support ZANU again.

By 2000, with Mugabe and his cronies fully ensconced in power, more than 70 percent of Zimbabweans lived in deep poverty. Nearly half the population was unemployed, and the economy was wracked with astronomical inflation. Average life expectancy had fallen from fifty-two years to forty-one years, while fuel and food lines became a regular part of people's lives. The government could no longer afford money for educational or social services. Essential drugs could only be found on the black market. Land lay abandoned. Victoria Falls, once an international tourist designation, had become a ghost town. The promised socialist utopia had turned into a living hell for the people Mugabe had promised to liberate.

Mugabe remained in power another seventeen years. The world no longer looked at him as a new African leader. In 2017, the ninety-three-year-old, cancer-ridden, and dying Mugabe still sought to keep power beyond the grave by having First Lady Grace Mugabe succeed him. Mugabe faced opposition from a faction led by First Vice President Emmerson Mnangagwa, who was backed by elements around the Zimbabwe Defence Forces (ZDF), the unified command system of the army and air force. Grace Mugabe accused him of plotting a coup. As it turned out, he was. On November 14, 2017, ZDF troops seized control of the Zimbabwe Broadcasting Corporation and surrounded the capital, Harare. Robert Mugabe was placed under house arrest. Threatened with impeachment and a trial, Mugabe resigned from office on November 21. He went into exile with Grace, only to die a few months later. Reports were that the couple were allowed to keep $100 million of their ill-gotten gains.

Emmerson Mnangagwa, who replaced Mugabe, came into office with a well-deserved reputation as a monster. He had gained the nickname "the Crocodile" because of his cold and ruthless personality. He had joined the war of liberation as a teenager, rising in the ranks to become Mugabe's bodyguard and then eventually intelligence chief in the new government. He had received his training in China. He had orchestrated the massacre of tens of thousands of the Ndebele people. Mnangagwa was outspoken in his support of seizing white farmers' lands. In ousting Mugabe, he promised new economic reforms and the expansion of the one-party system to allow other voices within the party. He professed to be a Maoist, so his call for dissident voices to be heard within the party appeared to echo Mao's "Let a Hundred Flowers Bloom"—a trap to get dissidents to expose themselves before cutting them down.

Robert Mugabe liberated his country from colonial rule, only to create a one-party state and terrorize it himself. He left his nation a failed state for those he had promised to liberate. Whatever his youthful ideals, his suit for power in the name of revolution brought tragedy, death, and sorrow to an African people that deserved more after having suffered under an oppressive colonial regime.

One ex-combatant told an interviewer in the early '90s when asked whether he would fight all over again, "What I just appreciate is that Zimbabwe is independent. It's no longer in the hands of foreigners," then adding, "If I could start again at the [age of thirteen], I would not join."

He concluded, "Many of those who thought they were going to get something nice after Independence are crying."[28]

This war veteran learned about the false promises of revolutionary liberation too late, but Mugabe's story is a cautionary tale for those seduced by prophets driven by their own will to power.

CHAPTER 5

Khomeini: God and the State

When the seventy-eight-year-old Sayyid Ruhollah Khomeini returned to Tehran on February 1, 1979, he told the mass of delirious Iranians who greeted him, "I am the truth and the people."[1] He had been in exile for fourteen years, and, as so many revolutionaries before him, he declared himself a liberator.

Khomeini appeared as all things to all people, and his supporters included religious clerics, students, secular liberals, and leftist revolutionaries. Only two weeks before, Mohammad Reza Pahlavi, the Shah of Iran, had fled the country. Over time, Iranians were to discover in Khomeini a man of tyrannical ambition who claimed to speak on behalf of God. Soon after his arrival, Khomeini announced in a press conference that he was the holy guardian of the lawgiver, the prophet Mohammed. As supreme leader, he established the Council of the Islamic Revolution that declared Iran an Islamic Republic. The council appointed Mehdi Bazargan as president of the provisional government. Khomeini declared, "The nation must obey him [Bazargan]. This is no ordinary government. It is a government based on the sharia [Islamic law]. . . . Revolt against God's government is a revolt against God. Revolt against God is blasphemy."[2] Opposition to Khomeini thus became an act against God himself.

Under a new constitution, approved in a popular referendum in 1979, Khomeini officially assumed the position of supreme leader (or supreme guide), which gave him virtually unlimited powers. As supreme leader, Khomeini was given the power to appoint heads of the armed services, the joint chief of staff of the armed services, and the head of national television and radio. The supreme leader was also charged with approving all candidates before they could run for office, and he could dismiss a president once elected. A 12-man Guardian Council, dominated by the supreme leader, needed to approve all legislation before it could become law.

The supreme leader remains the central institution in the Islamic Republic of Iran as a representative of the divine power on earth. The supreme leader (also considered the chief *faqih*, or jurist, of sharia law—the "grand jurist") serves as a conduit for the mind of God and the will of the people. He acts on behalf of God until the world is finally redeemed by the return of the final Imam (a descendant of the prophet Mohammed), at which time all nonbelievers and infidels will be destroyed. Until this time, the supreme leader represents God's sovereignty in the world and fulfills, as the preamble to the new constitution declares, "the ideological mission of jihad [struggle against the enemies of Islam] in God's path; that is, extending the sovereignty of God's law throughout the world."[3]

The creation of the title supreme leader reflected Khomeini's belief that through religious contemplation and self-discipline, a man such as himself could develop his soul until he takes on the form of the divine in the "Perfect Man." Khomeini described the Perfect Man as "the holder of the chain of existence. . . . He is God's great sign, created in God's image. Whoever knows the Perfect Man has known God."[4] Khomeini believed that the Perfect Man would guide society toward absolute perfection.

Khomeini was outspoken in his opposition to the concepts of democracy and constitutional government. For him, such concepts were alien to Islam. They were concepts thrust on Muslim people by Zionist and Western imperialists to denigrate the religion of Islam. While in exile, he claimed, in a series of lectures later published in a book called *Islamic Government*, that this plot to undermine Islamic civilization was begun by Jews "about three hundred years ago."[5] In pursuit of satanic materialism and moral corruption, Jews and other plotters had infiltrated alien beliefs—Western ideas—into Islam through agents in educational, religious, and governmental institutions. He labeled the United States the "Great Satan." He meant it literally. In his 10-year reign, thousands of Iranians—political opponents, former allies, and dissidents—were imprisoned, tortured, and executed as spies and agents of Israel, American and European imperialists, Masons, and even Satan himself.

If the promise of the revolution—a better and more equal and free society—was betrayed by Khomeini, it was a result of the dynamics of revolution and his vision of himself as a self-proclaimed prophet assured of the trajectory of history. Khomeini assumed for himself the role of the second Mohammed, with a mission to revive a moribund Islam. His religious followers accepted his claim. Some claimed an even more exalted status for Khomeini. One contemporary Iranian poet praised Khomeini as literally a "celestial being" to whom even angels bowed and prayed.[6] True believers accepted Khomeini's apocalyptic vision of the world, in which final redemption came through destruction and the triumph of Islam. When the Soviet empire collapsed in 1991, two years after Khomeini's death, his followers saw this as a clear sign of Islam's triumph promised by the prophet Mohammed.

Khomeini returned to Iran in 1979 supported by an uneasy coalition of fundamentalist Muslims, students, liberals, and radical leftists. All claimed to be Muslim, even his Marxist supporters. Step by step, Khomeini eliminated his rivals in the name of true Islam. In this regard, the Iranian Revolution followed a pattern seen in the French and Russian revolutions: overthrow of the existing regime, eradication of enemies of the revolution through revolutionary terror, and final consolidation of power.

The full extent of Khomeini's human rights violations in Iran are not fully known. The total number of deaths ordered by Khomeini can only be gleaned from Iranian and international human rights reports.

In the first years of his regime from 1981 to 1985, at least ten thousand people were executed. In 1988, he ordered political prisoners executed. Children as young as thirteen were slowly hanged from cranes. The number of political prisoners executed is estimated between twenty to thirty-five thousand. We know that religious and ethnic minorities have been persecuted through arrests, torture, and execution. Alleged homosexuals and those women accused of adultery have been stoned to death publicly. Khomeini's intelligence services have conducted widespread assassinations of political opponents. The regime conducts and sponsors international terrorism. As the supreme leader in revolutionary Iran, Khomeini revealed a ruthlessness equal to Lenin, Mao, Castro, and Mugabe. He called not for a "dictatorship of the proletariat," but a dictatorship in the name of God. Lenin, Mao, Castro, and Mugabe spoke in the name of the workers; Khomeini spoke in the name of God. All shared in a certainty that the result of history was a millennial age in which the Perfect Man arises. In preparing for the millennium to come, they welcomed apocalypse.

Khomeini: From Quietism to Activism

In the first days of the revolution, a romanticized image of Khomeini developed in the West. President Jimmy Carter wrote to Khomeini as "one man of God to another," while Andrew Young, the U.S. ambassador to the United Nations, hailed him as a "twentieth-century saint," and U.S. ambassador to Iran William Sullivan depicted Khomeini as a "Gandhi-like figure."[7] He was depicted as a man of simple virtue, modesty, erudition, and vision. Khomeini held a deserved reputation for his piety and ascetic lifestyle, but Westerners overlooked his political views that suggested theocratic rule by a single supreme leader.

When he returned to Iran from exile in 1979, he was a man in his late seventies with his worldview fully formed. He was a devout Shia Muslim who had spent a lifetime studying religious texts. He had carefully avoided direct opposition to the Shah's government until the early

1960s. His vociferous opposition to the Shah's call for women's rights made Khomeini into a national figure. He saw the Shah's program to modernize Iran as a plot by Israel and Western imperialists to subvert Islamic civilization. His opposition led the government to exile him. In exile, a powerful personality cult had formed around Khomeini, and he genuinely believed that he was "chosen" to save Islam from destruction. Those few religious leaders, mullahs, who challenged his political leadership and declaration of being "supreme leader" were targeted by Khomeini's political gangs. His power derived from a network of students and city merchants he had developed as a seminary teacher in Iran and later in exile.

Born in 1900, Khomeini grew up in a small village—Khomein—in the vast semi-arid plains of central Iran, approximately 180 miles south of Tehran. He came from a family of religious scholars. When his father was killed over a land dispute, Khomeini had to be brought up by a relatively wealthy uncle. Khomeini's son later recalled, "Even as a youngster, my father always wanted to be the Shah in the games he played."[8] His religious education consisted of memorizing Koranic verses and Shia history, which both imprint on young minds, such as his, a view of the world in black and white. At the age of seven, he began attending a public school established as part of the government effort to modernize the nation. When he was sixteen, he was sent to a seminary, where he studied under a leading Shia teacher, Abdul-Karim Haeri Yazdi. In seminary, he developed a specialty in Islamic mystical philosophy and ethics. In his study of mysticism, he focused on Irfan, a type of mysticism that explored the possibility of unity with the divine one and the inner universal self of the true believer. Most Shia theologians condemned this kind of mysticism as pantheism in that individual union with God suggested deification of mortal souls. (Khomeini recognized that his study of mysticism was unorthodox, and he did not publish much directly on mysticism until after 1979. He studied and taught mysticism privately.) Ironically, Plato's *Republic*, as transmitted through various Arabic texts, provided the intellectual foundations for his mysticism. Through Platonic and neo-Platonic thought, Khomeini examined knowledge of eternal truth and development of the Perfect Man in union with the divine.

Whether at this point Khomeini saw himself as such a man is unclear. He understood that few men could attain such a status. In *The Light of Guidance*, published in 1931, written to reconcile the original neo-Platonic theory of divine manifestation and the Shia tradition, Khomeini wrote, "Anyone who has the quality of a perfect man, that is the quality of the divine essence, is a caliph in this world as he was in the origins."[9]

After he received his diploma, Khomeini became a teacher in jurisprudence and philosophy at the seminary in the small city of Qom. At the age of twenty-seven, he requested the hand of a fifteen-year-old daughter of a prominent family. As a teacher, Khomeini found a large following among Iranian students of Islam, but he did not consider himself Iranian by blood. Instead, he claimed to be a descendant of the Prophet, thus of Arabian stock. As a teacher, he developed a large student following as well as connections with artisans and small shopkeepers in Tehran. He received a small income from teaching, as well as income from his father's property, administered by his older brother, another cleric.

Khomeini's arrogance in claiming to be the direct voice of God can only be understood within the context of Shia Islam. Iran was unique in the Middle East for having a Shia majority population. Most Middle Eastern countries were Sunni. On the surface, the theological differences between Sunni and Shia appear to be based on a dispute over of the prophet Mohammed's legitimate successor. Underlying this historical debate were far deeper issues. Sunni and Shia Muslims accused each other of being apostates. The Shia claimed that Mohammed's three immediate successors, or caliphs (rulers), were usurpers intent on destroying Islam. The charge explicitly condemned all later Sunni governments as illegitimate and representing dark forces in history. This meant that 88 percent of those claiming to be Muslim (Sunnis) were in fact unbelievers.

Shia clergy (mullahs) were held responsible for applying sharia (traditional Islamic law) in their communities. In the Shia tradition, clergy trained in Islamic law (*mujtahidun*) were obligated to provide general guidance to the government without holding direct political power. From this small group of *mujtahidun*, one or two might emerge in a generation to serve as supreme guide to the community. Even the most learned among them should not directly hold office, however. Thus, when Khomeini claimed to be the supreme leader—not just for the community of believers, but for the nation itself and to hold governmental power—some Shia theologians considered him an "innovator" (a term of abuse in Islamic polemics) and his system a "satanic novelty."[10]

Without a church hierarchy, Khomeini's claim to be the supreme leader could only be disputed by individual mullahs. The title "mullah" is given to mosque leaders, but there is no official certification to become a mullah. In 1977, shortly before the revolution, the Iranian government found that of the 250,000 men claiming to be mullahs, 20 percent were "illiterate" or "semiliterate." There were those who switched back and forth between religious and civilian life. For example, Akbar Hashemi Rafsanjani, who became a president of the Islamic Republic of Iran, was a small building contractor and pistachio grower in the early 1970s but in 1978 claimed the role of a middle-level mullah. Mohammad Khatami, another future president of Iran, was a director of a travel agency in Tehran, but in the late 1970s, he grew a beard, began wearing a turban, and claimed a religious title.

Clerical opposition to the Shah did not develop as a political force until after the Second World War. As a clerical student and teacher in the 1920s, Khomeini did not express overt political positions, even when Reza Pahlavi, the father of Mohammad Reza, sought to secularize Iran at the expense of the mullahs. During his 16-year reign, Reza Shah sought to modernize Iran along the lines of Mustafa Kemal Atatürk's Turkish government. European laws were introduced, and judges were required to hold a law degree from the newly established Tehran University. This reduced the power of clergy within the judicial system. Schools and universities were created as rival centers of power. This agenda drew opposition from the mullahs, who were directly challenged by the Shah's programs. Confrontation between the clergy and the government turned violent when government troops entered a holy shrine in the city of Mashhad where protesters had gathered. The troops opened fire, killing dozens and wounding hundreds. This event appears to have left a deep mark on the young Khomeini, who often spoke about the incident later in the 1960s. In 1935, however, Khomeini expressed little anger. Eventually, Reza brought the clergy under control through patronage and brutal suppression of opponents. In 1941, British and Russian troops invaded Iran and ousted Reza Pahlavi, whom they considered too favorably disposed to German commercial interests. The Allied troops placed the Shah's son, Mohammad Reza Pahlavi, on the throne.

For the next two decades, Khomeini remained circumspect in directly criticizing Mohammad Reza Shah. There were signs, though, found in his 1942 book, *The Unveiling of Secrets*, of his developing political views. In the book, published anonymously, Khomeini denounced Mohammad Reza Shah as a usurper aligned with Western imperial interests in an attempt to subvert Islamic civilization. He called upon the defenders of Islam and the clergy to "smash in the teeth of this brainless mob with their iron fist" and "trample upon their heads with courageous strides."[11] Khomeini's polemics equaled Lenin's when it came to invective.

Khomeini argued further that the prophet Mohammed had brought to the people the promise of freedom, justice, salvation, and perfection. Khomeini viewed Western democracy, representative government, constitutionalism, and separation of church and state as antithetical to Islam. In *The Unveiling of Secrets*, he projected Islam as an all-embracing system of life and government. Before his death, the prophet Mohammed had delegated authority to Imami (clergy) to fulfill this prophecy. Within the Shia tradition, some held that the Twelfth Imam, Mohammed ibn al-Hasan al-Mahdi, mysteriously disappeared while still young in the Iranian city of Samarra twelve centuries earlier. He concealed himself, awaiting the day when he would return to establish the reign of order and justice promised in the prophecy. During the great occultation of the Twelfth Imam, or Hidden Imam, and while the world awaits the Imam's awakening, moral men—learned Muslims—are charged with combating tyranny and enlightening the masses. Through enlightenment, Muslims will choose the most just and most learned leader to represent them on behalf of the Hidden Imam. Khomeini's book suggested, without fully stating it, that the fulfillment of the Prophet's promise was a "deputy" to represent the prophecy until the return of the Hidden Imam.

Nonetheless, during this period, Khomeini avoided direct political involvement. He kept quiet when the elected prime minister of Iran, Mohammad Mosaddegh, was overthrown in a military coup orchestrated by the CIA and British intelligence. Khomeini remained quiet about the coup probably because most of the senior clergy actually supported it. They thought Mosaddegh was too closely aligned with the Marxists.

The Shia tradition in Iran believed that clergy should guide government but that they should abstain from direct governance. Shia clergy opposed the concept of a clergy-led government. Khomeini appears to have shared this view of tempered state-church separation until he published *Islamic Government* in 1970, based on his earlier lectures. The book was a polemic, with shallow scholarship, composed of short chapters ranting about Western imperialist and Zionist efforts to undermine Islamic civilization. In his "Lessons on Jurisprudence in Islam," a series of lectures delivered in 1969–70 to his students in Iraq, he maintained, "Since its inception, the Islamic movement was afflicted with the Jews when they started their counter-activity by distorting the reputation of Islam, by assaulting it and by slandering it." He added, "This has continued to our present day. Then came the role of groups that can be considered more evil than the devil and their troops."[12] He declared that the Jews and Christian colonialists were not trying to convert Iranian youth. Their goals were more sinister, because they were "working to corrupt them and make them disavow religion and to become indifferent."[13] He claimed that this campaign to poison Iranian youth had been going on for "hundreds of years."[14]

In the book, Khomeini proposed that good Islamic government should require compliance with traditional Islamic law (sharia) and that this required political "guardianship" through a leading Islamic clerical jurist (*faqih*). Good laws were not enough in themselves to preserve Islam. He wrote, "A collection of laws is not enough to reform society. For law to be an element for reforming, and making people happy, it requires executive authority."[15] This ruler, the Imam, should be well versed in Islamic law. He asserted that it was an acknowledged fact that the scholars of jurisprudence were rulers over kings. This was a clear articulation of the need to create a theocracy under a strong executive leader, not democratically elected, in order to save Islam from subversion. The exact role of the *faqih* was not fully developed in the text, but it was suggested this role could be performed by a single man, or perhaps by a committee of mullahs. He made clear that this theocratic ruler, a scholar of Islamic jurisprudence, held duties beyond that of judges or courts.

Khomeini's call for the creation of a theocracy was not accepted by most leading mullahs in Iran, but given his popularity, especially among young, religious students, few were willing to publicly repudiate this clear break with Shia political tradition. Khomeini's doctrine of *faqih*-headed government found expression in the 1979 constitution of the Islamic Republic of Iran, which created the first *faqih* as "guardian" in the position of the supreme leader—in this case Khomeini.

The 1979 Revolution

Like his father, Mohammad Reza Pahlavi sought to modernize Iran through the creation of a prosperous middle class. He wanted women to find a new place in Iranian society. Also like his father, he confronted an entrenched clergy. But unlike his father, he ultimately failed to intimidate them. The Shah found himself caught on the shoals of a modernizing

Iran and the Islamic tradition. He came under American pressure for his clear violations of human rights.

Beginning in the early 1960s, Mohammad Reza Shah launched what he called the "White Revolution," an intensified campaign to modernize the country through land reform, local elections, secular education, and providing rights to women. The Shah proposed land reform, privatization of some state industry, infrastructure construction, and education. In seeking modernization—without liberalization of political institutions— the Shah inadvertently unleashed a small, organized Left that undertook guerrilla attacks. He contained mullah opposition for a while by modifying his reform program and, like his father, directing funds to the mullahs. As for the Left's opposition, it remained a security threat but lacked a popular base to win a revolution on its own. As a result, by the end of the decade, the Shah appeared to have won the political battle over his White Revolution.

The Shah's proposal in 1961 to break up large land holdings and redistribute the land created the first signs of tension. On the surface, land reform appeared necessary to foster the economic betterment of peasants. In some cases, large-scale landowners had control of dozens of villages. In other cases, clerics themselves were the large-scale landowners. Most clergy, whether owning land or not, relied on landowners for financial support. As a result, the Shah's land reform challenged the economic and political order in rural areas.

Further tensions arose over the government's educational reforms. But the most heated issue became the government's decree providing for the elections of local councils. Behind local council elections lay the larger issue of the role of women in Islamic society. The law allowed women to vote for the first time, allowed for elected village and city councils to be sworn in on a holy book (rather than the Koran specifically), and allowed non-Muslims to serve in office. Religious leaders saw this as a direct attack on the Islamic community and their power. Throughout the land reform debate, Khomeini had kept relatively quiet. Not so with the council election mandate. Khomeini stepped forward as the Shah's most vociferous critic, accusing the government of plotting against the Islamic faithful. He described the measure as an attempt "to corrupt . . . chaste women."[16] He warned, "The court of the oppressor wants to give equal rights to women and men, and trample on the precepts of the Koran and the sharia, and to take [eighteen]-year-old girls into compulsory military service."[17] He attacked the Shah for encouraging Western dress among women and men, declaring, "They have put chamber-pot-shaped hats over your head and gladdened your hearts with naked women in the middle of streets and swimming pools."[18]

Khomeini accused the government of trying to denigrate Muslim women by encouraging education and work outside the home. By 1979, 160,000 women worked in government at all administrative levels; 317 served as judges or advocates, including one female judge on the 9-justice supreme court. Khomeini and other traditional clergy saw these advances as the further subversion of Islam. He charged the Shah with "aping the [W]est."[19] He warned that the local council law was "perhaps drawn up by spies of Jews and Zionists," saying, "The Koran and Islam are in danger. The independence of the state and the economy are threatened by a takeover by Zionists, who in Iran have appeared in the guise of the Baha'is."[20] Liberal moderates welcomed the attack on the Shah: The government did not respect the right of men to vote, so why should it respect the right of women to vote?

Tensions between the clergy and the government were again exacerbated when the Shah revised a land reform law in 1963. The law included provisions that covered religious and other endowments. Khomeini stepped forward once again to voice clerical opposition by declaring, "In the interests of the Jews, America[,] and Israel, we must be jailed and killed; we must be sacrificed to the evil intentions of foreigners." He declared in another sermon, "Love of the Shah means rapine, violations of the rights of Muslims[,] and violation of the commandments of Islam." He warned that the Iranians were "not prepared to see the country crushed beneath the Jewish boot."[21]

On June 3, 1963, Khomeini stepped up his attacks with even greater ferocity in a widely broadcast sermon. He attacked the Shah (calling him an "unfortunate wretch") for refusing to listen to the larger community of believers; instead, the Shah served foreign interests intent on destroying Islam. He alleged, "Israel does not want the Koran to survive in this country." Israel sought, he claimed, to "crush" the Iranian people, crush the nation, take over the economy, and "destroy [Iranian] commerce and agriculture."[22] Khomeini's message spread to Tehran and other cities. Khomeini showed an ability to mobilize vast numbers of people through his powerful speeches and through his organizational ability. He began to reach out to other anti-Shah groups and mobilized merchants. The devotion of his followers was stunning. One merchant declared, "If you give the order[,] we are prepared to attach bombs to ourselves and throw ourselves at the Shah's car to blow him up."[23]

The Shah responded by ordering Khomeini's arrest. As word spread of the arrest, rioting broke out across Iran. Ten months later, Khomeini was released with his promise to stay out of politics. He broke this promise within months by addressing students at Tehran University, delivering a speech that renewed his attack on the Shah as a lackey of foreign interests. In the fall of 1964, he escalated his attacks on the Shah and the parliament for the passage of a bill that extended diplomatic immunity to American military personnel residing in Iran. Khomeini called the law another sign that Western powers, along with Israel, sought to colonize Iran. His recorded sermon was sold in bazaars and spread through word of mouth. The government had had enough of Khomeini. He was rearrested, exiled to Turkey, and later permitted to settle in Najaf, a Shia holy site in Iraq. Here he continued writing, speaking, and teaching his followers to prepare themselves for resistance. In exile, he developed a network of supporters throughout Iran. This ensured his primacy as the opposition leader in the religious community in Iran. Throughout Khomeini's opposition to the Shah, he never denounced armed resistance, which would have been unpopular within the growing resistance movement. Thus when the first violent protests against the Shah broke out in 1978, Khomeini stood ready to step forward as the leader of the revolution.

The Shah's repressive measures through his secret police drew heavy criticism in the Western press. Yet Khomeini's persistent use of anti-Semitic rhetoric went unreported. Khomeini's rhetoric, both in its appeal to base prejudices, as well as wealth inequality and corruption in the political system, struck a chord in Iranian society. The breakdown in traditional society that had come with urbanization and a growing consumer society had created deep cultural anxiety. Between 1956 and 1976, the urban population rose from six to sixteen million. Older, more traditional Muslim adults were shocked by young Iranians drinking, young women wearing skirts, and young people rejecting Islam. At the same time, young students found within political Islam an outlet for their idealism.

Political Islam and the Iranian Left

In the early 1960s, no one could have predicted a revolution led by Khomeini. Ironically, though, the political Left captured much of the angst within Iranian youth in this period. Fears of *Gharbzadegi* (toxic Westernization) found expression on the Left through intellectuals who sought to fuse Western radical political ideology, including Marxism, with traditional Islamic culture.[24] Political Islam, as it was later called, seeped its way into the minds of young Iranian students anxious to find a voice in Iranian society. Political Islam emerged in an environment of global student unrest in the 1960s. Young Iranians were influenced by the Cuban Revolution (1953–1959), the Algerian War for Independence (1954–1962), the Vietnam War (1955–1979), and the Palestinian Liberation Organization, founded in 1964. In this revolutionary atmosphere, the idea of armed resistance began to take shape. Mehdi Bazargan, a Muslim social democrat and the first prime minister appointed by Khomeini after the fall of the Shah, recalled, "All opposition groups and organizations, with their differing ideologies, reached a single conclusion. . . . [T]he only means of struggling against the regime was through armed struggle."[25]

Political Islam first found expression in the 1930s with writers such as Hasan al-Banna, the founder of the Egyptian Muslim Brotherhood, and other authors who sought to define Islam as primarily a political system. They argued that Muslim law, sharia, remained the sole source of the law for the state, the people, and the individual. Sovereignty rested only in God. In their eyes, the separation of the public and the private realm was a Western concept. The concept of the nation-state was rejected for the universal ideal which included all believers, the community of the faithful (the *ummah*). Inherent in the rhetoric of Political Islam was a strong tendency toward a conspiracy theory in which the European powers, working or aligned with Jews, sought to subvert Islam on behalf of Satan. The early authors of such a theory were fundamentalist Sunnis. Political Islam took a turn in the post–World War II era when authors, clearly influenced by European political concepts, began warning that the greatest threat to Islamic nations was Western imperialism.

Leading in this critique of Western imperialism and the call for the restoration of Islamic culture were Iranian writers such as Ali Shariati Mazinani, a French-educated political author deeply influenced by French West Indian revolutionary thinker Frantz Fanon. Shariati translated Che Guevara's *Guerrilla Warfare* (1961) into Farsi. Although Shariati died in 1977 before the Iranian Revolution, he became for many the revolution's leading ideologue. A lyrical writer, he combined utopian politics with spiritual symbols that captivated the youth. Shariati's contribution was to bridge Shia Islam with secular revolutionary thought. He confronted what appeared to be a contradictory dilemma of reconciling Western-oriented modernity with traditional Islam. He called for a revolution to create a new universal Islamic order to fulfill the promise of social justice. He told students in 1972, "We are living in a transitional stage[,] and if anyone wants to do anything, this is the time to make one's move."[26] He claimed that the corruption of Islamic culture was a result of the deliberate importing of a Western culture of "drink and drugs, violence and sex through television and cinema, its philosophy and ideology which alters as frequently as fashion."[27]

Shariati called for a restoration of a "golden age" of Islam in the face of European colonialism. He proclaimed it was the responsibility of the young to resist Western imperialism. The mullahs, he argued, had acquiesced to the Shah's agenda of Westernizing Iran. In the absence of clerical opposition, he maintained, the faithful should act through the politics of the street. His critique of imperialism grafted European leftist thought onto an Islamic tradition while rejecting basic Western concepts of liberty and democracy. He called democracy "a veil of chastity worn by a whore." He asked, "What is the value of the votes of people who sell it for a ride or a bellyful of soup? And that is without mentioning the votes of the enslaved sheep, the votes of donkeys and cows." The masses, he held, needed to be led by an Imam, "who [would choose] his goals based on the Truth. Which Truth? The Truth revealed by Islamic ideology."[28] He remained ambivalent about Marxism, only later siding against Marxist factions within the militant Iranian resistance.

He and other authors found an enthusiastic audience among young Iranian students. Anti-imperialist sentiment had grown in Iran following a military coup in 1953 that had ousted Mohammad Mosaddegh, the elected prime minister of Iran, when he had attempted to nationalize Iranian oil. Anti-American sentiment ran strong, especially among Iranian students living in urban areas who had little prospect for upward mobility. When the 1979 revolution occurred, half of the population lived in urban areas. Those declaring themselves revolutionaries included both males and females.

By the late 1960s, armed-resistance guerrilla groups formed and began training for organized military action. On February 8, 1971, Iran was stunned when a small band of 9 Marxist-Leninist guerrillas attacked a police post in Siahkal, killing three policemen and freeing two previously arrested guerrilla soldiers. Iranian security forces hunted them down, eventually leading to the arrest, conviction, and execution of 13 guerrilla soldiers. Nonetheless, the attacks continued. From 1971 to 1977, 341 members of different guerrilla organizations lost their lives. Most were young intellectuals under the age of 35. Many had trained in Palestinian Liberation Army boot camps. They launched violent attacks, including the bombings of 10 major buildings and the assassinations of American and Iranian officials. They were able to infiltrate army units and worker organizations and played a major role through the Confederation of Iranian Students, which brought attention to their cause outside of Iran. Photos of Iranian students protesting with their faces masked to hide their identity from security forces appeared regularly in the Western press.

While abroad, many of these students aligned themselves with American and European student revolutionary groups—Maoist and Trotskyist. But the situation could not have been more different for Westerners and Iranians. American and Western European students who declared themselves revolutionaries eventually graduated, entered the middle class, and went on to lead comfortable, privileged lives. The Iranian Left, while undertaking terrorist activity and making some gains among the young, was thrown into an existential struggle against the Iranian state, one in which it failed to gain mass popular support. The clergy would prove critical to the mobilization of the masses.

As late as 1977, the opposition to the Shah remained fragmented, and most observers believed the Shah remained secure on his throne. Indeed, in 1978, President Jimmy Carter, hardly the most prescient figure in foreign affairs, described Iran as an island of stability. Behind this illusion of stability rested rising inflation, deep corruption, and accusations of police and security force brutality. An antiprofiteering campaign launched by the Shah against shopkeepers and members of the bazaar caused massive resentment among small-scale as well as some wealthy businessmen, especially when corruption ran rampant through the political system.

The Shah's government came under heavy criticism from human rights groups. In early 1977, the Shah relaxed some controls over press censorship and freed over three hundred political prisoners. These measures failed to satisfy reformers. In October, liberal democratic reformers led by Shapour Bakhtiar, Mehdi Bazargan, Karim Sanjabi—all of whom later played important roles in the coming revolution and postrevolutionary period—called on the United Nations to investigate human rights violations.

Khomeini remained on the offensive throughout this period. In November 1977, Ayatollah Khomeini's elder son, Mostafa, died of a heart attack in Iraq, where his father was in exile. The Khomeini camp in Iran whipped up anti-Shah protests, which were joined by secular opposition in solidarity. In the past, the Shah had successfully kept the opposition divided. No longer. Khomeini emerged as the leader of the revolution, as anti-Shah factions united around him. In response the government heightened its propaganda campaign against Khomeini by accusing him of being of Hindu descent, being a former British spy, and having homosexual tendencies as expressed in his erotic poetry. The attack on Khomeini only outraged the clerical establishment. The bazaar and seminaries closed in Qom. Demonstrators went to the streets demanding the government offer a public apology and return Ayatollah Khomeini from exile. Security forces reacted in force, opening fire on the demonstrators. The opposition reported seventy deaths and more than five hundred injured. This incident led clerics to call for demonstrations across the country. The second phase of the revolution had begun, led by clerics.

Most of the marches that followed were peaceful, but in the city of Tabriz they turned violent following a shooting that had killed one demonstrator. This killing caused mobs to attack government and public buildings in the city. In the days that followed, over three hundred were killed. The rioting ended when the Iranian military moved in and declared martial law. In the process, troops entered the house of a cleric, killed two theological students, and further outraged the clergy. As the news traveled, violence broke out in other cities.

The Shah tried to quell the rebellion. He removed the longtime head of the security forces and announced that the upcoming elections set for August 5 would be free and fair. Even with the removal of the head of state security, the security forces began organizing their own vigilante groups to violently attack demonstrators. These attacks fueled popular anger, already inflamed by declining economic growth, with budget cuts, announced earlier, being made by the government in an attempt to control rampant inflation. These budget cuts hurt both the urban poor and bazaar merchants in a government-induced recession.

In August 1978, the situation exploded when a fire and explosion at the Cinema Rex in Abadan left over four hundred men, women, and children dead. The government blamed the fire on the opposition, and the opposition accused SAVAK, the regime's security and intelligence service, of setting the fire. As street protests intensified, the Shah responded by replacing the prime minister with a close ally, Jafar Sharif-Emami. In order to appease the clerics, the new prime minister ordered casinos and gambling houses closed, raised salaries of government workers and military personnel, and freed many political prisoners. He dismissed politicians and generals accused of having Baha'i connections. (The Baha'i faith arose in Persia in the nineteenth century proclaiming the universality of humankind and equated Jesus, the Buddha, and Mohammed as equal prophets. The Baha'i faithful were condemned as heretics by Shia clerics.)

These concessions defused the situation momentarily, but in the fasting months of Ramadan in the fall of 1978, a quarter of a million demonstrators gathered in the major public square in Tehran to protest against the government. Protesters included workers, merchants, bearded mullahs dressed in black, veiled women, and dissident students in jeans. In response, the Shah ordered martial law in Tehran. Newspapers were closed, and arrest warrants were issued for Sanjabi, Bazargan, and other liberal anti-Shah leaders. The following day protestors gathered in Jaleh Square, many of them not realizing that public demonstrations and marches had been banned. In the clashes that followed, hundreds of people were killed. The opposition claimed over four thousand had been killed; the military said it was fewer than a hundred. But no matter how many died that day, Friday, September 8, 1978, became known as "Black Friday." Any hope of reconciliation was ended.

Matters worsened when seven hundred oil refinery workers in Tehran went on strike. The strike spread to other industrial cities. An earthquake in the Khorasan region left thousands dead. Khomeini's calls for more strikes and his demand that the Shah step down were widely disseminated by BBC news bulletins broadcast in Persian, even though Khomeini still remained under house arrest in Iraq. In late 1978, the Iraqi government, with the support of Iran, decided to expel Khomeini from the country. After attempting to enter Kuwait and other Arab countries, Khomeini agreed to move to Paris. In Paris, Khomeini found unlimited access to the world media. Hundreds of reporters gathered each day to hear him. He was joined by secular Iranian opposition leaders who served as translators for him in multiple meetings with reporters. These translators downplayed his more radical statements. Khomeini played to reporters and his liberal allies by speaking of a progressive Iran in which women would have the right to vote. He promised an Islamic Republic to ensure freedom, independence, and social justice. He promised a true democracy in which everyone's voice would be heard.

The Shah responded to the Khomeini groundswell by seeking to create a coalition government. He invited Khomeini to enter the government. Khomeini refused and continued to encourage massive street protests and countrywide strikes. He had become a kind of saint who could save the country. When a rumor spread that people could see Khomeini's face on the moon, thousands of people gathered in Tehran to watch the moon. Mullahs, liberals, and Marxist revolutionaries rallied behind him. Placed on the defensive, the Shah proceeded to form a coalition government under Shapour Bakhtiar. A moderate, Bakhtiar accepted the call to form a new government on the condition that the Shah leave the country. On January 16, the Shah left Iran for Egypt, where he was welcomed by President Anwar Sadat. Iranians were jubilant. Thousands of people danced in the cities. The Bakhtiar government invited Khomeini and other exiled opposition leaders to return to Iran. Bakhtiar hoped that Khomeini's return might restore peace. His hopes were soon dashed.

After fifteen years in exile, Khomeini returned to Tehran on February 1, 1979. The *New York Times* reported, "A Prophet Returns to His Own Land—With Honor." He was greeted by millions of Iranians who lined the route. Khomeini proceeded to a holy cemetery where he denounced the Bakhtiar government. He declared, "I will strike with my fists at the mouths of this government. From now on it is I who will name the government. . . . I tell you it's up to all of us to maintain the revolution until we choose the government."[29] The Bakhtiar government was finished. On February 5, only a few days before his return, Khomeini announced the formation of the provisional government of the Islamic Republic of Iran under Mehdi Bazargan, a devout religious intellectual, as prime minister. Khomeini warned that any action against the new government would be considered "an uprising and under Islamic law guilty of blasphemy."[30]

Bazargan appealed to the democratic aspirations of the intellectuals and moderate clerical forces who sought a constitutional order. He stepped forward as a moderate and a gradualist in a country clamoring for radical change. Bazargan tried to reassure the middle classes that he did not see himself as a bulldozer tearing down the old order but that he intended to build a democracy on established institutions. He appointed middle-class professionals and technocrats to his cabinet. He sought to restore order, only to find it impossible. Bazargan faced a parallel government of revolutionary committees, makeshift courts, and revolutionary street fighters.

In the next few years, a half million people fled the country, mostly from the professional and middle classes. For those that remained, tragedy followed. Thousands of people were executed in the next few years as Khomeini began to consolidate power.

Revolutionary Chaos

Khomeini, who claimed to be the supreme leader of the regime, unleashed a wave of terror across the country. Attempts by Bazargan to restore order were further undermined by revolutionary courts, established by the Khomeini-controlled Council of the Islamic Revolution, to administer Islamic justice. The first trials began with four top generals, who were tortured by the Islamic Revolution Committees before they were brought to court. Khomeini told the court prosecutor, "These people are guilty in any case." Khomeini instructed the prosecutor to hear what they had to say "then execute them."[31] After the generals were executed, seventy others were brought to court and ordered executed. Meanwhile, Khomeini ordered that homosexuals, prostitutes, adulterers, and petty criminals be tried and publicly flogged and executed. In July 1979, Bazargan prevailed upon Khomeini to offer a general amnesty to all members of the old regime that had not been involved in killing or torture. Tribunals ignored the decree, however, and Bazargan had no way of enforcing their closure. The Islamic Revolutionary Guard Corps, an armed militia organized by Khomeini, conducted its own courts, harassed reluctant mullahs who appeared opposed to the new regime, and launched attacks against radical leftists. Khomeini's Revolutionary Guard Corps—storm troopers, in effect—wielded their power in the streets through execution, tribunals, and intimidation.

Bazargan found his authority further undercut by the Islamic Revolution Committees that sprang up around district mosques. Hundreds of such committees had formed around local mosques, serving to impose their own authority. More than 1,500 committees operated in Tehran alone. These revolutionary committees, like the Revolutionary Guard Corps, confiscated property, conducted trials, and executed their enemies. Khomeini declared that there was a great need for these committees.

Adding to this chaos were armed groups aligned with mullahs and revolutionary factions. For example, Hojjat ol-Eslam Ghaffari, an influential cleric in Tehran, organized networks of "club-wielders" who appeared en masse on the streets, sometimes numbering more than two hundred thousand people. Ghaffari organized other groups as well that became known informally as Hezbollah, the "party of God" (distinct from the Lebanese group of the same name), which terrorized opponents, newspaper editors, and anyone who questioned the regime. In addition, the government faced well-armed revolutionary gangs that roamed cities, towns, and villages tracking down alleged counterrevolutionaries, former security officials, and high-ranking military and government officials of the previous government.

Political parties and factions sprang up across the country. In the chaos of revolution, different factions emerged with agendas of their own. Two major groups emerged, one of which was a cluster of groups into which the Organization of Iranian People's Fedai Guerrillas (Marxists) had split, and the other of which was the People's Mujahedin of Iran (leftist Muslims). In order to consolidate power among the clerics, Khomeini and his followers organized the Islamic Republican Party (IRP). The goal of the party was to establish an Islamic state and government based on Khomeini's concept of a leader to represent the Hidden Imam until the awaking. The IRP never fully functioned as a party, but through *hezbollahi* it was able to exert power on the streets. To the left was an array of secular leftist parties including the Soviet-aligned Tudeh Party, the Democratic Party of Iranian Kurdistan, and a collection of Marxist self-proclaimed workers' parties. These parties called for a democratic government, but their loyalty to democracy was thin. Centrist support for constitutional representative government came from Bazargan's Freedom Movement of Iran and remnant factions of the National Front led by Karim Sanjabi.

The drafting of a new constitution fell initially to the Bazargan government. The first draft of the constitution was generally secular and created a democratically elected parliament. Khomeini made it clear from the outset that he opposed parliamentary government. For him, this was a Western concept designed to undermine Islamic civilization. While in exile he had articulated his vision of an Islamic state based on the "rule of divine law over man" and a belief that "sovereignty belongs to God alone[,] and law is His decree and command." God's law, Khomeini proclaimed, had "absolute authority over all individuals and Islamic government." Islamic government should be headed by a ruler who must surpass all others in knowledge.[32] He had repeated such beliefs in Paris, but his allies, secular moderates and revolutionaries, had then ignored his statements. When the first draft of the new constitution came to him, however, Khomeini did not take exception to the establishment of a parliament, which would have alienated him from the general Iranian public, especially the middle classes. At this point in the revolution, Khomeini did not have complete control of his coalition. He was too powerful for moderates to oust, but not yet so powerful to oppose the newly drafted constitution outright.

Instead, he made two requests: women should be excluded constitutionally from holding the presidency and serving in the judicial system, and the draft constitution should be approved in a popular referendum. Moderates rejected the proposal to bring the constitution to a popular vote. They feared that Khomeini might rally the streets in opposition to a more secular constitution. As a compromise, they agreed to the formation of an elected assembly of experts to debate and approve the draft constitution. This proved an immense miscalculation.

Fundamentalist mullahs swept the August 1979 elections to the "assembly of experts." Over 80 percent of the thousand delegates elected were fundamentalists who were instructed by Khomeini thus: "[Do not] sit back while foreignized intellectuals, who have no faith in Islam, give their views and write the things they write."[33]

The Assembly of Experts for Constitution convened on August 18, 1979. From the outset fundamentalist clerics and Islamic parties dominated. The assembly thoroughly revamped the first draft of the constitution and created the foundation for a theocratic state. The final draft of the new constitution, completed in mid-November amid anti-American demonstrations, created a theocratic state with only a modest veneer of democracy. The draft of the new constitution enshrined Islam as the basis of government. They declared that sovereignty belonged only to God and through him to the Prophet, the Imami, and the jurists. Twelver Shi'ism was embodied in the constitution through the establishment of the supreme leader, who was empowered to appoint the heads of the military, the government, and the judiciary. The supreme leader was charged with ensuring that "All civil, penal, financial, economic, administrati[ve], cultural, military, political and other laws be in accordance with Islamic criteria."[34] The constitution established a 12-man Council of Guardians (composed of clerics and lawyers) with the power to veto any legislation that it considered contrary to Islam. The supreme leader was charged with selecting six of the Islamic jurists, with the other members to be selected by the Iranian parliament after nomination by the head of the judiciary, who, in turn, was appointed by the supreme leader.

In short, the new constitution created a theocratic dictatorship without an explicitly defined dictator. The constitution established a supreme leader, an Islamic jurist (*faqih*), with immense powers. This position was insisted upon by Khomeini and was to be assumed by him. The *faqih* was to appoint jurists on the Council of Guardians, chief judicial officials, the chief of staff of the armed forces and heads of military branches, and the commander of the Revolutionary Guard Corps, and he would also approve candidates running for office.

The constitution established an elected constituent assembly, the Majles, a parliament with limited power. All candidates seeking office in this body were required to undergo vetting by the Council of Guardians and be approved by the supreme leader before taking office. Real power was held by the supreme leader—Khomeini. As one moderate exclaimed during the debate on the constitution, the doctrine of a supreme leader created "a sovereignty and guardianship without parallel, an authority to rival the authority of the government that is unacceptable in today's world."[35]

The constitution imparted a duty for the new republic to unify global Islam. In this way, it proclaimed Iran the redeemer nation. The preamble to the constitution charged that the responsibility of the Iranian Republic had a duty to extend God's sovereignty throughout the world. Article ten of the constitution reiterated this ideological mission by stating, "The government of the Islamic Republic has the duty of formulating its general policies with a view to the merging and union of all Muslim peoples, and it must constantly strive to bring about the political, economic, and cultural unity of the Islamic world."[36] Khomeini emphasized this obligation when he insisted, "Today we need to strengthen and export Islam everywhere. You need to export Islam to other places, the same version of Islam which is currently in power in our country."[37] Khomeini saw his divinely ordained rule as necessary to world liberation, echoing the pretensions of the French revolutionaries and Lenin.

With the constitution for the new Islamic Republic of Iran, Khomeini took a critical step in consolidating his power. He still faced, however, opposition from secular moderates, more moderate mullahs, and an armed Left. In the next few years, Khomeini would remove any threat from these forces.

External Enemies and the Fall of Iran's First President

External enemies, in this case the United States and Iraq, allowed Khomeini to complete final consolidation of power by crushing moderate and leftist opposition. Khomeini used the U.S. Embassy hostage crisis to further churn anti-American sentiment in the country. At the same time, the war with Iraq, which began when Saddam Hussein launched an attack on Iran in September 1980 over disputed territories, provided further opportunity for Khomeini and his allies to crack down on both the People's Mujahedin of Iran (the Iranian revolutionary Left) and moderate opponents.

Anti-American fears ran high in revolutionary Iran. Khomeini artfully employed anti-U.S. paranoia to maintain control over hard-line factions among the Iranian Revolutionary Guard Corps, the mullahs, Marxist revolutionaries, and the moderates. When 500 young Iranian revolutionaries, calling themselves Student Followers of the Imam's Line, stormed the U.S. Embassy in late 1979, seizing 66 U.S. diplomats, the eventual outcome was the collapse of the Bazargan government. The hostage crisis lasted 444 days. Americans watched on their television sets as blindfolded American diplomats were paraded before angry student revolutionaries. Khomeini's exact role in the takeover remains uncertain, but once the crisis began, he gave his support to the students. He explained, "This action has many benefits. . . . This has united our people."[38] He understood that the hostage crisis rallied his supporters while providing an instrument to incite anti-American popular sentiment—all of which assured the passage of the referendum. In brief, the hostage crisis neutralized the secular moderate opposition to the constitution.

For the Bazargan government, the hostage crisis was a no-win situation. The hostage crisis, the seizure of an embassy, made Iran into an international pariah in Europe, but any attempts at a diplomatic resolution to the crisis gave the appearance of negotiating with satanic powers to the public in Iran. After failing to end the hostage crisis—revealing just how weak his powers were—Bazargan submitted his resignation. His resignation came in the midst of the country's first presidential election. Khomeini shrewdly banned Massoud Rajavi, the brother of the leftist People's Mujahedin leader, from standing for office. Abolhassan Banisadr, a member of the Council of the Islamic Revolution, won the election as the country's first president, stepping into office on February 4, 1980.

Banisadr, although from a clerical family, had been educated at Tehran University. At the university, he had become a student leader in the National Front, a pro-Mosaddegh organization. Upon graduation, he traveled to Paris to continue his studies, where he encountered critiques of American imperialism. He became a revolutionary and called for a government combining social justice and Islamic principles. He feared absolute rule by one man. Nonetheless, as anti-Shah demonstrations broke out, he aligned himself with Khomeini and became one of his chief representatives in Paris. His close association with Khomeini allowed him to win the presidency. Consequently, he relied on Khomeini for legitimacy. When Banisadr confronted a fundamentalist-controlled 270-seat parliament (Majles), he learned that Khomeini's support was unreliable. In the parliamentary election, fundamentalist clergy—Khomeini's allies—took control of the parliament and appointed Mohammad-Ali Rajai as prime minister. The clash between fundamentalist clergy and Banisadr's government was inevitable. To restore order, Banisadr sought to revive the regular military, police force, and judiciary. This meant confronting the multiple centers of power created by revolutionary forces under control of the clergy. Banisadr found himself at war with parliament, the clergy, militant organizations which controlled the streets, and ultimately Khomeini.

Banisadr discovered, as had his predecessor Bazargan, that ultimate power rested in the clergy, under Khomeini's control. He thus faced the daunting task of overseeing a war with Iraq while fighting a political battle with a fundamentalist-controlled parliament. Banisadr tried to rally moderates and the middle class, only to fail. He then tried to win hard-liners and popular opinion by calling for a "cultural revolution" against the secular Left, especially among students at Tehran University. In 1982, the regime passed legislation making the hijab (a woman's head-covering) mandatory for all females above six years of age. Violating the code was punishable by one hundred lashes of the cane and six years of imprisonment. The regime demanded that women cover themselves to restrain the lust of Muslim men. A year earlier, Banisadr announced that scientific research had shown that women's hair emits rays that drive men insane with lust. Tehran University had become a hotbed of political activity. Thousands of students, for example, turned up to hear Massoud Rajavi, the People's Mujahedin leader, deliver a series of lectures that combined Islam, Darwinism, and Marxism. He warned, "The struggle is over two kinds of Islam. One, an Islam of class, which ultimately protects the exploiter; and a pure[,] authentic[,] and popular Islam, which is against classes and exploitation."[39] On April 18, 1980, Khomeini attacked the universities by declaring, "What we are afraid of is Western universities and the training [of] our youth in the interests of West or East."[40] As a response, Hezbollah gangs attacked students at universities across the country. Banisadr showed up a few days later to proclaim a "cultural revolution" and the need to Islamize education. Dozens of students and faculty were arrested for subversion against the Islamic Republic.

As part of the cultural war, Banisadr also launched an antinarcotics campaign headed by Sadegh Khalkhali, a hard-line Islamic judge. Khalkhali's campaign unleashed a bloodbath, as he ordered the execution of hundreds of people for drug and sex offences as well as plotting counterrevolution and spying for Israel. Among them was Farrokhroo Parsa, a leading women's rights activist and former minister of education. Meanwhile, under Khomeini's orders, the government was purged of suspected "royalists." When Khalkhali was finally forced from office because of corruption (not brutality), the damage had already been done.

The terror would come at great political cost to Banisadr. While the campaign cost him heavily among liberals, Banisadr failed to win over the hard-line clergy. He had made a bet that taking a strong stand in the cultural wars would give him a new lease on political life. He could not have been more wrong.

Tensions came to a head when the Majles impeached Banisadr in the summer of 1981. Khomeini appears to have instigated the impeachment. Even before Khomeini signed the impeachment papers, the Revolutionary Guard Corps had seized the presidential buildings and begun executing allies of Banisadr. Khomeini ordered all political parties, except his own, the Islamic Republican Party, banned. Opposition leaders from the People's Mujahedin and the Soviet-aligned Tudeh Party were arrested and imprisoned. Banisadr went into hiding, where he formed an alliance with the militant Massoud Rajavi, leader of the People's Mujahedin party. Concluding that opposition to Khomeini inside Iran was impossible, they fled into exile in Paris. Later Massoud would join People's Mujahedin military forces in Iraq.

Banisadr accused Khomeini of conducting a coup d'état against democracy. But the crackdown on the opposition had begun well before Banisadr was ousted from the presidency. Even while the assembly was writing the new constitution and creating a theocracy, dozens of newspapers and magazines had been suppressed. When demonstrators gathered to protest the crackdown, they were violently attacked by Hezbollah militants wielding iron bars and chains. Opposition leaders were arrested.

Khomeini denounced his critics by declaring, "We thought we were dealing with human beings. It is evident we are not." He added that, "After each revolution several thousand of these corrupt elements are execut[ed] in public and burnt and the story is over. They are not allowed to publish newspapers."[41] Between January 1980 to June 1981, before Banisadr was impeached, an estimated nine hundred people were executed. The year following Banisadr's removal, approximately another three thousand people were executed.

Reign of Terror

From 1980 to 1982, the Islamic Republican Party consolidated its power by crushing People's Mujahedin armed resistance through guerrilla war and terrorism. Prior to the outbreak of war, People's Mujahedin opposition had made great gains within the military, universities, factories, and villages through an underground network. In 1979 and 1980, a full-scale purge of the Iranian armed services was undertaken. An estimated twelve thousand men were purged from the military, many of whom were arrested and executed. The disarray within the Iranian military had encouraged Saddam Hussein's invasion.

The suppression of the People's Mujahedin was especially severe. Attacks on People's Mujahedin rallies and student societies broke out in 1980. One fundamentalist cleric with a large following incited a mob against the People's Mujahedin for being Communists, taking part in a Kurdish uprising, and misleading young girls. He declared, "Even if they hide in mouseholes, we will drag them out and kill them. . . . We are thirsty for their blood. We must close off their jugular."[42] Once Banisadr was ousted from power, Khomeini unleashed the full force of Hezbollah thugs against People's Mujahedin opponents. In June 1980, Khomeini publicly denounced the People's Mujahedin as polytheists. The group retreated underground.

In late June 1981, a bomb exploded at the Khomeini-backed Islamic Republican Party headquarters in Tehran, killing seventy-three top party officials, including the second most powerful figure in the Iranian Revolution, Chief Justice Mohammad Beheshti. Khomeini publicly blamed the terrorist bombing on the People's Mujahedin of Iran. In August 1981, the People's Mujahedin stepped up violence with the assassinations of the newly elected second president of Iran and other high officials. The fury unleashed against them was intense in what can only be described as a reign of terror. An estimated twelve thousand political dissidents died in violent sieges, street confrontations, and public executions. The Soviet Union–aligned Tudeh Party, which had supported the crackdown on the People's Mujahedin, found that they were not protected from this reign of terror either. In January 1983, seventy leaders and central committee members of the Tudeh Party were arrested. Party leader Noureddin Kianouri was arrested, tortured, and forced to make a public confession on state television. The Khomeini regime ordered the party dissolved and all members to report to authorities.

By 1984, the regime was in full control. Khomeini, confident that the Left had been broken, sought to bring revolutionary courts, local committees, and the Revolutionary Guard Corps under control. Nonetheless, arrests, torture, and imprisonment continued. Prisons filled with those arrested as enemies of the state. In prisons, political dissenters were tortured and interrogated and underwent intense reeducation programs to turn "deviants" into proper "human beings."[43] The regime outlawed torture, but under Islamic law, prison authorities were allowed to apply 74 lashes until "honest" answers were given. Later, key dissident and political leaders who broke under interrogation appeared on public television to confess their sins. Dozens appeared on television in solo confessions, as well as roundtables involving up to 17 people in 90-minute sessions. Most notable was Mehdi Hashemi, the brother of the son-in-law of Ayatollah Montazeri, at one time Khomeini's designated heir. He confessed on television to "heresy, apostasy, and treason against the Imam, the Community, Islam, and Islamic Revolution." He was later executed for his "relations with Satan" and "his disease of eclecticism." At his trial, he thanked the court for saving him.[44]

In July 1988, an ailing Khomeini issued a decree: "Whoever at any stage continues to belong to the PMOI [People's Mujahedin Organization of Iran] must be executed. Annihilate the enemies of Islam immediately!" He ordered, "Those who are in prison throughout the country and remain steadfast in their support for PMOI are waging war on God and are condemned to execution. . . . It is naïve to show mercy to those who wage war on God."[45] No mercy was to be shown to teenagers or women. Exiled Iranians alleged thirty thousand political prisoners were subsequently executed; a UN commission placed the number at nineteen thousand. Over the next several months beginning in July 1988, hundreds of prisoners were hanged each day (many taking up to five minutes to die) and buried in mass graves.

Meanwhile the war with Iraq had continued. Initially, Khomeini saw the war as a chance to overthrow the militant secular Iraqi government but also as an opportunity to march on Israel itself and liberate the Palestinians. The slogan "Through Karbala to Jerusalem" became a mantra to enlist young Iranians in the war effort. They were encouraged to become "Volunteers for Martyrdom," necessary to liberate the Iraqi city of Karbala before carrying on to Jerusalem. The war itself reinforced extremist elements in the government. The Revolutionary Guard Corps grew in power. Thousands of young Iranians enlisted in the army to become martyrs on the Iraq front. As the war continued, it was a bloodbath on both sides. The war ended in stalemate in August 1988, when Khomeini was finally convinced that Iran could no longer afford the financial cost of the war. His decision was not humanitarian or an act of contrition for the estimated five hundred thousand soldiers on both sides who had died. He accepted the "poison chalice" of a cease-fire but could not understand why God had failed him. His son later recorded, "After accepting the cease-fire he could no longer walk. He kept saying, 'My Lord, I submit to your will.' He never again spoke in public."[46]

The United States remained a continuous target under Khomeini and his successors. At Tehran University and other universities, special courses in "Anti-American" studies were offered. "Death to America" has remained a popular slogan chanted in unison at mass rallies and found painted on city walls throughout the country. American military interventions in Iraq in the First Gulf War and the Second Gulf War encouraged anti-American sentiment and conspiratorial fears that the United States, through the CIA or Zionist agents, planned to overthrow the Iranian revolutionary regime. The regime decided that, while its navy and air forces were to be built up and a huge regular military and militia created, essential to Iran's survival was the development of a missile and nuclear weapons. Following the failure to win the war against Iraq, a major decision was made to develop a missile program. Through a partnership with North Korea, using Chinese and Russian technology, three generations of missiles were developed in the ensuing years. At the same time, a nuclear program was accelerated. The election of the militant Mahmoud Ahmadinejad as the sixth president hardened the regime's stance against nuclear disarmament.

U.S. sanctions, the war, and poor management and policies left Iran in economic tatters. Having crushed domestic opposition, the Iraqi government became factionalized between those wanting to undertake domestic reform and those seeking to further the international revolution. Behind the factionalism, Khomeini remained hard-line in suppressing enemies of the Islamic state. In 1988, Khomeini issued an execution decree condemning imprisoned People's Mujahedin members who refused to repent. That same year he issued a fatwa (decree) that Salman Rushdie, author of *The Satanic Verses*, and his publishers should be killed. He declared, "I call on all zealous Muslims to execute them quickly, wherever they find them, so that no one will dare to insult the Islamic sanctities."[47] Khomeini died of a heart attack in the summer of 1989, having been in ill health for over a year. A hastily convened Assembly of Experts convened to elect a new supreme leader, Ali Khamenei.

The New Ruling Class

The Islamic state created by Khomeini defies easy political classification. Maxime Rodinson, a French scholar of Islam, after visiting Iran in 1981, described Khomeinism as "fascism entering Iran, perhaps the Muslim world, in the guise of Islam[ic] revival."[48] The regime, though, is not completely monolithic in power, nor is it a typical dictatorship as found in Lenin and Stalin's Russia, Mao's China, or even Mugabe's Zimbabwe. Following Khomeini's death, current government decisions cannot be traced to one man nor to an easily identifiable group. This should not be taken as evidence, though, that this regime is not authoritarian or oppressive. Secret police operate with a ruthlessness rarely seen in any regime. The Iranian regime is an authoritarian system controlled by the clergy and a ruling clique. Those resisting the system are arrested, imprisoned, and executed. The supreme leader demands obedience. Leadership agitates the masses through anti-American and anti-Israeli propaganda. The regime sponsors dozens of international terrorist organizations, while it enjoys close relations with other authoritarian regimes, including North Korea and Venezuela. In turn, branches of Hezbollah are found as far away as Brazil, Argentina, Uruguay, and Paraguay.

By the time Khomeini died in 1989, Iran had created a new ruling class formed around powerful mullahs, leaders of the Revolutionary Guard Corps, and a clique of political and economic leaders. By 1979, the new Islamic Republic had taken over all Iranian banks. This source of wealth provides endless wealth for mullahs in control of banks. Mullahs assumed control of the insurance industry. Islamic tradition saw insurance as sinful because it preempted the will of Allah. Khomeini, however, declared insurance as a licit business, thereby benefiting his associates. As supreme leader, Khomeini created the Office of the Supreme Leader, which was not to be overseen by any other institution. Its annual budget reaches billions of dollars, and it employs thousands of people. This office accounts for a quarter of the private sector's economic activity. An estimated 113 foundations under its control exist, each headed by an influential mullah. Contracts for these businesses are awarded to mullahs and their families. When Khomeini died, the Assembly of Experts selected Ali Khamenei to become the country's supreme leader.

Khamenei, although not trained as an Islamic jurist, has proven adroit in maintaining his power as supreme leader. He navigated factional Iranian politics formed by rival ideological forces and political cliques. He served the revolution in many capacities, including as head of the Revolutionary Guard Corps. As supreme leader he has faced the protests of Iranian students in 1999, protests over the presidential election in 2009, general protests in 2011–12 and 2017–18, and general strikes from 2018 to 2020. During these protests thousands were arrested and imprisoned. In addition, hundreds of others have been arrested on charges of blasphemy against the supreme leader. In 2006, the government called for a second cultural revolution to remove Zionist and satanic influences in the universities. State propaganda projects Khamenei living an austere lifestyle. He is the object of a massive cult of personality, described as the "Divine Gift to Mankind" and the "Shining Sun of Imamate."[49] He believes that he is one of the chosen to save Iran, while he lives in a private court that includes six palaces.

The revolution extended primary education to rural areas. Consequently, Iran has a high literacy rate of 80 percent. Secondary schools include public and private schools. These private schools privilege the better-off. Education in public and private schools continues to inculcate Islamic ideology. The outbreak of university protest, however, reveals that many of the Iranian youth continue to question the values of the regime. In 2012 the Iranian government prevented women from attending university classes in engineering, computer science, English literature, and business studies at various universities. The regime cracked down on university dissent, but after thirty years in power, many in it recognized that the younger generation had lost confidence in the revolution. Across Iran, uncensored media can be found. Satellite dishes are carefully hidden to pick up European, Turkish, and Middle Eastern channels. One former Revolutionary Guard Corps member and prominent filmmaker declared, "The younger generation in our country does not understand our revolutionary language anymore. We're wasting our time with the media we make."[50]

Economic problems remain, including rampant unemployment and runaway inflation. An estimated 25 percent of the young are unemployed. Widespread poverty has led to a sharp decline in the birth rate. Prostitution and drug addiction are prevalent in the cities. These economic problems have created fissures in the government as technocrats pursue economic reform. Throughout the back-and-forth of domestic politics, government policy toward the press and dissidents has wavered between loosening restrictions and increasing state repression. Political opponents have been assassinated and arrested by the regime's secret police. Religious minorities remain oppressed.

State-supported terrorism continues. In August 1991 Shapour Bakhtiar, former prime minister when the Shah fell, was assassinated in his home in Paris. In March 1992 a suicide bomb at the Israeli Embassy in Buenos Aires killed thirty people. Kurdish opposition leaders have been assassinated in Berlin and Vienna. A bombing of the Khobar Towers in Saudi Arabia in June 1996 killed nineteen U.S. servicemen. Terrorist attacks on U.S. soldiers persisted in Iraq throughout the Second Gulf War.

Khamenei, as supreme leader, has close ties with the Islamic Revolutionary Guard Corps. The Revolutionary Guard Corps wields political and economic power. Militarily, it has its own ground, air, and naval divisions. Politically, it controls a 400,000-man militia called the Basij. Additionally, the Revolutionary Guard Corps's Karbala brigades are used to crush opposition that arises. Economically, the Revolutionary Guard Corps is the country's largest holding company. When Iran sought to privatize many of its corporations, an estimated one-third ended up in the hands of the Revolutionary Guard Corps or of individual commanders. Revolutionary Guard–affiliated businesses and corporations control major sectors of the country, including armaments, construction, petroleum and gas, shipping, and telecommunications. They directly control news outlets, including publications and websites, as well as filmmaking. Membership in the Revolutionary Guard Corps provides a fast-track ticket to economic and social advancement.

The Revolutionary Guard Corps is also in the business of exporting revolution, financing Hezbollah groups in at least twenty countries. In addition, it controls Iran's nuclear program. The mission of making Iran a vehicle for global Islamic revolution clashes with the interests of the country as a nation-state. This has created its own conflicts within the regime. Previous presidents sought to focus on economic and political reform, only to meet opposition from fundamentalist clergy, entrenched economic interests, and radicals seeking to pursue international revolution. Understanding the centers of power in Iran has created immense difficulties for Western and American diplomats seeking to negotiate with the regime to end its nuclear program and support of international terrorism.

In the 2004 elections, hard-liners captured the Iranian parliament; and in the presidential election of 2005, Mahmoud Ahmadinejad, a hard-liner with close ties to the Revolutionary Guard Corps, won the presidency. In office, he pursued an aggressive foreign policy, which included accelerating the country's nuclear program. He was a holocaust denier and claimed that the Hidden Imam's return might be imminent. His election marked a clear setback after more pragmatic leadership under the previous president, Akbar Hashemi Rafsanjani (in office 1989–1997), whose attempts at reform had been opposed by radicals in the parliament decreeing, "Democracy is nothing but the dictatorship of capital, consumerism, and selfishness. Democracy is reactionary."[51] In June 2021 Ebrahim Raisi, well known for his role in the 1988 massacre of an estimated thirty thousand political prisoners, became Iran's new president.

The current regime continues to operate in the interests of a small clique that denies political freedoms through repression. Political debate occurs within the parameters of an authoritarian regime and within a confined religious ideology. The regime awaits the appearance of the

Hidden Imam, at which time the world will be redeemed, following the apocalypse. Revolutionary Iran, following the dictates of Khomeini, claims to be the representative of the Hidden Imam and the rightful ruler of the world. This mentality allows no dialogue between civilizations, because there is no civilization outside Islam.

Khomeini's vision came from a mystic belief that a mortal man such as himself, through piety, could become one with God. His mysticism prevented him from shedding tears for the death of infidels. God's anger was his anger. Khomeini created a regime with a messianic mission that vied with the dreams of former Communist leaders. Lenin, Mao, and Castro believed in the eventual utopia for the proletariat. They envisioned the creation of the New Socialist Man. Mugabe envisioned a pan-African utopia. Khomeini's vision was grander: a final apocalypse with the death of all infidels. His vision was the creation of a heaven on earth. For many in Iran today, the regime is hell on earth.

Conclusion:
Lessons Learned?

Monsters walked amongst us in the twentieth century. Monsters remain in the twenty-first century—dictators in power and those seeking power. These monsters beguiled their followers with their illusions that the past could be cleansed and a new beginning made. They convinced enough people that their chains of privation could be broken through revolution. These revolutionary monsters promised, at least for the purposes of gaining power, that a new age, the millennium, was about to begin for humankind. They dreamed of the creation of a perfect world, the New Man, in a once imperfect world. The utopian promise of absolute justice, as entrancing as it is, leads, as has been the experience of social revolutions in the modern age, to disastrous social consequences.

The guilt of their hubris can be measured in the millions of people who died under these revolutionary regimes. The suffering they inflicted on their people is immeasurable. Yet dreams of revolution persist. Lessons of the past are denied or ignored. Is history to repeat itself?

The nineteenth and twentieth centuries can be characterized as ones of war and revolution. The irony is that they were also centuries of great material progress, the eradication of many diseases that had plagued mankind, and extraordinary technological advancements. Do such advancements belie the inevitability of war and revolution in our current century? In the twentieth century, the fear of a nuclear holocaust cautioned world leaders from unleashing forces of massive destruction. Similarly, will perhaps revolutions in the future be prevented by new mechanisms of social control enabled by technology and genetic engineering, as predicted in Aldous Huxley's *Brave New World* (1932)?

Whatever the case, from our study of social revolutions, we know the general stages of revolution. Revolutionary conditions gestate a long time before a spark sets off the conflagration of revolution. As the revolution gains momentum, a faction emerges to take control. Essential to the success of this faction in its quest for power is a leader who articulates with clear vision and profound idealistic sentiment the glorious promise of revolution. A prophet is born, often from relative obscurity, welcomed as the embodiment of the revolution: a liberator, a savior. In the leader, consciousness of power produces a vanity, a recognition within him of moral superiority, and a conviction that without him the revolution, both in the making and once gained, will fail.[1] A psychological metamorphosis occurs in the act of assuming power: the prophet, once born, awakens as a monster.

Most social revolutions have failed in the modern era: the revolutions of 1848, the Paris Commune in 1871, the Hungarian and German revolutions in 1919, the Salvadoran peasant uprising in 1932, and many others. Yet the constants of history—social equity and class rule—remain ever present as critical factors necessary for revolution in every modern society, liberal and authoritarian. Revolutions begin first with intellectual revolutions, cultural deterioration, the loss of confidence of the people in the ruling elite, and the weakening of the ruling elite itself. Within this deteriorating environment, prerevolutionary conditions are set, but they are not enough to spark a revolution themselves. A regime's strength is found in its culture, its ability to endure and prosper.

Youth are attracted naturally to new ideas and calls for change. Most often, these attractions are trivial—such as in fashion, music,

language, or behavior intended to shock their elders. Youthful intellectual fads often prove passing and not meaningful. Beatniks in the
1950s did not present much of a challenge to society. Challenges by the
youth can take positive forms, as evident in religious awakenings in
America in the 1740s, the Second Great Awakening in the early 1800s,
and the abolitionist movement in the 1850s that all attracted many of
the young. These intellectual movements occurred within the confines
of a liberal society. More insidious was the growth of Marxist thought
in Russia beginning in the 1860s and China at the turn of the century.
Political Islam attracted the Iranian youth in the 1960s. These intellectual movements sowed the seeds for revolution in Russia, China,
and Iran, as well as Cuba and Zimbabwe.

These movements reflected a loss of confidence among the youth and
intellectuals in the prevailing social order. In and of themselves, these
intellectual trends were not enough to undermine regimes. More important was the loss of confidence in the ruling elites themselves, as corruption and greed replaced social responsibility. Revolutionary thought
attracted their sons and daughters and seeped into the elite culture itself.
The political and social elites, lacking confidence in their own ability to
rule or a rationale for their rule other than to maintain power, collapsed
when faced by revolutionary upheaval. They doubted their own claim to
represent the people.

In all societies, it can be argued, there are those who rule and those
who are ruled. Ultimately those who rule in whatever regime—aristocratic,
authoritarian, or liberal—need the tacit support of the governed to remain
in power. This support can be maintained through social deference seen
in aristocratic regimes, coercion in authoritarian regimes, or representation in a liberal society. Liberal representative government became such
a powerful concept in the eighteenth and nineteenth centuries that even
the most authoritarian regimes in the twentieth century claimed to be
"people's republics." Communist leaders such as Lenin, Stalin, Mao,
Castro, and Mugabe, who despised bourgeois democracy, were pressured
to accept constitutions, parliaments, and elections, however formalistic

and feeble these institutions were in practice. Khomeini, who had denounced the concept of constitutional government and parliaments as little more than Western ploys to subvert Islamic civilization, accepted in the end a constitution that recognized a parliamentary body. Even an authoritarian theocratic state such as Iran had to proclaim itself a republic.

Thus lay the great and tragic irony of these revolutionaries who seized power cloaked in the rhetoric of liberal democracy. They persuaded the masses, at least enough of them, to believe that they were democrats, at least of a sort, qualified by those they claimed to represent, the proletarian or the religious faithful. In power, even as they implemented policies of terror and repression, they established republics, if in name only. Their regimes, however, were nothing more than tyrannies. They were social revolutionaries driven by the will to power. Their dreams of a new millennium, the creation of a perfect world, and abstract justice inevitably failed. Their failure came because theirs was an illusion that the Perfect Man or the Perfect World can be created by fallible man. Their greatest sin, however, was not just their disregard for "humanity," but their contempt of individuals, who could be sacrificed en masse to fulfill an imputed design of history. In their hubris, these monsters claimed to understand a design to history and its end, known only to them.

Political revolutions, as opposed to social revolutions, succeeded, although not always, in the modern era because they sought individual rights, not social equality. These political revolutions sought liberty, not just freedom, for the individual. Liberty meant that individuals were protected from arbitrary and capricious coercion from the state and those in power. True liberty rested in the recognition of individual rights. Tyranny, they understood, comes when a single person or group of people makes its will permissible without the due process of law. A liberal political order requires impersonal restrictions on those in power and protections for all individuals to act according to their own consciences providing they do not harm others. It means that individuals have rights—natural rights, as the Founders held—to life, liberty, and property. This means that they have the right to follow their religion of choice, to assemble, and to express, in public forums or through the press, criticisms of the government. Liberty means that an individual is protected from arbitrary arrest and conviction without legal representation. Judicial courts were thus required by the Founders to act as arbitrators in legal disputes that inevitably arise when matters of property and wealth and rights arise. Power is to be feared, whether from a political elite or an unrestrained majority. The most powerful argument made on behalf of liberal government is that a free society is a product of conflict and differences of individual opinion, not a contrived harmony or uniformity of belief imposed by the state.

These ideals of liberty and a free society are not easily realized in actuality, yet these were the ideals which allowed for progress toward a *more* perfect society—not a *perfect* society. The potency of this noble dream of liberty rests in the dignity of the individual from which the collective good is realized. This is the primary lesson of history.

Acknowledgments

A pologies are offered for not listing people in order of their helpfulness in this project.

Two readers brought their expertise in reading the chapter on Mao: John Carroll at the University of Hong Kong and Le Duan, a former colleague of mine at Arizona State University who is now at Sam Houston University. Entrepreneur Dean Riesen, an avid reader of history, read and commented on the entire manuscript. My wife, who is a soldier in her own right, read and edited drafts of the manuscript too often to keep count.

Although they were not readers, I want to thank those who listened to me on many occasions talk about the book: my teaching colleagues at Arizona State University, including Professor Jonathan Barth, Dr. Mark Power Smith, and Roxane Barwick, manager of the Program in Political History and Leadership at Arizona State University, which I lead. Amy Shepard, who serves as national outreach specialist for the program, deserves my appreciation as well. My friend Professor Gregory Schneider directed me to some good literature on the Russian and Chinese revolutions.

Three undergraduate research assistants, Nathan Callahan, Noah Olnsorg, and Nico Pacioni warrant heartfelt thanks. They did more than just collect many books and articles; they offered their insights throughout the entire project.

Support for this project came from the Katzin Family Trust, which has been generous in its support of my research and teaching. ASU Foundation officer Clay Tenquist introduced me to two members of the Katzin family, David and Bob Katzin.

My literary agent Alexander Hoyt arranged for a contract for the book, and my good friend Irv Gellman continued to offer his wise advice at various stages of writing the book. My late and dear friend Bill Rorabaugh helped me think through the organization and subject matter. Over the years, Bill has read nearly every book manuscript I have produced. Unfortunately for me, his passing left me without his guiding hand; fortunately, I found two excellent editors at Regnery Publishing: Paul Choix, who did the bulk of editing, and Harry Crocker, who edited the first chapter and saved me from the inevitable prolixity of an academic historian. Regnery's Tadeusz Wójcik also brought his fine editorial eye to the copyediting process.

My grandson Alex Critchlow did yeoman's work organizing and creating the Selected Reading List for each chapter.

Donald T. Critchlow
Katzin Family Professor
Arizona State University
Tempe, Arizona

Selected Readings

General Readings

Arendt, Hannah. *On Revolution.* New York: Viking Press, 1963.

Aron, Raymond. *The Opium of the Intellectuals.* London: Secker & Warburg, 1957.

Burnham, James. *The Machiavellians: Defenders of Freedom.* New York: John Day, 1943.

Burke, Edmund. *Edmund Burke on Revolution.* Edited by Robert A. Smith. New York: Harper Torchbooks, 1968.

Dikötter, Frank. *How to be a Dictator: The Cult of Personality in the Twentieth Century.* London: Bloomsbury Publishing, 2019.

Edwards, Lyford P. *The Natural History of Revolution.* Chicago: University of Chicago Press, 1927.

Greene, Thomas H. *Comparative Revolutionary Movements.* New Jersey: Prentice-Hall, 1937.

Kolakowski, Leszek. *Main Currents of Marxism: The Founders, the Golden Age, the Breakdown.* New York: W. W. Norton & Company, 2005.

Michels, Robert. *Political Parties: A Sociological Study of the Oligarchical Tendencies of Modern Democracy.* Translated by Eden and Cedar Paul. New York: Hearst's International Library Company, 1915.

Moore, Barrington, Jr. *Social Origins of Dictatorship and Democracy: Lord and Peasant in the Making of the Modern World.* Boston: Beacon Press, 1966.

Newell, Waller R. *Tyrants: A History of Power, Injustice, and Terror.* New York: Cambridge University Press, 2016.

Chapter 1: Lenin

Chernyshevsky, Nikolai. *What is to be Done?* Translated by Michael R. Katz. Annotated by William G. Wagner. Ithaca, New York: Cornell University Press, 1989.

Clark, Ronald W. *Lenin: A Biography.* New York: Harper and Row, 1988.

Cohen, Stephen F. *Bukharin and the Bolshevik Revolution: A Political Biography, 1888–1938.* New York: Alfred A. Knopf, 1973.

Daniels, Robert V. *The Rise and Fall of Communism in Russia.* New Haven, Connecticut: Yale University Press, 2007.

D'Encausse, Hélène Carrère. *A History of the Soviet Union, 1917–1953.* Volume 1, *Lenin: Revolution and Power.* Translated by Valence Ionescu. London: Longman, 1982.

Deutscher, Isaac. *Lenin's Childhood.* London: Oxford University Press, 1970.

Ferro, Marc. *The Russian Revolution of February 1917.* Englewood Cliffs, New Jersey: Prentice-Hall, 1972.

Figes, Orlando. *A People's Tragedy: The Russian Revolution: 1891–1924.* New York: Penguin Books, 1996.

Fischer, Louis. *The Life of Lenin.* New York: Harper & Row, 1964.

Fowkes, Ben. *Communism in Germany under the Weimar Republic.* London: Macmillan Press, 1984.

Haimson, Leopold H. *The Russian Marxists and the Origins of Bolshevism.* Cambridge, Massachusetts: Harvard University Press, 1955.

Harding, Neil. *Leninism.* London: Macmillan Press, 1996.

Kenez, Peter. *Civil War in South Russia, 1919–1920: The Defeat of the Whites,* Berkeley: University of California Press, 1977.

Lenin, V. I. *The April Conference.* London: Lawrence & Wishart, 1938.

———. *Materialism and Empirio-Criticism: Critical Comments on a Reactionary Philosophy.* Moscow: Progress Publishers, 1970.

———. *State and Revolution: Marxist Teaching about the Theory of the State and Revolution.* New York: International Publishers, 1932.

———. *The Unknown Lenin: From the Secret Archive.* Edited by Richard Pipes, with the assistance of David Brandenberger. Translated by Catherine A. Fitzpatrick. New Haven, Connecticut: Yale University Press, 1996.

———. *What is to be Done? Burning Questions of Our Movement.* Edited by V. J. Jerome. Translated by J. Fineberg and G. Hanna. New York: International Publishers, 1969.

Lih, Lars T. *Lenin Rediscovered: What is to Be Done? In Context.* Leiden, Netherlands, and Boston: Brill, 2006.

Luxemburg, Rosa. *The Russian Revolution and Leninism or Marxism?* Ann Arbor, Michigan: University of Michigan Press, 1961.

Mawdsley, Evan. *The Russian Civil War.* New York: Pegasus Books, 2005.

Meyer, Alfred G. *Leninism.* New York: Frederick A. Praeger, 1962.

Mitchell, Allan. *Revolution in Bavaria, 1918–1919: The Eisner Regime and the Soviet Republic.* Princeton, New Jersey: Princeton University Press, 1965.

Pearson, Michael. *The Sealed Train.* New York: G. P. Putnam's Sons, 1975.

Pipes, Richard. *The Russian Revolution.* New York: Alfred A. Knopf, 1990.

Radzinsky, Edvard. *Stalin: The First In-Depth Biography Based on Explosive New Documents from Russia's Secret Archives.* Translated by H. T. Willetts. New York: Doubleday, 1996.

Read, Anthony. *The World on Fire: 1919 and the Battle with Bolshevism*. New York: W. W. Norton & Company, 2008.

Sebestyen, Victor. *Lenin the Dictator: An Intimate Portrait*. London: Weidenfeld & Nicolson, 2017.

Service, Robert. *Lenin: A Biography*. London: Macmillan Press, 2000.

———. *Stalin: A Biography*. Cambridge, Massachusetts: Belknap Press of Harvard University Press, 2004.

Shub, David. *Lenin: A Biography*. New York: Mentor Book, 1950.

Trotsky, Leon. *The Defence of Terrorism*. London: The Labour Publishing Company, 1921.

Volkogonov, Dmitri. *Lenin: A New Biography*. Edited and translated by Harold Shukman. New York: Free Press, 1994.

———. *Trotsky: The Eternal Revolutionary*. Edited and translated by Harold Shukman. New York: Free Press, 1996.

Watt, Richard M. *The Kings Depart: The Tragedy of Germany: Versailles and the German Revolution*, New York: Simon & Schuster, 1968.

Zubok, Vladislav, and Constantine Pleshakov. *Inside the Kremlin's Cold War: From Stalin to Khrushchev*. Cambridge, Massachusetts: Harvard University Press, 1996.

Chapter 2: Mao

Chen, Jack. *Inside the Cultural Revolution*. London: Sheldon, 1976.

Clark, Paul. *The Chinese Cultural Revolution: A History*. Cambridge, United Kingdom: Cambridge University Press, 2008.

Cohen, Arthur A. *The Communism of Mao Tse-tung*. Chicago: University of Chicago Press, 1964.

Harrison, James P. *The Communist and Chinese Peasant Rebellions: A Study in the Rewriting of Chinese History*. New York: Atheneum, 1969.

Isaacs, Harold. *The Tragedy of the Chinese Revolution*. London: Secker & Warburg, 1938.

Johnson, Chalmers A. *Peasant Nationalism and Communist Power: The Emergence of Revolutionary China, 1937–1945*. Stanford, California: Stanford University Press, 1962.

Leys, Simon. *The Chairman's New Clothes: Mao and the Cultural Revolution*. New York: St. Martin's Press, 1977.

Li Zhi-sui. *The Private Life of Chairman Mao: The Memories of Mao's Personal Physician*. New York: Random House, 1994.

Liang Heng and Judith Shapiro. *Son of the Revolution*. New York: Alfred A. Knopf, 1983.

MacFarquhar, Roderick, and Michael Schoenhals. *Mao's Last Revolution*. Cambridge, Massachusetts: Belknap Press of Harvard University Press, 2006.

Schwartz, Benjamin I. *Chinese Communism and the Rise of Mao*. Cambridge, Massachusetts: Harvard University Press, 1951.

Snow, Edgar. *Red Star Over China*. New York: Random House, 1938; Grove Press paperback edition, 1961.

Wu Yiching, *The Cultural Revolution at the Margins: Chinese Socialism in Crisis*. Cambridge, Massachusetts: Harvard University Press, 2014.

Yang, Rae. *Spider Eaters: A Memoir*. Berkeley: University of California Press, 1997.

Zhai Zhenhua. *Red Flower of China*. New York: Soho, 1992.

Chapter 3: Castro

Attwood, William. *The Reds and the Blacks: A Personal Adventure*. New York: Harper & Row, 1967.

Bonsal, Philip W. *Cuba, Castro, and the United States*. Pittsburgh, Pennsylvania: University of Pittsburgh Press, 1971.

Casuso, Teresa. *Cuba and Castro*. New York: Random House, 1961.

Coltman, Leycester. *The Real Fidel Castro*. New Haven, Connecticut: Yale University Press, 2003.

DePalma, Anthony. *The Cubans: Ordinary Lives in Extraordinary Times*. New York: Penguin Random House, 2020.

Dorschner, John and Roberto Fabricio. *The Winds of December*. New York: Coward, McCann & Geoghegan, 1980.

Draper, Theodore. *Castro's Revolution: Myths and Realities*. New York: Frederick A. Praeger, 1962.

Encinosa, Enrique. *Unvanquished: Cuba's Resistance to Fidel Castro*. Los Angeles, California: Pureplay Press, 2004.

Fagen, Richard. *The Transformation of Political Culture in Cuba*. Stanford, California: Stanford University Press, 1969.

Fernandez, Alina. *Castro's Daughter: An Exile's Memoir of Cuba*. New York: St. Martin's Griffin, 1998.

Fontova, Humberto. *Exposing the Real Che Guevara: And the Useful Idiots Who Idolize Him*. New York: Sentinel, 2007.

Foss, Clive. *Fidel Castro*. Stroud: Sutton Publishing, 2000.

Galvez, William. *Che in Africa: Che Guevara's Congo Diary*. Melbourne, Australia, and New York: Ocean Press, 1999.

García-Pérez, Gladys Marel. *Insurrection and Revolution: Armed Struggle in Cuba, 1952–1959*. Boulder, Colorado: Lynne Rienner Publishers, 1998.

Geyer, Georgie Anne. *Guerrilla Prince: The Untold Story of Fidel Castro*. Boston: Little, Brown & Company, 1991.

Habel, Janette. *Cuba: The Revolution in Peril*. London and New York: Verso, 1991.

Halperin, Maurice. *The Rise and Decline of Fidel Castro: An Essay in Contemporary History*. Berkeley, California: University of California Press, 1972.

———. *The Taming of Fidel Castro*. Berkeley: University of California Press, 1981.

Hansen, Jonathan M. *Young Castro: The Making of a Revolutionary*. New York: Simon & Schuster, 2019.

Harnecker, Marta. *Fidel Castro's Political Strategy: From Moncada to Victory*. New York and London: Pathfinder Press, 1987.

Johnson, Scott. *The Case of Cuban Poet Heberto Padilla*. New York: Gordon Press, 1977.

Karol, K. S. *Guerrillas in Power: The Course of the Cuban Revolution.* Translated by Arnold Pomerans. New York: Hill and Wang, 1970.

Latell, Brian. *After Fidel: The Inside Story of Castro's Regime and Cuba's Next Leader.* New York: Palgrave Macmillan, 2002.

LeoGrande, William M. *Policy Papers in International Affairs.* Berkeley, California: University of California Press, 1955.

Leonard, Thomas M. *Fidel Castro: A Biography.* Westport, Connecticut: Greenwood Press, 2004.

Lindop, Edmund. *Cuba.* New York: Franklin Watts, 1980.

Mitchell, Allan. *Victors and Vanquished: The German Influence on Army and Church in France after 1870.* Chapel Hill, North Carolina: University of North Carolina Press, 1984.

Oppenheimer, Andres. *Castro's Final Hour: The Secret Story Behind the Coming Downfall of Communist Cuba.* New York: Simon & Schuster, 1992.

Pflaum, Irving Peter. *Tragic Island: How Communism Came to Cuba.* Englewood Cliffs, New Jersey: Prentice-Hall, 1961.

Phillips, R. Hart. *The Cuban Dilemma.* New York: Ivan Obolensky, 1962.

Quirk, Robert E. *Fidel Castro.* New York: W. W. Norton & Company, 1993.

Ratliff, William E. *Castroism and Communism in Latin American, 1959–1976: The Varieties of Marxist-Leninist Experience.* Washington, D.C.: American Enterprise Institute for Public Policy Research, 1976.

Taibo, Paco Ignacio. *Guevara, Also Known As Che.* Translated by Martin Michael Roberts. New York: St. Martin's Press, 1997.

Sánchez, Germán. *Cuba and Venezuela: An Insight into Two Revolutions.* Melbourne, Australia, and New York: Ocean Press, 2007.

Sánchez, Juan Reinaldo. *The Double Life of Fidel Castro.* New York: St. Martin's Press, 2015.

Skierka, Volker. *Fidel Castro: A Biography.* Malden, Massachusetts: Polity Press, 2004.

Smith, Wayne S. *Castro's Cuba: Soviet Partner or Nonaligned?* Washington, D.C.: Woodrow Wilson International Center for Scholars, 1984.

Suárez, Andrés. *Cuba: Castroism and Communism, 1959–1966.* Translated by Joel Carmichael and Ernst Halperin. Cambridge, Massachusetts: Massachusetts Institute of Technology Press, 1967.

Szulc, Tad. *Fidel: A Critical Portrait.* New York: William Morrow & Company, 1986.

Tetlow, Edwin. *Eye on Cuba.* New York: Harcourt, Brace & World, 1966.

Valls, Jorge. *Twenty Years and Forty Days.* New York: Americas Watch Committee, 1986.

Varona, Manuel Antonio. *The Drama of Cuba before America.* Florida: Revolutionary Pro-Democratic Rescue Organization, 1962.

Werlau, Maria C. *Cuba's Intervention in Venezuela: A Strategic Occupation with Global Implications.* Washington, D.C.: Free Society Project, 2019.

Young, Allen. *Gays under the Cuba Revolution.* San Francisco, California: Grey Fox Press, 1981.

Chapter 4: Mugabe

Alexander, Jocelyn. *The Unsettled Land: State-Making and the Politics of Land in Zimbabwe, 1893–2003.* Athens, Ohio: Ohio University Press, 2006.

Bhebe, Ngwabi, and Terence Ranger, eds. *Soldiers in Zimbabwe's Liberation War.* London: James Currey, 1995.

Birmingham, David. *Frontline Nationalism in Angola and Mozambique.* Trenton, New Jersey: Africa World Press, 1992.

Barber, James. *Rhodesia: The Road to Rebellion.* London and New York: Oxford University Press, 1967.

Blair, David. *Degrees in Violence: Robert Mugabe and the Struggle for Power in Zimbabwe.* London: Continuum, 2002.

Blake, Robert. *History of Rhodesia.* New York: Alfred A. Knopf, 1978.

Bowman, Larry W. *Politics in Rhodesia: White Power in an African State*. Cambridge, Massachusetts: Harvard University Press, 1973.

Clements, Frank. *Rhodesia: The Course to Collision*. London: Pall Mall Press, 1969.

Compagnon, Daniel. *A Predictable Tragedy: Robert Mugabe and the Collapse of Zimbabwe*. Philadelphia, Pennsylvania: University of Pennsylvania Press, 2011.

Flower, Ken. *Serving Secretly: An Intelligence Chief on Record: Rhodesia into Zimbabwe, 1964 to 1981*. London: John Murray, 1987.

Gerety, Rowan Moore. *Go Tell the Crocodiles: Chasing Prosperity in Mozambique*. New York: New Press, 2018.

Goodwin, Peter, and Ian Hancock. *"Rhodesians Never Die": The Impact of War and Political Change on White Rhodesia, 1970–1980*. Oxford, United Kingdom: Oxford University Press, 1993.

Linden, Ian. *The Catholic Church and the Struggle for Zimbabwe*. London: Longman, 1980.

Martin, David and Phyllis Johnson. *The Struggle for Zimbabwe: The Chimurenga War*. London: Faber and Faber, 1981.

Meredith, Martin. *The Fate of Africa: From the Hopes of Freedom to the Heart of Despair: A History of Fifty Years of Independence*. New York: PublicAffairs, 2005.

———. *Our Votes, Our Guns: Robert Mugabe and the Tragedy of Zimbabwe*. New York: PublicAffairs, 2003.

———. *Mugabe: Power, Plunder, and the Struggle for Zimbabwe*. New York: PublicAffairs, 2007.

Norman, Andrew. *Robert Mugabe and the Betrayal of Zimbabwe*. Jefferson, North Carolina: McFarland Publishers, 2004.

Vambe, Lawrence. *From Rhodesia to Zimbabwe*. Pittsburgh, Pennsylvania: University of Pittsburgh Press, 1976.

Wrong, Michela. *In the Footsteps of Mr. Kurtz: Living on the Brink of Disaster in Mobutu's Congo*. London: Fourth Estate, 2000.

Young, Kenneth. *Rhodesia and Independence*. New York: James H. Heineman, 1967.

Young, Crawford. *Politics in the Congo: Decolonization and Independence.* Princeton, New Jersey: Princeton University Press, 1965.

Chapter 5: Khomeini

Abrahamian, Ervand. *Tortured Confessions: Prisons and Public Relations in Modern Iran.* Berkeley, California: University of California Press, 1999.

Amuzegar, Jahangir. *The Dynamics of the Iranian Revolution.* Albany, New York: State University of New York Press, 1991.

Arjomand, Said Amir. *After Khomeini: Iran under His Successors.* New York: Oxford University Press, 2009.

———. *The Shadow of God and the Hidden Imam: Religion, Political Order, and Societal Change in Shi'ite Iran from the beginning to 1890.* Chicago: The University of Chicago Press, 1984.

Axworthy, Michael. *Revolutionary Iran: A History of the Islamic Republic.* New York: Oxford University Press, 2013.

Bakhash, Shaul. *The Reign of the Ayatollahs: Iran and the Islamic Revolution.* New York: Basic Books, 1984.

Bajoghli, Narges. *Iran Reframed: Anxieties in the Islamic Republic.* Stanford, California: Stanford University Press, 2019.

Cole, Juan R. I., and Nikki R. Keddie. *Shi'ism and Social Protest.* New Haven, Connecticut: Yale University Press, 1986.

Cooper, Andrew Scott. *The Fall of Heaven: The Pahlavis and the Final Days of Imperial Iran.* New York: Henry Holt & Company, 2016.

Daneshvar, Parviz. *Revolution in Iran.* New York: St. Martin's Press, 1996.

Engineer, Asghar Ali. *Islam and Revolution.* Delhi, India: Ajanta Publications, 1984.

Keddie, Nikki R., and Eric J. Hooglund. *The Iranian Revolution and The Islamic Republic.* New York: Syracuse University Press, 1986.

———. *Religion and Politics in Iran: Shi'ism from Quietism to Revolution.* New Haven, Connecticut: Yale University Press, 1983.

Khomeini, Ayatollah Ruhollah. *Islamic Government*. New York: Manor Books, 1979.

Kurzman, Charles. *The Unthinkable Revolution in Iran*. Cambridge, Massachusetts: Harvard University Press, 2004.

Martin, Vanessa. *Creating an Islamic State: Khomeini and the Making of a New Iran*. London: I. B. Tauris, 2000.

Milani, Mohsen M. *The Making of Iran's Islamic Revolution: From Monarchy to Islamic Republic*. Boulder, Colorado: Westview Press, 1988.

Moin, Baqer. *Khomeini: Life of the Ayatollah*. London: I. B. Tauris, 1999.

Montazam, Mir Ali Asghar. *The Life and Times of Ayatollah Khomeini*. London: Anglo-European Publishing, 1994.

Mozaffari, Mehdi. *Islamism: A New Totalitarianism*. Boulder, Colorado: Lynne Rienner Publishers, 2017.

Naraghi, Ehsan. *From Palace to Prison: Inside the Iranian Revolution*. Translated by Nilou Mobasser. Chicago: Ivan R. Dee, 1994.

Nasr, Seyyed Vali Reza. *The Vanguard of the Islamic Revolution: The Jama'at-I Islami of Pakistan*. Berkeley, California: University of California Press, 1994.

Ostovar, Afshon. *Vanguard of the Imam: Religion, Politics, and Iran's Revolutionary Guards*. New York: Oxford University Press, 2016.

Rahnema, Ali. *Call to Arms: Iran's Marxist Revolutionaries: Formation and Evolution of the Fada'is, 1964–1976*. London: Oneworld Academic, 2021.

———. *An Islamic Utopian: A Political Biography of Ali Shari'ati*. London: I. B. Tauris, 2000.

Roy, Olivier. *The Failure of Political Islam*. Translated by Carol Volk. Cambridge, Massachusetts: Harvard University Press, 1994.

Stempel, John D. *Inside the Iranian Revolution*. Bloomington, Indiana: Indiana University Press, 1981.

Taheri, Amir. *The Persian Night: Iran under the Khomeinist Revolution*. New York: Encounter Books, 2009.

Wright, Martin, ed. *Iran: The Khomeini Revolution*. Harlow: Longman, 1989.

Zabih, Sepehr. *The Communist Movement in Iran*. Berkeley, California: University of California Press, 1966.

Notes

Introduction The Revolutionary Mind

1. Hannah Arendt, *On Revolution* (New York: Viking Press, 1965 paperback edition), 61.
2. Ibid., 106.
3. Richard Pipes, "Afterward," *The Unknown Lenin: From the Secret Archive*, (New Haven, Connecticut: Yale University Press, 1998 paperback edition), 183.
4. Revelation 18:12

Chapter 1 Lenin

1. Dmitri Volkogonov, *Lenin: A New Biography*, trans. Harold Shukman (New York: The Free Press, 1994), 181.
2. Richard Pipes, *The Russian Revolution*, (New York: Alfred A. Knopf, 1990), 791.
3. Ibid.
4. Isaac Steinberg, *Gewalt und Terror in der Revolution* (Berlin, 1974), 22–25, quoted in Pipes, *Russian Revolution*, 793.
5. Pipes, *Russian Revolution*, 813.
6. Orlando Figes, *A People's Tragedy: The Russian Revolution: 1891–1924* (London: Jonathan Cape, 1996), 628.
7. Robert Service, *Lenin: A Biography* (New York: Macmillan Publishers, 2000 paperback edition), 5–7. Service provides a brief overview of Lenin historiography. This chapter relies heavily on Service's superb biography of Lenin, as well as the other biographies of Lenin, other Bolshevik revolutionaries, and histories of the Russian Revolution here, including those by Victor Sebestyen, Stephen Kokin, Richard Pipes, Orlando Figes, and others listed in the Selected Readings section of this book.
8. Dmitri Volkogonov, *Trotsky: The Eternal Revolutionary* (New York: The Free Press, 1996), 218.

9. Robert V. Daniels, *The Rise and Fall of Communism in Russia* (New Haven, Connecticut: Yale University Press, 2007), 182.
10. Stephen Kotkin, *Stalin* (New York: Penguin Books, 2014), 427.
11. Edvard Radzinsky, *Stalin* (New York: Random House, Penguin edition, 1997), 65.
12. Volkogonov, *Lenin*, 197.
13. Vladislav Zubok and Constantine Pleshakov, *Inside the Kremlin's Cold War: From Stalin to Khrushchev* (Cambridge, Massachusetts: Harvard University Press, 1996).
14. Pipes, *Russian Revolution*, 137.
15. Victor Sebestyen, *Lenin the Dictator* (London: Weidenfeld & Nicolson, 2017), 46.
16. Leopold H. Haimson, *The Russian Marxists and the Origins of Bolshevism* (Cambridge, Massachusetts: Harvard University Press, 1955), 103.
17. Sebestyen, *Lenin the Dictator*, 47.
18. Haimson, *Russian Marxists*, 67.
19. Edmund Wilson, *To the Finland Station* (New York: Harcourt, Brace & Company, 1940), 390, quoted in Neil Harding, *Leninism* (New York: MacMillan Press, 1996), 5.
20. Volkogonov, *Lenin*, 20.
21. Quoted in Michael B. Katz, "Introduction," Nicolai Chernyshevsky, *What Is to Be Done?*, trans. Michael B. Katz (Ithaca, New York: Cornell University Press, 1989), 33.
22. Sergey Nechaev, *Catechism of a Revolutionist*, 1869, https://pages.uoregon.edu/kimball/Nqv.catechism.thm.htm.
23. V. I. Lenin, *What Is to Be Done? Burning Questions of Our Movement* (New York: International Publishers, 1961 edition), 22, 41.
24. Ibid., 78.
25. Ibid., 81.
26. Ibid., 121.
27. Ibid., 133
28. Ibid., 29.
29. Lars T. Lih, *Lenin Rediscovered: What Is to Be Done? in Context* (Leiden, Netherlands, and London: Brill, 2006), 442. Although *Revolutionary Monsters* avoids endnoting every reference, party membership is obscure and deserves citation.
30. Haimson, *Russian Marxists*, 178.
31. Sebestyen, *Lenin the Dictator*, 149.
32. Figes, *A People's Tragedy*, 331.
33. Neil Harding, *Leninism*, 38–39.
34. Rosa Luxemburg, *The Russian Revolution and Leninism or Marxism* (Ann Arbor, Michigan: The University of Michigan Press, 1961).
35. Sebestyen, *Lenin the Dictator*, 151.
36. Ibid., 286.
37. Volkogonov, *Lenin*, 119.
38. Harding, *Leninism*, 103.
39. Volkogonov, *Lenin*, 220
40. Ibid., 76.
41. Figes, *A People's Tragedy*, 641.
42. Service, *Lenin*, 351.
43. Service, *Lenin*, 365.
44. Robert Royal, *The Catholic Martyrs of the Twentieth Century* (New York: Herder & Herder, 2000), 44.
45. Service, *Lenin*, 388.
46. Volkogonov, *Trotsky*, xxx.
47. Anthony Read, *The World on Fire: 1919 and the Battle with Bolshevism* (New York: W. W. Norton and Company, 2008), 191.

48. Richard M. Watt: *The Kings Depart: The Tragedy of Germany* (New York: Simon & Schuster, 1970), 326.
49. Service, *Lenin*, 411.
50. Volkogonov, *Lenin*, 238.
51. Service, *Lenin*, 465.
52. Ibid., 489.

Chapter 2 Mao

1. Ian Johnson, "Who Killed More: Hitler, Stalin, or Mao?" *New York Review of Books*, ✓ February 5, 2018.
2. Jack Gray, "Mao in Perspective," *The China Quarterly*, September 2006.
3. Jung Chang and Jon Halliday, *Mao: The Unknown Story* (New York: Random House, Anchor edition, 2006), 13.
4. Quoted in Robert Payne, *Portrait of a Revolutionary: Mao Tse Tung* (London: Abelard-Schuman, 1950), 34.
5. Quoted in Jonathan Spence, *Mao Zedong* (New York: Viking Press, 1999), 15.
6. Quoted in Payne, *Portrait of a Revolutionary*, 27.
7. Payne, *Portrait of a Revolutionary*, 37.
8. Ibid., 60.
9. Spence, *Mao Zedong*, 36.
10. Chang and Halliday, *Mao*, 33.
11. Payne, *Portrait of a Revolutionary*, 74.
12. Chang and Halliday, *Mao*, 44.
13. Ibid., 52.
14. Ibid., 111.
15. Ibid., 91.
16. Spence, *Mao Zedong*, 99.
17. Chang and Halliday, *Mao*, 137
18. John E. Rue, *Mao Tse-tung in Opposition, 1927–1935* (Stanford, California: Stanford University Press, 1966), 131.
19. Lucien Bianco, *Origins of the Chinese Revolution, 1915–1949*, trans. Muriel Bell, (Stanford, California: Stanford University Press, 1971), 159.
20. Chang and Halliday, *Mao: The Unknown Story*, 191.
21. The full story of journalistic bias and Mao's manipulation of these journalists has not been fully told. Agnes Smedley, though, has attracted a sympathetic biography. New Zealand journalist James Bertram interviewed Mao extensively. Following the Second World War, in which he was interned as a Japanese prisoner of war, Bertram remained active in left-wing causes, including the Society for Closer Relations with Russia and the New Zealand–China Friendship Society. In the 1970s he was a guest of honor for Zhou Enlai. Haldore Hanson, a later State Department official, became a victim of the McCarthy Red Scare, but he clearly was a man of the Left. Anna Louis Strong was another journalist who interviewed Mao favorably. She lived in the Soviet Union from 1921 through 1940. T. A. Bisson, a journalist in the 1930s, later became a professor at the University of California, Berkeley, from where he was let go in the 1950s for clear Communist sympathies. There were dozens of other journalists who offered sympathetic portraits of Mao, the humble peasant democrat. In fairness, some of these journalists turned to work later for the Nationalist government in Taiwan. This journalism was not a conspiracy, but a mobilization of left-leaning journalists willing to avoid tough questioning of Mao.

22. Charles B. McLane, *Soviet Policy and the Chinese Communists, 1931–1946* (New York: Columbia University Press, 1958), 3.
23. Chang and Halliday, *Mao*, 201.
24. Ibid., 241.
25. Ibid., 230.
26. John Haynes and Harvey Klehr, *Venona: Decoding Soviet Espionage in America* (New Haven, Connecticut: Yale University Press, 1999).
27. Frank Dikötter, *The Tragedy of Liberation: A History of the Chinese Revolution, 1945–1957* (London: Bloomsbury Publishing, 2013, 2017 paperback edition), 12.
28. Chang and Halliday, *Mao*, 201.
29. Dikötter, *Tragedy of Liberation*, xi, 4.
30. Ibid., 25.
31. Rae Yang, *Spider Eaters: A Memoir* (Berkeley, California: University of California Press, 1997), 9.
32. Robert Loh, *Escape from Red China* (New York; Coward-McCann, 1962), 38, 41.
33. Loh, *Escape from Red China*, 13.
34. Frank Dikötter, "The People's Republic of China was Born in Chains," *Foreign Policy*, October 2019.
35. Chang and Halliday, *Mao*, 352.
36. Ibid., 353. For Stalin's views on the inevitability of war, discussed in Chapter 1, see Vladislav Zubok and Constantine Plekhanov, *Inside Kremlin's Cold War: From Stalin to Khrushchev* (Cambridge, Massachusetts: Harvard University Press, 1996).
37. Dikötter, *Tragedy of Liberation*, 131.
38. Spence, *Mao Zedong*, 116.
39. Ibid., 127.
40. Chang and Halliday, *Mao*, 403.
41. Ibid., 375, 385.
42. Ibid., 387.
43. Frank Dikötter, *Mao's Great Famine: The History of China's Most Devastating Catastrophe, 1958-1962* (London: Bloomsbury Publishers, 2010, 2017 paperback edition), 19.
44. Dikötter, *Tragedy of Liberation*, 283.
45. Li Zhisui, *The Private Life of Chairman Mao: The Memories of Mao's Personal Physician* (New York: Random House, 1994), 200, quoted in Dikötter, *The Tragedy of Liberation*, 291.
46. Chang and Halliday, *Mao*, 411.
47. Ibid., 431.
48. Ibid., 433.
49. Ibid., 477.
50. Li, *Private Life of Chairman Mao*, 469, quoted in Frank Dikötter, *The Cultural Revolution: A People's History, 1962-1976* (London: Bloomsbury Publishing, 2016, 2019 paperback edition), 71.
51. Chang and Halliday, *Mao*, 507.
52. Quoted in Dikötter, *Cultural Revolution*, 77.
53. Gao Yan, *Born Red: A Chronicle of the Cultural Revolution* (Stanford, California: Stanford University Press, 1987), 39.
54. Yang, *Spider Eaters*, 113, 115.
55. Ibid., 119, 121.
56. Chang and Halliday, *Mao*, 575.
57. Dikötter, *Cultural Revolution*, 318.

Chapter 3 Castro

1.   Robert E. Quirk, *Fidel Castro* (New York: W. W. Norton, 1993), 221; Tad Szulc, *Fidel: A Critical Portrait* (New York: William Morrow & Company, 1986), 459, 469.
2.   Brian Latell, *After Fidel: The Inside Story of Castro's Regime and Cuba's Next Leader* (New York: Macmillan, 2005), 63.
3.   Jonathan M. Hansen, *Young Castro: The Making of a Revolutionary* (New York: Simon & Schuster, 2019), 77.
4.   Ibid., 117.
5.   Leycester Coltman, *The Real Fidel Castro* (New Haven, Connecticut: Yale University Press, 2003), 39.
6.   Hansen, *Young Castro*, 143.
7.   Coltman, *The Real Fidel Castro*, 65.
8.   Ibid.
9.   Quoted in Marta Harnecker, *Fidel Castro's Political Strategy from Moncada* (New York: Pathfinder Press, 1987), 11.
10. Georgie Anne Geyer, *Guerrilla Prince: The Untold Story of Fidel Castro* (Boston: Little, Brown & Company, 1991), 110.
11. Coltman, *The Real Fidel Castro*, 79.
12. Geyer, *Guerrilla Prince*, 126–27.
13. Ibid., 133.
14. Ibid., 145.
15. Coltman, *The Real Fidel Castro*, 114.
16. Geyer, *Guerrilla Prince*, 165.
17. Ibid., 169.
18. The Sierra Manifesto is reprinted in its entirety in Harnecker, *Fidel Castro's Political Strategy*, 49–51.
19. Geyer, *Guerrilla Prince*, 189–90.
20. Ibid., 204.
21. Ibid., 205.
22. Coltman, *The Real Fidel Castro*, 152.
23. Ibid.
24. Maurice Halperin, *The Rise and Decline of Fidel Castro: An Essay in Contemporary History* (Berkeley, California: University of California Press, 1972), 21.
25. Quirk, *Fidel Castro*, 218.
26. Hansen, *Young Castro*, 403.
27. Coltman, *The Real Fidel Castro*, 148.
28. Teresa Casuso, *Cuba and Castro* (New York, Random House, 1961), 193.
29. Ibid., 198.
30. Quirk, *Fidel Castro*, 326.
31. Coltman, *The Real Fidel Castro*, 145.
32. Geyer, *Guerrilla Prince*, 244–5.
33. Ibid., 215.
34. Ibid., 216.
35. Quirk, *Fidel Castro*, 255.
36. Geyer, *Guerrilla Prince*, 272.
37. Ibid., 281.
38. James G. Blight and Janet M. Lang, "How Castro Held the World Hostage," *New York Times*, October 28, 2012; James G. Blight and Janet M. Lang, *The Armageddon Letters: Kennedy, Khrushchev, Castro in the Cuban Missile Crisis* (Lanham, Maryland: Rowman & Littlefield Publishers, 2012).

39. Halperin, *Rise and Decline of Fidel Castro*, 129.
40. Quirk, *Fidel Castro*, 522.
41. Geyer, *Guerrilla Prince*, 310.
42. Ibid., 313.
43. Volker Skierka, *Fidel Castro: A Biography* (Cambridge, England, and Malden, Massachusetts: Polity, 2004), 189.
44. Quirk, *Fidel Castro*, 611.
45. Coltman, *The Real Fidel Castro*, 233; Skierka, *Fidel Castro*, 215.
46. Quirk, *Fidel Castro*, 828.
47. Andres Oppenheimer, *Castro's Final Hour: The Secret Story Behind the Coming Downfall of Communist Cuba* (New York: Simon & Schuster, 1992), 19.
48. Skierka, *Fidel Castro*, 303.
49. Anthony DePalma, *The Cubans: Ordinary Lives in Extraordinary Times* (New York: Random House, 2020), 533.
50. Ibid., 5.
51. Ibid., 533.
52. Sally H. Jacobs, "Castro Steps Down as Díaz-Canel Assumes Cuban Presidency," Pulitzer Center, April 19, 2018, https://pulitzercenter.org/stories/castro-steps-down-diaz-canel-assumes-cuban-presidency.
53. Janette Habel, *Cuba: The Revolution in Peril* (London: Verso, 1991), 193.

Chapter 4 Robert Mugabe

1.   Quoted in Martin Meredith, *Our Votes, Our Guns: Robert Mugabe and the Tragedy of Zimbabwe* (New York: PublicAffairs, 2002), 28–29.
2.   Frank Clements, *Rhodesia: The Course to Collision* (London: Pall Mall Press, 1969), 199.
3.   Quoted in Kenneth Young, *Rhodesia and Independence: A Study in British Colonial Policy* (London: Dent, 1969), 106.
4.   James Barber, *Rhodesia: The Road to Rebellion* (London, New York: Oxford University Press, 1967), 199.
5.   Ian Linden, *The Catholic Church and the Struggle for Zimbabwe* (London: Longman, 1980), 183.
6.   Quoted in Young, *Rhodesia and Independence*, 291.
7.   Quoted in Meredith, *Our Votes, Our Guns*, 3.
8.   David Martin and Phyllis Johnson, *The Struggle for Zimbabwe: The Chimurenga War* (Harare, Zimbabwe: Zimbabwe Publishing House, 1981), 257.
9.   Quoted in Andrew Norman, *Robert Mugabe and the Betrayal of Zimbabwe*, (Jefferson, North Carolina: McFarland Publishers, 2004), 73.
10. Martin Meredith, *Mugabe: Power, Plunder, and the Struggle for Zimbabwe* (New York: PublicAffairs, 2007), 7.
11. Ibid., 8.
12. Ibid., 9.
13. Ibid.
14. Ibid., 10.
15. Martin Meredith, *The Fate of Africa: From the Hopes of Freedom to the Heart of Despair: A History of Fifty Years of Independence* (New York: PublicAffairs, 2005), 618.
16. David Blair, *Degrees in Violence: Robert Mugabe and the Struggle for Power in Zimbabwe* (London: Continuum International Publishing Group, 2002), 24.
17. Meredith, *Mugabe*, 17.
18. Quoted in Meredith, *Our Votes, Our Guns*, 17.
19. Meredith, *Mugabe*, 52

20. Ibid., 63.
21. Ibid., 70.
22. Ibid., 57.
23. Meredith, *Our Votes, Our Guns*, 92.
24. Meredith, *Mugabe*, 125.
25. Ibid.,131.
26. Quoted in Norman, *Robert Mugabe*, 133.
27. Meredith, *Mugabe*, 97.
28. Quoted in Teresa A. Barnes, "The Heroes' Struggle: Life after the War for Four Ex-Combatants in Zimbabwe," in *Soldiers in Zimbabwe's Liberation War*, Ngwabi Bhebe and Terence Ranger, eds. (London: J. Currey, 1995), 133, 138.

Chapter 5 Khomeini

1. Michael Axworthy, *Revolutionary Iran: A History of the Islamic Republic* (New York: Oxford University Press, 2013), 142.
2. Ibid., 5.
3. Ibid., 163.
4. Baqer Moin, *Khomeini: Life of the Ayatollah* (London: I. B. Tauris, 1999), 48.
5. Axworthy, *Revolutionary Iran*, 137.
6. Amir Taheri, *The Persian Night: Iran under the Khomeinist Revolution* (New York: Encounter Books, 2009), 4.
7. Ibid.
8. Moin, *Khomeini*, 2.
9. Vanessa Martin, *Creating an Islamic State: Khomeini and the Making of a New Iran* (London: I. B. Tauris, 2003), 39.
10. Taheri, *Persian Night*, 21.
11. Moin, *Khomeini*, 63.
12. Ruhollah Komeini, *Islamic Government*, trans. Joint Publications Research Service (New York: Manor Books, 1979), 5.
13. Ibid., 95.
14. Ibid., 104.
15. Ibid., 17.
16. Shaul Bakhash, *The Reign of the Ayatollahs: Iran and the Islamic Revolution* (New York: Basic Books, 1984), 24.
17. Martin, *Creating an Islamic State*, 61.
18. Afshon Ostovar, *Vanguard of the Imam: Religion, Politics, and Iran's Revolutionary Guards* (New York: Oxford University Press, 2016, 2018 paperback edition), 31.
19. Moin, *Khomeini*, 57.
20. Bakhash, *Reign of the Ayatollahs*, 26.
21. Ibid., 29
22. Ibid.
23. Moin, *Khomeini*, 80.
24. Parviz Daneshvar, *Revolution in Iran* (New York: St. Martin's Press, 1996), 82.
25. Ali Rahnema, *Call to Arms: Iran's Marxist Revolutionaries: Formation and Evolution of the Fada'is, 1964–1976* (London: Oneworld Academic, 2021), 2–3.
26. Ali Rahnema, *An Islamic Utopian: A Political Biography of Ali Shari'ati* (London: I. B. Tauris, 2000, 2014 edition), 297.
27. Daneshvar, *Revolution in Iran*, 83–85.
28. Bakhash, *Reign of the Ayatollahs*, 47, 52.
29. Daneshvar, *Revolution in Iran*, 124.

30. Ibid., 125.
31. Ibid., 135.
32. Ibid., 141; Bakhash, *Reign of the Ayatollahs*, 78.
33. Daneshvar, *Revolution in Iran*, 143; Bakhash, *Reign of the Ayatollahs*, 78.
34. Daneshvar, *Revolution in Iran*, 144.
35. Bakhash, *Reign of the Ayatollahs*, 85.
36. Axworthy, *Revolutionary Iran*, 163.
37. R. K. Ramazani, "Shi'ism in the Persian Gulf," in *Shi'ism and Social Protest*, Juan R. I. Cole and Nikki R. Keddie, eds. (New Haven, Connecticut: Yale University Press, 1986), 35.
38. Moin, *Khomeini*, 228.
39. Bakhash, *Reign of the Ayatollahs*, 121.
40. Ibid., 122.
41. Moin, *Khomeini*, 219.
42. Bakhash, *Reign of the Ayatollahs*, 123.
43. Ervand Abrahamian, *Tortured Confessions: Prisons and Public Recantations in Modern Iran* (Berkeley, California: University of California Press, 1999), 138.
44. Abrahamian, *Tortured Confessions*, 164.
45. Struan Stevenson, "The Forgotten Mass Execution of Prisoners in Iran in 1988," *The Diplomat*, July 31, 2013, https://thediplomat.com/2013/07/the-forgotten-mass-execution-of-prisoners-in-iran-in-1988/; Shamsi Saadati, "International Condemnation of Iran's 1988 Massacre," National Council of Resistance of Iran, December 13, 2020, https://www.ncr-iran.org/en/iran-1988-massacre-of-political-prisoners/international-condemnation-of-irans-1988-massacre/; Majid Rafizadeh, "Iran's Massacre and Rising Crimes against Humanity," Gatestone Institute, October 5, 2016, https://www.gatestoneinstitute.org/9062/iran-massacre.
46. Axworthy, *Revolutionary Iran*, 281.
47. Ibid., 298.
48. Bakhash, *Reign of the Ayatollahs*, 76.
49. Taheri, *Persian Night*, 235.
50. Narges Bajoghli, *Iran Reframed: Anxieties in the Islamic Republic* (Stanford, California: Stanford University Press, 2019), 1.
51. Said Amir Arjomand, *After Khomeini: Iran Under His Successors* (New York: Oxford University Press, 2009), 67.

Conclusion Lessons Learned?

1. James Burham, *The Machiavellians: Defenders of Freedom: A Defense of Political Truth against Wishful Thinking* (New York: John Day, 1941), 150–51, quoting Robert Michels, *Political Parties: A Sociological Study of the Oligarchical Tendencies of Modern Democracy* (New York: International Library Company, 1915), 206–7. This conclusion drew heavily from both Burnham and Michels.

Index

26th of July Movement, 79–80, 88, 90
1848 Revolutions, 174
1871 Paris Commune, 174
1905 Russian Revolution, 15–16
1917 Russian Revolution. *See* October Revolution (1917 Russian Revolution).
1919 German revolution, 174
1919 Hungarian revolution, 174
1932 Salvadoran peasant uprising, 174

A

Abadan, 153
Agrarian Reform Bill (Cuba), 87
Ahmadinejad, Mahmoud, 167, 171
Algerian War for Independence, 148
Allende, Salvador, 99–100
American Revolution, xi–xv
Angola, 95, 100–2
anti-Communism, 24, 44, 82, 88
anti-imperialism, 73, 87, 150
anti-Semitism, 148
apartheid, 114–15
Argentina, 73–74, 80, 95–96, 168
Atatürk, Mustafa Kemal, 141
Authentic Cuban Revolutionary Party, 72
Autumn Uprising, 40

B

Baha'i faith, 146, 153

Bakhtiar, Shapour, 151, 154–55, 170
Bakunin, Mikhail, 10
Banisadr, Abolhassan, 161–64
Banna, Hasan al-, 149
Bastidas, Adina, 87
Batista, Fulgencio, 67, 71–72, 75, 77, 79–85, 89
Bay of Pigs invasion, 91–93
Bayo, Alberto, 80
Bazargan, Mehdi, 135, 148, 151, 153, 155–57, 160–62
Beatniks, 175
Beauvoir, Simone de, 33, 58
Beheshti, Mohammad, 165
Beijing, 36–37, 45, 47, 49, 51–52, 57, 59–60, 64
Bertram, James, 45, 196n21
Bisson, T. A., 45, 196n21
Black Friday, 153
Blanqui, Louis Auguste, 9
Bo Gu, 42
Bolivia, 68, 96–97
Bolsheviks, xiv, xv, 2, 4–5, 14–23, 27, 29, 117
Bosch, Juan, 73
Buddhism, 34, 51, 153
Bush War (Rhodesia/Zimbabwe), 119

C

Cardona, Miró, 85

201

Carrington, Lord Peter, 120
Carter, Jimmy, 138, 151
Castro, Fidelito, 67–68, 75, 84, 105
Castro, Raúl, 67, 70–71, 75–76, 79, 81–82, 85–86, 88–90, 102, 104–05
Casuso, Teresa, 88
Catholic church, xii, 23–24, 51–52, 70, 86, 109, 114, 118, 126, 131
Central Intelligence Agency (CIA), 57, 84, 91–93, 100, 143, 167
Central Intelligence Organisation (Rhodesia/Zimbabwe), 122
Central Powers, 21
Chakaipa, Patrick, 131
Chávez, Hugo, xvii, 87, 103
Cheka, 2–3, 20, 26
Chen Duxiu, 36–37, 48
Chernyshevsky, Nikolai, 10–11
Chiang Kai-shek, 40, 42–45, 47–49, 60
Chibás, Raúl, 82
Chile, 95, 99–100
Chimurenga, 116
Chinese Communist Party (CCP), 33, 37–50, 54
Chinese Nationalist Party. See Kuomintang.
Chiyangwa, Phillip, 124
Christianity, xii, 22, 109, 118
Cienfuegos, Camilo, 91
Colombia, 73–74, 95, 102
Colombian Liberal Party, 74
Comintern, 23, 25, 38, 44, 46, 54
Committees for the Defense of the Revolution (Cuba), 89
Confederation of Iranian Students, 151
Confucianism, 37
Congo, 96, 115–16
Conservative Alliance (Zimbabwe), 127. See also Rhodesian Front.
Contras, 100
Costa Rica, 95
Council of the Islamic Revolution, 135, 155, 161
Cuban Communist Party, 67, 71, 73, 88
Cuban missile crisis, 68, 91, 93–94
Cultural Revolution (China), 31–32, 45, 58–59, 63, 65, 97
Currie, Lauchlin, 47
Cewale River, 126
Czechoslovakia, 90, 97

D
Deng Xiaoping, 63–64
Díaz-Balart, Mirta, 68, 74, 79
Díaz-Canel Bermúdez, Miguel, 105
Dominican Republic, 73, 87
Dorticós, Osvaldo, 89, 94
Duma, 15–17
Duvalier, François, xvii
Dzerzhinsky, Felix, 20

E
Eastman, Max, 2
Echevarría, José Antonio, 81
Educational Reform Law (Cuba), 86
Eisenhower, Dwight D., 91
Eisner, Kurt, 24
El Salvador, 95, 174
Emergency Powers Act (Rhodesia/Zimbabwe), 123
Engels, Friedrich, 6, 36
Ethiopia, 100–2

F
Fanon, Frantz, 123, 149
Fedai. See Organization of Iranian People's Fedai Guerrillas.
Field, Winston, 112–13
Fifth Brigade (Zimbabwe), 125–26
Finland, 17–18
First Five-Year Plan. See Superpower Program.
First Gulf War, 167
First Sino-Japanese War, 36
First World War. See World War I.
Flower, Ken, 122–23
Fort Hare, 109
Founding Fathers, xii–xiii, 177
Franqui, Carlos, 88–89
French Revolution, xi–xii, xiv, 9, 106, 160

G
Gaitán, Jorge Eliécer, 74
Gapon, Georgy, 15
García Márquez, Gabriel, 105
German Social Democratic Party, 14, 23
Geyer, Georgie Ann, 84
Ghaffari, Hojjat ol-Eslam (clerical title), 156
Ghana, 110, 116
Gharbzadegi. See Westernization.
glasnost', 101–2
Glorious Revolution, xi
Gorbachev, Mikhail, 101–3

Gorky, Maxim, 19
Granma, 81
Grau, Ramón, 72
Great Britain, xii, 5, 23, 35, 55, 57, 64, 73,
    111–16, 119–22, 124, 142–43, 152
Great Leap Forward (Second Five-Year
    Plan), 31, 54, 56, 58
Great Revolutionary Offensive (Cuba), 97
Grenada, 100
Guardian Council (Iran), 136
guerrilla warfare, 44, 46, 80, 83, 87, 89, 91,
    95–97, 112, 115–19, 123, 125, 127, 145,
    149–50, 157, 164
Guevara, Alfredo, 193
Guevara, Che, 68, 80, 84, 86, 91, 96, 149
gulag, 3, 25, 29, 56

H
Haeri Yazdi, Abdul-Karim, 139
Hamilton, Alexander, xiii
Hammer, Armand, 23
Hanson, Haldore, 196n21
Harare (Salisbury), Zimbabwe 108, 113,
    118, 121–22, 127, 129, 131, 133
Hashemi, Mehdi, 165
Havana, Cuba, 67, 70–75, 79, 81–82,
    84–90, 92–94, 96–97, 101
Hayfron, Sally, 110, 131
Hernández, Melba, 76
Hezbollah (Iran), 156–57, 162–64, 168, 171
Hidden Imam, 136, 142–44, 150, 157, 160,
    165, 169, 171–72
"History Will Absolve Me," 78–79
Hitler, Adolf, xvii, 5, 31–32, 130
Ho Chi Minh, xvii
homosexuality, 92, 94, 99, 129, 138, 152, 156
Honduras, 95
Hunanese Socialist Youth League, 37–38
Hunzvi, Chenjerai, 130
Hurley, Patrick, 45
Hussein, Saddam, 160, 164
Huxley, Aldous, 174

I
Insurrectional Revolutionary Union
    (Cuba), 72
Iranian hostage crisis, 160–61
Iraq, 143, 147, 152, 154, 160, 162–63,
    166–67, 170
Irfan, 139

Islam, 136–37, 139–40, 142–44, 146–50,
    158–62, 165–66, 168–72, 175. *See also*
    Political Islam; Shi'ism; Sunnism.
Islamic Republican Party, 157, 163–64
Islamic Revolution Committees, 156
Islamic Revolutionary Guard Corps, 156,
    159–60, 163, 165–66, 168–71
Isle of Pines prison, 78
Israel, xi, 137, 139, 146–47, 163, 166,
    168, 170

J
Jacobin clubs, xii, xiv
Japan, 36, 42–44, 45–49
Jesuits, 71, 108–9, 115, 118
Jews, 5, 7, 137, 143, 146, 149. *See also*
    anti-Semitism.
Jinggang mountains, 40
Johnson, Hewlett, 79

K
Kalanga people, 125
Kaunda, Kenneth, 117
Kennedy, John F., 91–93
Kenya, 116
Kerensky, Alexander, 17–18, 23
Kerensky, Fedor, 8–9
Khalkhali, Sadegh, 163
Khamenei, Ali, 167, 169–70
Khatami, Mohammad, 141
Khrushchev, Nikita, 54–55, 63, 93–95
Kianouri, Noureddin, 165
Kidd, Benjamin, 35
Kim Il-sung, xvii, 52
Kissinger, Henry, 63–64, 119
Kombayi, Patrick, 128
Koran, 139, 145–47
Kornilov, Lavr, 18
Krupskaya, Nadezhda, 1, 9
kulak, 3, 5, 21, 26
Kun, Béla, 25
Kuomintang (Nationalists; KMT), 35,
    37–40, 43
Kuwait, 154

L
Lancaster House Agreement, 120–21,
    123, 127
Law and Order (Maintenance) Act (Rhode-
    sia/Zimbabwe), 110, 123
League of Nations, 42
Left Opposition, 26

Leninism, 4, 10, 13, 15, 27, 33, 39, 43, 90, 92, 123, 150
"Let a Hundred Flowers Bloom," 56, 98, 133
Li Zhisui, 56
Liebknecht, Karl, 23–24
Lin Biao, 49, 57
Lipp, Franz, 24
Little Red Book, 33, 59
Liu Shaoqi, 62
Loh, Robert, 50
Long March, 40–43
Lumumba, Patrice, 115
Lusaka, 109, 117
Luxemburg, Rosa, 15, 23–24
Lvov, Prince Georgy, 17–18

M

MacArthur, Douglas, 53
Machado, Gerardo, 71, 78
Machel, Samora, 117, 121
Madame Mao. See Qing, Jiang.
Maduro, Nicolás, 104
Majles, 159, 161, 163
Marshall, George, 48
Martí, José, 80, 92
Martov, Julius. See Zederbaum, Yuliy.
Marufu, Grace, 131
Marx, Karl, 6, 8, 14, 36, 109, 123
Marxism, 4, 6, 10–12, 15–16, 22, 27, 33, 36, 38–39, 43, 71, 75, 78, 92, 107, 109–10, 120, 121, 129–30, 137, 143, 148, 150, 154, 157, 160, 162, 175
Marxism-Leninism, 4, 33, 92, 123, 150
Mashhad, 142
Matabeleland, 125, 130
Matos, Huber, 89
Matthews, Herbert, 82
Mensheviks, 15–17, 20, 117
Mif, Pavel, 38
Mnangagwa, Emmerson, 132–33
Mobutu, Joseph, 115–16
Mohammed (prophet), 135–37, 140, 142, 153
Molotov, Vyacheslav Mikhailovich, 22
Moncada barracks attack, 76–79
Monje, Mario, 96
Montazeri, Ayatollah (clerical title), 165
Mosaddegh, Mohammad, 143, 150, 161
Movement for Democratic Change (Zimbabwe), 130
Mozambique, 116–21, 127
Mugabe, Sally. See Hayfron, Sally.

Mujahedin. See People's Mujahedin of Iran.
mujtahidun, 141
mullah, 139, 141–42, 144–45, 150, 153–54, 156, 158, 160, 168–69
Muslim Brotherhood (Egypt), 149
Mussolini, Benito, xvii
Muzorewa, Abel, 119–21

N

Najaf, 147
Nanjing, 40, 45–46, 49
National Agrarian Reform Institute (Cuba), 88
National Democratic Party (Rhodesia/Zimbabwe), 110–11
National Socialism (Nazism), 5, 130
Nazism. See National Socialism.
Ndebele people, 108, 125–26, 133
Nechayev, Sergey, 10–12
New Deal, 58
New Economic Policy, 26
New Jewel Movement, 100
Nicaragua, 100–2
Nicholas II, Czar, 10, 15–16
Nietzcheanism, 71
Nigeria, 123
Nipe-Sagua-Baracoa, 69
Nixon, Richard, 63–64, 87
Nkomo, Joshua, 110–13, 117, 119–23, 125–27
Nkrumah, Kwame, 110
Nolte, Gustav, 24
North Korea, 52–53, 125, 167–68
Northern Rhodesia. See Zambia.
Nyasaland, 112
Nyerere, Julius, 117

O

O'Hea, Jerome, 108–9
Ochoa Sánchez, Arnaldo, 100–2
October Revolution (1917 Russian Revolution), 2, 5, 15, 18, 25
Ogaden War, 101
one-party system, 1, 14, 27, 67, 88, 105, 107, 120, 123, 126, 128, 133
Organization of Iranian People's Fedai Guerrillas, 157
Orgburo, 20
Oriente Province (Cuba), 69, 73, 76, 80, 83, 149
Ortega, Daniel, 101
Ortodoxo Party, 72, 75–76, 82

P

Padilla, Heberto, 99

Pahlavi, Mohammad Reza (son of Reza Pahlavi), 135, 142, 144

Pahlavi, Reza (father of Mohammad Reza Pahlavi), 141–42

Palestinian Liberation Army. *See* Palestinian Liberation Organization.

Palestinian Liberation Organization, 148, 151

pan-Africanism, xvii

Panama, 87

Paris, 23, 75, 154, 157, 161, 163, 170, 174

Paulsen, Friedrich, 33

Paz, Octavio, 99

Pazos, Felipe, 82

Peng Dehuai, 57

People's Liberation Army, 49, 62

People's Mujahedin of Iran, 157, 160, 165

People's State of Bavaria, 24

perestroika, 103

Perón, Juan, 73

Peru, 95

Pflaum, Irving, 88

Philadelphia Convention, xii

Pilsudski, Josef, 25

Pino, Rafael del, 74

Pipes, Richard, xv

Plekhanov, Georgy, 13–15

Poland, 16, 25–26

Polish-Soviet War, 26

Politburo, 20, 28, 90

Political Islam, 148–50, 162, 175

Popular Socialist Party (Cuba). *See* Cuban Communist Party.

Prío, Carlos, 75, 80

Protestantism, 7, 23

Punto Cero de Guanabo, 87

Q

Qing dynasty, 34–36

Qing, Jiang (Madame Mao), 45, 59, 64–65

Qom, 140, 152

R

Rafsanjani, Akbar Hashemi, 141, 171

Raft, George, 84

Raisi, Ebrahim, 171

Rajai, Mohammad-Ali, 161

Rajavi, Massoud, 161–63

Reagan, Ronald, 101

Red Army (Chinese), 32–33, 41–42, 44, 47–49

Red Army (Soviet), 3–4, 20, 25–27

Red Guard (Chinese), 32, 49, 60–62, 126

Red Guard (Soviet), 18

Red Terror (Chinese), 41

Red Terror (Soviet), 2, 21

Rent Reduction Law (Cuba), 86

Revuelta, Natalia, 79

Rhodesian Front, 112, 114

Robespierre, Maximilien, xii, 9, 106

Rodinson, Maxime, 168

Roosevelt, Franklin, 32, 45, 47, 58

Rousseau, Jean-Jacques, 79

Rushdie, Salman, 167

Russian Orthodox church, 7, 15, 23, 34

Russian Revolution. *See* 1905 Russian Revolution; October Revolution.

Russian Social Democratic Labor Party, 13–14

Ruz, Lina, 69

S

Saint-Just, Luois Antoine de, 9

Salisbury, Rhodesia. *See* Harare (Salisbury), Zimbabwe.

Sánchez, Celia, 86

Sandinista National Liberation Front, 100

Sandinistas, 87, 100–1

Sanjabi, Karim, 151, 153, 157

Santiago, Cuba, 70, 76, 85

Sartre, Jean-Paul, 33, 58, 99

SAVAK, 153

Second Five-Year Plan. *See* Great Leap Forward.

Second Great Awakening, 175

Second Gulf War, 167, 170

Second World War. *See* World War II.

Sergeants' Revolt, 71

Shanghai, 37–38, 40–42, 44–45, 50

sharia, 135–36, 141, 144, 146, 149

Shariati Mazinani, Ali, 149

Shi'ism, 138–44, 147, 149, 153, 158

Shona people, 108, 116, 125–26

Siahkal, Iran, 150

Sierra Maestra, 68–69, 81, 83, 86, 101

Silveira House, 118

Sithole, Ndabaningi, 113, 118, 129

Smedley, Agnes, 44–45

Smith, Ian, 113–14, 120, 122–23, 127

Snow, Edgar, 40–41, 44, 82

Social Darwinism, 35–36, 72
Socialist Revolutionary Movement
  (Cuba), 72
Somoza, Anastasio, 100
Sorge, Richard, 44
Soto del Valle, Dalia, 105
South Africa, 101, 109, 114–16, 119,
  123–24
Southern Rhodesian African National Con-
  gress (SRANC), 110
Soviet Communist Party, 2, 4–5, 19–21, 29
Spanish Civil War, 80
Spartacus League, 23–24
St. Petersburg, 8–9, 15–16
Steinberg, Isaac, 3
Stowe, Harriet Beecher, 7
Strategic Arms Limitation Talks, 64
Strong, Anna Louis, 45
Student Followers of the Imam's Line, 160
Student Revolutionary Directorate, 84
Sullivan, William, 138
Sun Yat-sen, 34–35, 38–39, 169
Sunnism, 140, 149
Superpower Program (First Five-Year Plan),
  55
supreme leader (Iran), xiv, xvi, 135–36,
  138–39, 141, 144, 155, 158–59, 167–70
Switzerland, 12, 16, 24
Szulc, Tad, 88

T

Tanzania, 116–17, 119
Tehran, 135, 139–41, 147, 153–54, 156,
  161–62, 164, 167
Tekere, Edgar, 127–29
Thatcher, Margaret, 120
Tkachëv, Pëtr, 10
Toller, Ernst, 24–25
Treaty of Brest-Litovsk, 21
Trotsky, Leon, 3–4, 6, 15, 18–21, 23, 26–29
Trujillo, Rafael, 72, 87
Truman, Harry, 32, 47, 53
Tsvangirai, Morgan, 129–30
Tudeh Party, 157, 163, 165
Turkey, 93, 147

U

Uganda, 116
ummah, 149
United African National Council, 121–22
United Kingdom. See Great Britain.
United Nations, 64, 114, 119, 138, 152

United States, 5, 19, 23, 33, 45, 48, 50, 52,
  63–64, 98, 73–74, 80, 82, 84, 86, 89,
  91–93, 101, 114, 119–20, 124, 127, 137,
  160, 167
Urban Reform Law (Cuba), 86
Urrutia Lleó, Manuel, 84, 88–89

Vargas Llosa, Mario, 99
Venezuela, 87, 89, 95, 102–4, 168
Victoria Falls, 132
Vietnam War, 148
Vilá, Herminio Portell, 76

W

War Communism, 21
Westernization, 36, 148, 150
White Revolution (Iran), 145
Whitehead, Sir Edgar, 112
Wilhelm II, Kaiser, 23
Wilson, Edmund, 10
World War I, 16
World War II, 113, 116, 149

Y

Yalta Conference, 47
Yang, Rae, 61
Young, Andrew, 138

Z

Zambia, 109, 116–19
ZANU. See Zimbabwe African National
  Union (ZANU).
Zanzibar, 116
ZAPU. See Zimbabwe African People's
  Union (ZAPU).
Zederbaum, Yuliy (Martov, Julius), 9,
  14–15
Zhou Enlai, 64, 196n21
Zhu De, 41
Zimbabwe African National Union
  (ZANU), 113, 15, 117–19, 121–22,
  124–28, 132
Zimbabwe African People's Union (ZAPU),
  112–13, 117–19, 125–26
Zimbabwe Defence Forces, 133
Zinoviev, Grigory, 3, 20
Zionism, xi, 136, 143, 146, 167, 169